# Shadow Marriage

# Shadow Marriage

✦

## A Descent into Intimacy

*Paul Dunion*

iUniverse, Inc.
New York  Lincoln  Shanghai

# Shadow Marriage
## A Descent into Intimacy

iUniverse books may be ordered through booksellers or by contacting:

iUniverse
2021 Pine Lake Road, Suite 100
Lincoln, NE 68512
www.iuniverse.com
1-800-Authors (1-800-288-4677)

ISBN-13: 978-0-595-38849-3 (pbk)
ISBN-13: 978-0-595-83227-9 (ebk)
ISBN-10: 0-595-38849-3 (pbk)
ISBN-10: 0-595-83227-X (ebk)

Printed in the United States of America

Dedicated to my wife, Connie Jones Dunion, who boldly and courageously steps into the initiation created by our marriage, calling me to uncharted regions of my soul, where I am inevitably unprepared to go.

# Contents

Introduction . . . . . . . . . . . . . . . . . . . . . . . . . . . . . . . . . . . . . . . . . . . . .1

CHAPTER 1    An Immense Arousal of the Heart . . . . . . . . . . . . . . .7

CHAPTER 2    Shadow Marriage. . . . . . . . . . . . . . . . . . . . . . . . . . . . .22

CHAPTER 3    Nuptial Initiation . . . . . . . . . . . . . . . . . . . . . . . . . .36

CHAPTER 4    The Shame Shadow. . . . . . . . . . . . . . . . . . . . . . . . . .51

CHAPTER 5    Dark Night of Marriage. . . . . . . . . . . . . . . . . . . . . .71

CHAPTER 6    The Shadow of Power . . . . . . . . . . . . . . . . . . . . . . .86

CHAPTER 7    The Soul of Intimacy. . . . . . . . . . . . . . . . . . . . . . .102

CHAPTER 8    Nuptial Diversity and Accompanying "Isms" . . . . .131

CHAPTER 9    The Shadow Dance of Sex. . . . . . . . . . . . . . . . . . .152

CHAPTER 10    The Mystery of Marriage. . . . . . . . . . . . . . . . . . . .177

# *Acknowledgments*

I am deeply grateful for the critical reading of the manuscript by Dr. George Rogers, and for his continued reminders of when I step away from myself. I am grateful to Dr. Tom Daly, Jeffrey Duvall, and Jane Downey for their critical feedback. Many thanks to Cliff Barry for his promotion of *Shadow Marriage*. I am also thankful for the editorial commentary I received from my friends Gary Blaser and Michael Chell; I am especially thankful for their soulful commitment to understanding the nature of intimate relationships and their willingness to enter into long and involved discussions aimed at teasing out the subtleties surrounding human intimacy. Much gratitude to my friends Thom Allena, Clive West, James Sullivan and Norbert Gauthier for holding me in compassion when I have lost my way. I am grateful for the support and criticism I have received from Connie Jones Dunion, whose feedback strips the abstraction from many of my ideas, rendering them relevant and applicable, and for her many reminders of the times that I want to give up and move into bad faith. Lastly, I want to express my indebtedness to all the couples who have chosen to invite me into the privacy of their marriages, where I have both taught and learned about the depth of nuptial mystery.

A writer who creates meaningful works does not want to become happy, he wants to be creative. Likewise married people can seldom enjoy happy, harmonious marriages, as psychologists would force it upon them and lead them to believe. The image of the "happy marriage" causes great harm.

—*Adolf Guggenbuhl-Craig*

# *Introduction*

## A Major Disturbance

Marriage can be a deeply disturbing experience. It may be fitting that we have been fooled into believing marriage is about happiness, comfort, and security. The reality is that marriage can be extremely disappointing, uncomfortable, and insecure. If we knew the truth, most of us might find remaining single to be the favorable alternative. Although this book was originally intended for anyone curious about surrendering to and navigating a committed relationship, it will particularly serve anyone who is married or intending to be married.

If you are reading this book, it is extremely likely that you have already been disillusioned about marriage. You are probably wondering if there is something inherently wrong with you, your spouse, or the way you relate to each other. I would suggest that there is likely nothing wrong with either of you.

You have stepped into one of the most powerful spiritual experiences known to humanity: marriage. It is deeply mysterious, insecure, and unpredictable. It is likely that you have not been given any of the competencies necessary to support yourself and your relationship through such a baffling and challenging experience. Consequently, you will find yourself either denying the bewilderment of it all or feeling fairly overwhelmed. I encourage you not to blame yourself. Get the help you need, and remember that you have been tricked into believing that you were taking a simple walk in the park.

## Tricked and Disillusioned

Aphrodite is the goddess of love and beauty in Greek mythology. We are told that laughter and hoaxes are amongst her charges. One of her greatest hoaxes is that the beloved will bring everlasting joy, love, and sexual fulfillment. Normally, within one year of marriage we begin to understand that the chosen one is not delivering promised bliss.

It is common for couples to generate a great deal of drama around the experience of being disillusioned. Maybe it is a way to bring credence to crumbling beliefs, or maybe it reflects a need to protest broken dreams. Rather than generating excessive histrionics as we watch our dreams fall short of our original plan, we can begin to surrender to the possible gifts of disillusionment.

This book is about the disillusionment that inevitably accompanies marriage; it is not a cynical attack upon marriage. Marriage is an opportunity for us to process our illusions. Marriage provides extraordinarily favorable circumstances for unveiling beliefs founded upon naïveté and idealism. It is a chance to let go of convictions that fall short of shedding any light upon our experiences of love, intimacy, and sexuality. Growing up means that our beliefs actually reflect the reality of our humanity. Marriage provides an excellent opportunity for growing up. It may be that the current divorce rate is not a reflection of some negative attitude about partnering, but rather a testimony of our resistance to stepping into maturity.

## Initiatory Potency

This book portrays marriage as a deeply powerful initiation. Marriage has the power to push us out of childhood and pull us into adulthood. Marriages often move into crisis and dissolve when one party feels severely victimized by the other, or if the feeling is mutual. We believe our partners have the ability to either grant us happiness or obstruct us from attaining satisfaction and serenity. We are often left with the choice to either stay in a marriage as a victim or run off as a victim; in either case, we are doing our best to avoid the push and the pull. Or we can stay and allow the power of marriage to initiate us.

There are two compelling forces in a marriage that have the strength to drive us to our depths. These dynamic impulses begin to energize once we decide to place *two feet* in a relationship and not hold back. The first of these powers is the fear of losing one's partner and the second is the fear of losing oneself.

The constellation of these fears creates the container for nuptial initiation. These fears will either drive us to exhibit excessive loyalty to our partners and betray ourselves or become self-indulgent to the exclusion of our spouses. When we speak of fearing intimacy, what we fear is placing ourselves fully in a relationship and allowing ourselves to be pounded and shaped by the fear of losing the beloved and the fear of losing ourselves; yet there may not be a more profound way of coming into ourselves.

These two fears may be the most powerful catalysts for arousing self-examination in the human psyche. Once they are engaged, we are often driven into a frenzy as we attempt to prevent the loss of the beloved or the loss of self. As we do what we believe will prevent the occurrence of one loss, we begin to hear the voice of the other.

This book identifies how we can surrender to these fears and their accompanying initiation. It will identify how to remain focused during the initiatory process. It will discuss the inevitability of something dying and something being born during the initiation, and what it means to access viable support.

In essence, getting married means stepping into a powerful initiation. It means allowing ourselves to be vulnerable to deception, betrayal, neglect, and abuse while learning how to empower ourselves. A nuptial initiation will ask us to allow some part of ourselves to die, irrespective of our readiness for such an event. It will also invite us to attend to the gestation of what needs to be born within us. We will explore the key to enduring a marital initiation by learning to let go of a need to protest our initiation (or a need to run).

## A Descending Path

Similar to all honorable initiations depicted in ancient myths, marriage requires a willingness to walk the descending path; that is, before we can ascend to new insight accompanied by joy and delight, we will need to go down. Marriage requires that we be open to moving down into our bodies: into grief, fear, hurt, anger, and shadow. The descending path calls for a willingness to be lost.

Intimacy is not an elevated experience; it calls for the depth available to us as we embark upon a descent. As we move down into ourselves, we let go of pretense and begin to make peace with shadows. We learn how to welcome what has been designated as socially unacceptable, and we become receptive to the most brilliant parts of ourselves.

The welcome we extend to ourselves sets the stage for what we will be able to offer our partners. The goal is a kind of psychological ecology, where we find a place for as much of ourselves as we can embrace. Nothing is allocated to the junk heap! The more magnanimous we are with our own foibles, the greater the space created in our hearts to receive the frailties of our partners.

The descent is about depth. To walk this path means we are willing to drop into ourselves and into our humanity. The descending path points us away from personal victimization and our attempts at occupying high moral ground. This path does not encourage us to explain who we are by citing what our spouses have done or have failed to do. There is no depth in depicting ourselves as victims of our spouses. Victimization is an extremely simplistic explanation reflecting our childhood experiences, and it points us away from our adult selves.

## Radical Self-Responsibility

The descending path champions the depths available to us when we engage in radical self-responsibility. This level of responsibility refuses to explain who we are by offering an account of our spouse's choices. Radical self-responsibility defines our marital situation as a result of our own creation. Radical self-responsibility strives to eliminate victimization.

By remaining self-referenced, we stay focused in the only place where we have control: ourselves. Radical self-responsibility is a great way to grow some adulthood. It means we ask ourselves self-responsible and self-empowering questions: How did I contribute to this situation? How have I colluded with my partner's abuse or neglect of me? What choices have I made that were self-sabotaging? How have I inadequately supported myself? Does any of my behavior suggest a tendency to be masochistic? In what ways may I have set myself up?

Betrayal is a natural part of childhood. Many of us were abused and neglected by caregivers who were unable to give real care. We had no real power to do anything about it, and therefore we were genuinely victimized. When these childhood betrayals are placed in the unconscious, they have a way of reproducing themselves—in many cases, with our help.

Unless we introduce some level of self-responsibility when we are betrayed by our spouses, we simply reproduce the betrayal of childhood; we remain victims. We experience our marriages as though we are children our spouses have wronged. Our marriages are unable to reflect the vision and values of empowered adults. The tragedy is that many marriages end because someone feels deeply victimized and decides to leave the bad spouse-parent and search for a good spouse-parent. Of course, the past and its accompanying victimizations are likely to be reproduced in the next relationship.

## Good Cosmology

Marriages would likely be more enduring and resilient if spouses practiced good cosmology. We all believe in some form of cosmology; that is, we have beliefs about the nature of life and the afterlife. One cosmology might be intended to keep us bound to childhood, where we can remain immune to the challenges and responsibilities of adulthood; while another cosmology invites us to take our place in the adult community.

Each culture has its own origin myth that customarily sheds light upon the essence of life. The story of the Garden of Eden is our origin myth. Religions have found it necessary to interpret this story as one about disobedient children who are appropriately punished. Of course, we are then left with the obvious choices of disobedience and punishment or obedience and reward. Obedience is defined as adherence to the dogma of some church, with the reward being heaven.

It is curious that our religious institutions invite us to hold a cosmology that calls us back to childhood. A more mature interpretation of our origin myth might suggest that the story is telling us something important about growing up and about life itself. We could say that the story is about wanting to be bigger than we are and taking some action (eating the apple) that leads to loss and separation. We could also say that psychological separation from our parent is necessary, moving us from an obedience-based orientation to an ethical one, where we make our choices based upon our own values.

As long as we hold a cosmology that refers us back to childhood dynamics (such as disobedience and punishment), we will be ill-equipped to effectively cope with life and unprepared for the vicissitudes of marriage. Our origin myth suggests that life is about loss, and that it is mysterious, unpredictable, and insecure.

Once we get our cosmology right, we can begin asking some important questions about what it means to leave childhood and welcome our emotional and spiritual maturity. This book suggests that human maturation is mostly about learning to make peace with the mystery, unpredictability, and insecurity of life. It also contends that marriage maximizes our opportunities to make peace with life and find our way to our own personal depths. The more willing we are to make peace with life's mystery and to practice radical self-responsibility, the more likely that our marriages will surrender to the repose of authentic intimacy.

# 1

# *An Immense Arousal of the Heart*

Nothing uplifts the human spirit and electrifies the heart like falling in love. No amount of economic gain or social status can compete with falling in love as a reason to consummate a relationship through matrimony. Has this power that drives two people together in a romantic frenzy always been part of the human condition?

Maybe it started when *homo erectus* males witnessed females giving birth, which vaulted them to celestial status. Maybe it was when ancient woman discovered that her security depended upon her affiliation with a male who sported enough brawn to protect her from a long list of predators. In any case, a time came when men and women began to see their connection as larger than an attempt to secure safety or economic stability. At some point, the human heart became intrinsically involved in transforming the bond between men and women into something hot and tumultuous.

Some say it all began when European troubadours returned from the Holy Land, enthralled by the prayerful melodies of the Sufis. Constrained by an abstract theology that could not embrace the romance and sensuality of Sufism, the troubadours directed their musical innovations toward women, rather than God. These melodic images may very well have placed men on the quest for romantic love.

What is falling in love? Have we made it into something inhuman? Why does Hollywood make millions out of the idealization of falling in love? Should we ignore the experience as an emotional aberration, one best forgotten? Is there a difference between falling in love and loving someone? Should we search for our soul mate and the eternal bliss associated with procuring this special someone?

Few things constellate our psychic energies more powerfully than falling in love. We do ourselves a great disservice if we attempt to run from it or deny it when it occurs. From a surface perspective, we can say that falling in love calls us to someone in a big way—a way so big that we describe it as "falling." "Falling" implies that we are out of control. The forces of love push against us like the force of gravity, and we find ourselves both excited and scared.

From a deeper perspective, we might say that we are being called to ourselves in an immense way. Our psyches are rushing us to an encounter with ourselves by way of an intense attraction to the beloved. It is this potential rendezvous with ourselves that makes falling in love so trustworthy.

Falling in love is a grand invitation to discover who we are. The discovery may be delightful or ominous, causing us to be weary as we go; nonetheless, falling in love may be a great cradle for self-discovery. Before we turn to a discussion of these possibilities, let's examine the kind of expectations we have placed upon the experience of falling in love.

## Transference Beatification

Some social scientists have viewed falling in love as an encounter with everything we define as positive. It is as if everything we have dreamed of as wholesome and good suddenly stands before us in the flesh. In clinical terms, this process of meeting the "holy one" is identified as "transference beatification".

Joining the divine partner is not only about purging oneself of limitations and shortcomings, but it is also about sharing in the purity of the other. We are excited and delighted by the possibility of releasing the diminishing aspects of our personalities by being chosen by him or her who is without blemish.

Who knows the actual origin of romantic love? What we do know is that men can easily transform women into goddesses. And women, not finding a reason to protest, must have easily found their deification quite appealing. After years of being second-class citizens, and before the thought of equality passed through anyone's mind, women were vaulted to angelic status. Why wouldn't they take some joy in the trip?

Men can attempt to find such goddesses, seeking some form of redemption or salvation from the divine female. The search for the goddess is often undaunted by prior disappointments, where women proved their sheer mortality over and over again. Men are convinced that the divine one remains in waiting, and with a little luck, will surely be found. Rituals, prayers, visions, and a fervent devotion reflect the religion of the quest.

What we usually call falling in love is another description of being in the presence of the divine Other. What a man knows is that *she's the one*. Once that identification is branded in a person's heart and brain, there's no turning back. "The one" may be a convicted ax murderer; it doesn't matter. We believe that we are finally in the presence of the one who offers salvation, and that's all that matters.

Women have also found their way to romantic transcendentalism. If men are going about the business of searching for a female savior, then women will join them, seeking the Male Messiah, or the Divine Father. After all, Mary Magdalene had one—why can't every woman?

Whose beatification is transferred to the beloved? Is it the divinity of God that we attribute to the beloved? Maybe it is our father's or mother's divinity that we ascribe to the object of our affection, or maybe it is our own divinity that we unhesitatingly transfer to our beloved.

I recently came across a greeting card containing the following message:

---

*Dear Love,*

*I celebrate and rejoice that God gave us breath, and I thank the forces of destiny that let us find each other. I venerate those forces and you, dear. Love, pressed tenderly, does not yield all of its juices, nor does the Holy Spirit awaken without complete awareness in all the senses. Love must be lived-lived-lived and shared all-ways with enthusiasm—always.*

*We voyage in our own deep awareness of spirituality respectful-grateful-thankful for each other's individuality. Sharing both sun and rain, hand in hand.*

*You are as much of me as I am of you. My fate is linked to your fate, my dear. Precious love, you are the nectar of ambrosia, the essence of joyous sensuality that embraces all nature: our living earth. The you/me, the she/he—we/us, one in transcendence, one in heart, mind, body, and soul.*

*Even when not touching, we caress each other's aura. Ours is a love beyond love, an open door to a heaven and earth paradise...and when we touch, the gentle warmth of you becomes a flame in me. We become—we are—god and goddess to each other.*

*I worship and adore you. The dawn of enlightenment in love was evident in our first kiss. In the garden of love, my beloved, you are all flowers, all suns and moons, all heavens. You are the pulse, the heartbeat of ecstasy. The center point of my universe, my treasure of life.*

*Within a single sigh of love lives the secret of all secrets, an eternity of love. I respect and adore you for the human being that is you.*

*I love you.*

The giver and the recipient of this card are likely in for a rude awakening! The sentiments expressed in the above message are a great example of transference beatification. This Hallmark version of love points upward, with the intent to grow a relationship on high, hallowed ground. Why does this upward direction attract us so?

## The Fool

Nothing is more human than acting foolish, and nothing gets us to act more foolishly than falling in love. How many of us have proclaimed that we would never do such-and-such again when it came to falling in love, only to enact the pattern repeatedly?

It's important not to strip falling in love of its mystery by being reductionist and suggesting that we can capture its true essence in a single formula. We can point toward it and create images that reflect our experience, and hopefully even come to know ourselves better as people who fall in love. But nowhere is the fool more evident than in the choice to surrender our own divinity to the beloved.

No longer do we have to struggle with the responsibility of choosing ourselves, which is inevitably obstructed by guilt, shame, and deep feelings of inadequacy. We only need to gaze into the eyes of the divine beloved, and all is forgiven. Our redemption becomes as simple as holding hands, and we are released from the burden of our failings. Or we might say that once beatification is transferred, we get to sit side by side with our own divinity, since our own essential goodness is just too much for us to claim within ourselves.

I encourage you not to see the transference of our divinity to the other as simply unfortunate. It may be a rich opportunity to renew our faith in our own divinity and the divinity of humanity! The idea that a divine spark dwells deep within all of us seems absurd, even to the most romantic, until the fool dares to fall in love. Suddenly, a being who makes life worth living appears before us, and we finally understand that the sanctification of the human race is possible!

The shadow work of falling in love may be twofold. First, we need to understand that the divine qualities we project to the beloved are in us, and these positive traits are often just too much for us to claim. We deny our own inner gold and let the other carry it for us. We can at least begin to ask ourselves: Am I also beautiful? Am I desirable? Do I possess qualities worth loving?

Secondly, as we get to know the beloved, we can allow ourselves to witness the erosion of our idyllic images and begin to welcome a real human being. We can let ourselves feel our disillusionment and the accompanying disappointment as we find ourselves in the arms of a fragile human being. But we may be called to another opportunity: the possibility of seeing the divinity of our beloveds in the depths of their humanity, including their blemishes.

The fool responds to this immense arousal of the heart, and is willing to risk pain and hurt. The fool vaults the beloved to celestial status. And only the fool would be willing to seek the faith to reclaim his or her own beauty, and in the midst of all the defects and failings of the beloved, continue to be receptive to his or her own divine spark.

There will be no way to demonstrate or prove our own divinity, no miracles or wondrous acts to show we are deserving of love. If we dare hold ourselves as worthy, we will hear the shaming voices of the past challenging our efforts to hold our own merit. We will also need to be ready to betray these demeaning voices from the past, and others who abused and neglected us, by slowly moving in the direction of self-benevolence, daring to treat ourselves differently than we were treated.

It is a true gift to ourselves when we allow the fool within us to hold love for our partners as they fall from grace. As our spouses shed the idyllic images we projected upon them, we have the opportunity to experience loving and being loved by an ordinary human being. We accept the invitation to be in a relationship with a real man or a real woman. We accept the opportunity to allow such a relationship to bring us to unexplored depths within ourselves. And it is the fool that ignites the power within us to witness the divine in the most mundane and ordinary of human undertakings.

Two members of one of my therapy groups recently experienced the loss of a mutual friend, and one of them also lost a son. Besides losing her friend, Gina had also lost her son in a car accident. Matt told the group that he had some grief work to do, and explained to Gina how he hesitated to do the work because she had lost her son as well as their mutual friend. Matt was minimizing his grief in the light of Gina's losses.

I asked one of the other group members to lie on the floor, eyes closed, playing the role of the dead friend. Matt lost no time expressing his anger: "I loved you, and you left me here! You said you wanted to be my friend, and you went away! I can't believe I allowed all this to happen! You tricked me!"

When Matt's anger was somewhat subdued, I asked him if he would do it all over again. He looked at me and began to wail, accessing deep grief and yelling, "Yes! Yes! I would do it again! What's wrong with me?" When he was finished crying, he locked his gaze with Gina's. In that moment, he and she knew one another with a clear accessibility, uncluttered by pleasantries.

I allowed for the silence of their encounter, and then softly said, "Each of you sits in admiration of the fool in the other, who chooses an open heart, knowing it will likely be broken."

## Just Want To Be Saved

It may be important to take a closer look at this idolatry we bring to our vision of one another. Why do we seek the perfect partner? Can a man or a woman feel satisfied with a mortal, or do we inevitably feel like we are settling for one? And what form of salvation do men and women hold for one another?

It appears that we may want to be saved. We want to be saved from some present demon or some old ghost that continues to haunt us. It's often easier for us to see the current demons, while the old ones remain somewhat mercurial.

Philip, a fifty-five-year-old literature professor, came to see me. His demons were in the present. He had been married to the same woman for twenty-two years. He reported a lengthy history of secretive affairs with students at the university.

"The affairs just aren't giving me what they once did. Even the younger women don't seem to give me any real fulfillment," explained Philip.

"Do you know what it is that you have been seeking from these women?" I asked.

"I thought I did. I just don't know anymore," said Philip.

"Do you have a best friend?" I asked.

"What's that got to do with anything?" he asked.

"I'm just wondering if there's a man or woman in your life with whom you feel a genuine connection," I suggested.

"No, there isn't. I haven't had a best friend in years," he responded, his voice dropping off.

Philip was experiencing an isolation common to many men. The combination of homophobia and sexualizing relationships with women can leave men estranged from both genders. Their answer is to find a goddess who will meet all of their affiliation needs. Of course, the strategy is doomed. No one person can meet all of a man's relational needs.

Philip began to understand that he was asking his student goddesses to save him from aging, and ultimately from dying. This is a popular request of goddesses who are ten or more years younger than a man. Unfortunately, this issue is often trivialized and thought of as ridiculous; however, in a culture where men have no permission to either age or die with dignity, even bright and educated men like Philip respond to the aging process with a deep desperation. On some primitive level, they actually believe that a lovely young woman can really save them from their ultimate decline.

Philip talked about experiencing a temporary reprieve from the loss of his youth as he lay next to a beautiful thirty-five-year-old woman. However, Philip was seeing that some of his disillusionment with his affairs was that these women were not saving him from aging. He also began to identify his real quest, which was to make peace with his own death, and began to realize that only he could make that happen.

The combination of homophobia and ageism also made it impossible for Philip to acknowledge his own beauty. Heterosexual men are not supposed to see the beauty of their own gender, which translates into a belief that they're not supposed to see the beauty of any man, including themselves. Men are dependent upon women, who are responsible for validating our attractiveness by choosing us, which quickly leads to desperation as we age.

There are several other ways in which Philip was asking the goddess to save him from himself. The first was that he spent most of his life denying his sensitivity and softness, since they did not fit with his masculine image of himself. Philip wanted these women to carry his sensitivity for him. He saw sensitivity as an honorable trait—but not one he could own and still be a real man. When he saw the goddess as loud, crass, intense, or intrusive, he decided that she was failing miserably in her role as savior. She was a goddess-turned-bitch and of no use to Philip.

Seeking the goddess also allows men to stay on the quest. Philip loved remaining on the quest, where he was essentially immune from all the folly that accompanies real love. On the quest, he was exempt from being accountable for what he gave and how he received. His questing allowed him to step beyond the inevitable vulnerability that characterizes genuine intimacy.

The quest allows us to postpone any real encounter with fear of abandonment, fear of inadequacy, fear of getting lost, and whatever other fears we associate with a real relationship. Men can remain on the quest, thus remaining in relationship with an idyllic image rather than with a real woman, insulating them from the hazards of genuine intimacy.

When Bruce, a forty-four-year-old investment broker, came to see me, he was complaining of a marriage he claimed was empty. Our sessions soon revealed that there was nothing specific bothering him about his wife, Nancy. However, he expressed a vague dissatisfaction, which alerted me to the possibility that Bruce might be in the market for a goddess.

"Bruce, I'm not sure what it is about Nancy that is bugging you," I pointed out.

"She's okay. She's very caring and very supportive. Something isn't quite right. I don't know what it is. Something is missing," Bruce explained.

"Are other women getting your attention?" I asked.

"Why, yes, they are," Bruce meekly responded.

Before long, Bruce was reporting that the goddess was located on the second floor of his office building. I almost never try talking a man out of his vision of Aphrodite. It's like telling Moses that he didn't really see a burning bush. Besides, my experience suggests that the goddess vision awakens something essential in a man's psychology, which might even be a rendezvous with his own divinity.

I've seen men become vital, passionate, adventurous, bold, and ready to experience life on new levels when encountering the goddess. It's safe to say that a goddess vision may very well imply that something critical in a man's psyche is beginning to awaken. The challenge is to allow for the goddess experience, and then with a little luck and support, to redirect our focus back to ourselves, where we can offer a helping hand to what awakens in us.

It can be very difficult for a man to mortalize a woman whom he has deified. Bruce needed to touch, smell, and taste the alleged goddess before he could truly see her humanity. An affair ensued, but it didn't take long for Bruce to become disillusioned with the goddess on the second floor. In his disillusionment, he was much more willing to look at himself and discover what was stirring within him.

Bruce discovered that he wanted his goddess to save him from his childhood. As long as he had hope for the arrival of Aphrodite, he could hold onto the belief that the mother he had always deserved was making her way to him. Bruce, like so many boys, coped with maternal neglect and abuse by deciding that these negative experiences were testimony that there was something inherently wrong with him.

The arrival of the goddess would be a clear sign that he was truly deserving of love and attention. This desire to prove his deservedness was coupled with a need to remain loyal to his mother by remaining in denial of her neglect of him.

Because there is no other place for the goddess to go but down, her failings become a way to remain loyal to the mother. The goddess's fall from grace reaffirmed that no one could actually attend to him better than his own mother. Men bring a painful pattern of deprivation upon themselves when they need a woman to help them prove that they are lovable, while also needing to demonstrate that no one can take the mother's place.

Bruce also realized that the fallen goddess gave him a great place to direct the anger he harbored toward his mother, without having to jeopardize his maternal relationship. He could maintain his maternal loyalty and medicate the depression that festered deep within his internalized anger. However, depression is inevitable when a man immerses himself in deprivation.

Bruce gradually became more willing to take responsibility for his childhood, realizing that the woman on the second floor couldn't save him. He decided to work on his marriage with Nancy and explore having a relationship with a mortal woman.

Philip and Bruce both decided to step away from the quest and closer to their own souls. Each grieved the end of his quest in his own unique way.

When men begin to see that they've been asking women to keep them alive forever, carry parts of themselves that they are afraid to carry, be their entire support system, and redeem a wounded childhood, they can begin to have authentic relationships with themselves and with women.

## The Benevolent Father

Alice had been dating Jason for about six months when she came into one of her sessions and reported that she was seriously thinking about ending the relationship.

"I definitely thought Jason was the one. He seemed gentle, sensitive, and thoughtful. Boy, was I wrong," said Alice.

"You seemed so happy with Jason. Tell me what happened," I suggested.

"I don't know. We were spending all this time together, which I thought he enjoyed as much as I did, and then things began to change," she said.

"What changed?" I asked.

"He started hanging out with his friends, watching sports on television, and just didn't seem to care anymore," explained Alice.

"So, let me get this straight. Jason hangs out with his friends and watches sporting events, and you decided he doesn't care for you," I said.

"Yeah, that's what happened," agreed Alice.

"Alice, I'm not sure what hanging out with his friends and watching television have to do with caring for you."

"Well, he's just not as available. We used to spend a lot of time together, and I thought he enjoyed it as much as I did," she insisted, beginning to tear.

"Jason may still value his time with you. And I'm wondering if you have told him what it is that you want from him," I remarked.

"Why would I have to tell him what I want? We've been together for six months!" Alice protested.

"Jason is not a mind reader."

"If he really cared, he would know," Alice argued.

Alice had defined Jason as the Benevolent Father, the one she had been awaiting for a long time. The Benevolent Father was supposed to know what she wanted and needed. There was no need for her to take any risks or ask for what she wanted. The father would know as part of his heavenly wisdom. And Jason was falling a long way from heaven.

I encouraged Alice to speak with Jason about what she wanted from him. After she got beyond the grip of her disillusionment, she decided it was worth taking the risk. She found Jason to be extremely receptive to her requests and discovered that he could spend time with his friends, watch sports, and love her too.

Alice's initial disillusionment with Jason was coupled with memories of how she felt neglected by her father. The minute Jason strayed from her side, she was convinced that she had made a serious mistake in judgment and that he would neglect her just like her father did.

Jenn, a thirty-six-year-old school teacher, had been divorced for a year when she came for her first session. Before long, Jenn declared she was ready to date, and soon met a young man, by whom she was much taken.

"I met Abe in a bar and I did something that I've never done before. I approached him and ended up taking him home with me," Jenn described, with a hint of embarrassment.

"How did it go?" I asked.

"Great! He's unbelievable!" she exclaimed.

"Well, what makes him so spectacular?"

"He's great in bed! The only drawback is that there's another woman involved in his life, but he's trying to move away from her," she explained.

Several weeks later, Jenn came to her session reporting her frustration over the fact that Abe had asked her not to call him. Consequently, she found herself hanging around the house, pining.

"I can't call him, because he lives with this woman! He doesn't call me when he says he will. Why am I so into this guy?" Jenn lamented.

"It's a great question. You don't know Abe; he doesn't know you; you can't trust his word; and you can't access him," I outlined.

"I must be really fucked up," she concluded.

"No, you're not fucked up. You're starving," I suggested.

I went on to remind Jenn that she had been in a ten-year marriage in which her sexual and emotional needs were hardly ever met. I described her as a woman walking out of the desert and meeting a man who gave her a morsel of pineapple. She was responding to this meager offering with great affection, gratitude, and hope. She laughed as I watched her body settle in with the analogy.

It took some time before Jenn would come to terms with her relationship with deprivation. She had deified her own father, who had withheld affection and warmth. She found herself attracted to men who would give little or nothing, thus securing her loyalty to a father whom she adored and had sworn to protect, at the cost of sacrificing herself.

Jenn had great resistance to betraying her father. She refused to see him as anything less than loving, warm, gracious, and generous. Jenn was determined to ignore her father's darkness, which would inevitably obscure her vision of all men. Subsequently, she could only explain her deprivation as a result of her own pathology.

The more I introduced the possibility of her father's blemishes, the more entrenched she became in her loyalty to him—she was not going to forsake this god! Her excessive loyalty condemned her to deprivation. Any man who would dare shower love and nurturance upon her would be a threat to her father's sanctification. Such a bounty would surely shed light upon her father's inaccessibility.

I finally asked her if she was familiar with the story of Adam and Eve. She said she was, and I suggested that there might be another way to approach the story, one that was not in keeping with traditional interpretations. I went on to describe Eve's eating of the apple as a significant act of betrayal, and possibly the only way that Eve could leave the subservience and dependency of childhood, the only way she could learn to be loyal to herself. Jenn gazed at me with a blank stare as our session came to an end.

She returned the following week and took a seat in my office, her head bent downward, her lip beginning to quiver.

"He was a good man! He loved me! He was a good man! He really loved me!" Jenn cried out over and over again, sobbing uncontrollably.

I am sure more was going on for Jenn than my story of the previous week; however, I like to believe that our origin myths lie somewhere deep within us, waiting to reveal their truths.

Jenn was ready to betray her father, to strip him and every man of their beatification. Her god (her father) had failed to save her, and so had every other man. Jenn was grieving the death of her god and feeling the joy of her own birth. Her exodus from the desert and all its deprivation was leading her back to an unavailable father, and back to herself.

We may all take circuitous routes to ourselves. Robert Johnson says it well in his book, *We*:

> *The appearance of romantic love in the West began a momentous chapter in this cosmic drama of evolution. Romantic love is the mask behind which a powerful array of new possibilities hides, waiting to be integrated into consciousness. But what has begun as a huge collective surge of psychic energy must be perfected at the individual level. It is always the role of the individuals to complete the task, to bring the divine process to fruition within the microcosm of our souls. It is up to us, as individuals, to take this raw unconscious energy of romantic love, this confusing array of impulses and possibilities, and transform it into awareness and relatedness.*

The actual nature of falling in love may continue to mystify us, and yet it deeply deserves our attention, for as Johnson points out, there is a powerful array of new possibilities hiding just beneath its mask. We have examined some of these possibilities hiding just beneath the mask. Ultimately, how we have turned against ourselves lies just beneath the mask, and romantic love becomes a huge opportunity to face what we have banished and victimized within ourselves. This immense arousal of the heart holds the possibility for the deepening of our awareness and our relatedness.

## Soul Mates and Spirit Mates

Seeking one's soul mate has become an enticing and popular endeavor. What most people describe as a soul mate might better be described as a "spirit mate". Our spirit mates are supposed to bring us into the light and help us transcend our pedestrian lifestyles. Life with our spirit mates is allegedly destined to be more fulfilling, more erotic, easier, and to probably assure us of living happily ever after. Spirit-mating appears to be about the search for gods and goddesses, while soul mating is about something quite different.

The soul man Thomas Moore describes the conditions of the soul as dark, wet, slow-moving, immanent, attached to beauty and love, and receptive to being lost. It hopefully will become obvious that soul-mating is not for everyone. It is challenging and deeply humanizing. For all the glamour presently surrounding the idea of soul mates, most couples coming to my office for counseling have a repugnant response to actually creating a relationship with their soul mate.

Let's begin with what Moore calls the soul's affinity for darkness. Soul mates visit darkness on a fairly regular basis. One form of darkness is the many initiatory tests that visit soul mates. These trials come in many forms. They might challenge an individual's capacity for sacrifice, for loyalty, integrity, the capacity to hold power, the ability to receive love, the employment of effective boundaries...the list is long. And of course there is the ordinary daily darkness, such as brooding, pouting, ridiculing, blaming, and sarcasm.

Another call to darkness for soul mates is regression. Regression occurs when we return to an earlier way of thinking, feeling, and acting. Our coping mechanisms are reduced to fight or flight, we think in extremes, and we can neither maintain a rational discussion nor make cogent decisions. When we are regressed, we are normally incapable of giving or receiving love. I refer to regression in a later chapter entitled "Dark Night of the Soul."

Soul mating is wet. Soul mates exchange fluids, including tears, perspiration, saliva, and genital fluids. Soul mates invite their grief and sadness into their relationship. The waters of deep sorrow are welcomed and allowed to flow. Soul mates experience their tears as renewing and deeply humanizing.

Their sweat, saliva, and genital fluids are ways to celebrate the concrete expression of their relationship. They are eager to create a myriad of opportunities to allow these bodily waters to find their way to one another. Sometimes spittle is exchanged in a passionate kiss, while other times it is spewed in an outburst of rage. Soul mates experience the depth of their connection by being immersed in their waters.

Soul mates want to be immanent or close. Their desire for closeness makes them easy prey for what is often described as enmeshment or fusion, whereby each individual may sacrifice some of their uniqueness in the name of creating closeness. Consequently, soul mates often get lost in their partners, sacrificing their own needs, values, and beliefs. They can be consistently challenged to let go of their partners and find their way back to themselves.

Soul mates may find themselves caught in a pattern of blaming one another when they lose their sense of self. In their desire to be close, soul mates struggle to find the kind of boundaries that allow them to be connected to their partners while maintaining a solid sense of self.

The soul is attached to being slow-moving. Soul mates are not heavily invested in going anywhere quickly. They're not concerned about being productive or efficient, which makes the experience of soul-mating countercultural. They enjoy puttering, napping, cuddling, making out, and getting lost in one another.

Soul mates are attached to beauty and love. They enjoy beautifying their bodies and their environment. They are acutely aware of their attraction (or lack thereof) when encountering one another. It can be quite important for soul mates to give a voice to what may be hindering their attraction to their partners. They are concerned about the quality of love communicated by their behavior. They want to know how to communicate love to their partners; they want to feel loved, and they want their partners to feel loved.

It is common for soul mates to become moody, jealous, or possessive as they attempt to maximize their experience of love. They easily become entangled in the nuances of one another's emotions, making it difficult to maintain a rational outlook about their relationship.

Soul mates are comfortable with unknowing, or mystery. The experience of their relationship is much more important to them than the understanding of it; however, they may find themselves comfortable with learning about themselves and each other. They experience their curiosity as an opportunity to get closer to themselves and their partners. Self-knowledge invites soul mates into their own depths, rather than creating the illusion of penetrating the mystery of their love.

Finally, soul mates are on a descending path, moving down and back. They are open to the influence of the past and its haunting impact. The way their parents related to one another will find its way into their lives, like water flowing under the guidance of a sloping terrain.

The descending path tells the story of loss being the only guarantee of love. Either someone will walk away from the relationship, or someone will die.

Soul mates walking the descending path welcome their grief, their fear, and their shame. They understand the potency of these three energies and how they significantly impact the best of relationships.

If a couple is mostly seeking happiness, then soul-mating is not for them. Soul mates are willing to surrender to the way of the soul, where the depths of their humanity are welcomed and they are willing to step into the darkness and the turbulence of the soul's journey. Happiness comes to soul mates as a by-product—as a consequence of the resiliency to unearth themselves and forgive their findings again, again, and again.

A fool's journey begins with an immense arousal of the heart. If we are willing to become self-referential, then a fool's venture is transformed into a lover's quest where our own divinity, as well as our partner's, begins to emerge from the ordinariness of our humanity.

When a couple decides to choose one another as the place where they will descend into their own depths and maybe discover intimate ways to relate to themselves and to each other, they create what I call a "shadow marriage" and create the possibility of descending into intimacy.

# 2

## *Shadow Marriage*

Our culture is overly zealous when it comes to hanging idealizations, images of perfectionism, and quixotic appeals to romance on the institution of marriage. These encumbrances have a crushing impact on marriage, resulting in the demise of thousands of marriages annually. Our nuptial dreams steer us off-course, until we find ourselves either wandering aimlessly or dashed upon some reef with a gaping hole in our hull, taking on water rapidly. It appears that we need to take a serious new look at marriage.

It may be important to consider the source of our excessive marital expectations. Hollywood promotes a popular marital myth: that there exists a perfect someone who will provide eternal bliss. The attractiveness of this position seems to have its roots in two powerful areas in the human psyche.

The first is that there very well might be a child within each of us who searches tirelessly for the perfect parent we never had. It is challenging to simply accept the childhood and parents we had, with all their foibles and faults. We just know that someone out there will eventually show up and finally love us the way we deserve to be loved. That someone may show up, and it behooves us to begin the process by giving love to ourselves.

The more we treat ourselves as deserving of love, the more likely it is that we will develop the capacity to effectively discern who is willing and able to love us, and cultivate the ability to receive love from another.

The second attitude that predisposes us to believe that the bearer of everlasting joy is out there somewhere is probably the single greatest failure of our educational system. We do not teach people that they are responsible for their own happiness. In my twenty-five years of doing couples counseling, I've never worked with a single couple who came into my office believing they were each responsible for their own happiness. In some cases, husbands or wives have been waiting several decades for their partners to make them happy!

"Shadow marriage" is a perspective of marriage that strives to shed from marriage what is unreal and unattainable. Shadow marriage is an invitation to identify and embrace the reality of marriage. It is an attempt to steal back from the gods this most human experience we call marriage and restore it to its rightful place, where we might see that marriage is frightening, messy, confusing, dangerous, and delightful.

The Jungian analyst Robert Johnson describes the nature of shadow in "Owning Your Own Shadow":

> *In the cultural process we sort out God-given characteristics into those that are acceptable to our society and those that have to be put away. This is wonderful and necessary, and there would be no civilized behavior without this sorting out of good and evil. But the refused and unacceptable characteristics do not go away; they only collect in the dark corners of our personality. When they have been hidden long enough, they take on a life of their own—the shadow life. The shadow is that which has not entered adequately into consciousness. It is the despised quarter of our being. It often has an energy potential nearly as great as that of our ego, it erupts as an overpowering rage or some indiscretion that slips past us; or we have a depression or an accident that seems to have its own purpose. The shadow gone autonomous is a terrible monster in our psychic house.*

Johnson describes shadows as those traits we deem unacceptable and avoid by pushing back into the dark corners of our personality. This is our way of coping with the tension created by shadow traits such as lust, arrogance, hatred, jealousy, greed, and vanity. Johnson doesn't limit shadow to our unacceptable traits; he also includes our exceptionally positive traits. People often ask how it is possible that we can see our greatest qualities as unacceptable and drive them deep into the unconscious.

Children are extremely sensitive to the pain and struggles of their parents, especially the self-loathing carried by a parent. When children decide that their more admirable traits might lead a parent to feel worse about themselves, those traits gradually are denied and kept in shadow, as if they did not even exist. As the meritorious elements of our personality are kept in shadow, we hope that our parents will feel better about themselves and have less reason to reject us.

We learn early to cope with the tension created when we witness either ourselves or our loved ones suffering the pangs of unworthiness. Most of us ease the tension by conveniently allowing whatever we deem unacceptable to slide into shadow, so it becomes easier for us to explain why we deserve our spouse's love and attention. The problem is that marriage is a most likely place for the appearance of shadow. Like a child who feels excluded because he has been scapegoated and identified as "the bad kid" in a family, our more repugnant attributes act out, seeking acknowledgment and integration into the system of the personality.

Johnson says that shadow gone autonomous is "a terrible monster in our psychic house." Continuing with the analogy of the bad kid who finds his way into the family by acting out and receiving negative attention, shadow also is inclined to act out in order to find its way into the psychic house of the personality.

Harvey and Louise came to see me for marriage counseling. Louise had found a note from a woman with whom Harvey had been having an affair for three years.

Louise emphatically described the emotional impact Harvey's betrayal was having upon her. "Harvey, I never dreamed that you could do something like this. I feel shocked, scared. I've lost my best friend. I can't imagine what will become of us. How will I ever trust you again?"

Harvey sat listening with an astonishing degree of reserve.

Finally, I addressed Harvey. "Harvey, how are you feeling about everything you're hearing from Louise?"

"Louise certainly has the right to be upset," he responded, as if her feelings were about some other man.

My hunch was that he was experiencing her feelings as if they were certainly about another man, some angry man whom he identified as a monster that dwelled in his psychic house.

"Harvey, I'm wondering if you might be angry at Louise and that it may not be easy for you to tell her about it," I suggested.

"I don't think that I allow myself to express my anger anywhere in my life," he reacted, his voice deepening and his fist clenching. Harvey began to explore his anger as a part of his shadow. He had banished his anger to the recesses of his personality, until it demanded the light of day by being acted out as an affair. Gradually, Harvey was able to talk about his affair as a way to be angry at Louise.

Louise began to admit that she was afraid of her own anger and that it had been a comfort to her that her husband was such a docile and gentle soul. She understood that she had colluded with Harvey to sequester his anger. In doing so, she knew that she had covertly collaborated in her own betrayal.

Some form of acting-out behavior that is not indicative of a person's general character is a common way that shadow makes its way into marriages. Another prevailing way that shadow expresses itself in marriages is through projection. Projection happens when our shadow breaks free from the "dark corner of the personality," and we refuse to accept the shadow characteristic as a reflection of ourselves. Rather than seeing the shadow trait as a statement about ourselves, the shadow quality is described as a statement about our spouses. Projection is like a game of hot potato, where one spouse grabs hold of some shadow trait, like selfishness, and quickly tosses it to the other spouse, exclaiming, "God! Are you selfish!"

I was working with Peter and Carol in couples counseling when Peter began to explain that he no longer had any tolerance for Carol's intensity.

"She's absolutely the most intense person I've ever known. She reacts intensely to anything; everything is a big deal for her. I don't think she has a mellow bone in her body!" Peter explained, with exaggerated energy.

"Peter, wouldn't you describe yourself as a fairly passionate man?" I asked.

"Yeah, I guess I would. I'm passionate, but she's always overreacting, loudly and intrusively!" Peter insisted.

Peter was discovering that although Carol was intense, so was he. He preferred to see himself as cool, calm, and collected, rejecting his own intensity and projecting it onto Carol. As Peter learned to reclaim his own intensity, he noticed it was much easier to live with Carol's.

When shadow is denied and shunned, we must live from our defenses, protecting ourselves from the possibility that someone might wander into the "dark corners of our personality" and discover who we really are. It's a full-time job to keep ourselves out of our own dark corners, and it is considerably more challenging to make sure it remains a restricted area for our spouses. With our elaborate defenses in place, attempting to make sure that our shadows remain off-limits to our partners, it becomes literally impossible to flourish emotionally and spiritually, individually and collectively.

## Shadows Protecting Shadows

Some shadows act as a defense protecting us from other shadows. "Inflation" and "deflation" are such shadows that we bring to our marriages. We each find more comfort in one than the other, with some spouses being proficient at both.

Inflation includes but is not limited to excessive narcissism, hubris, abuses of power, and grandiosity. Deflation is often expressed through timidity, withdrawal, false modesty, and abdication of power. The goal in both cases is to control the parts of ourselves—whether they are what we deem as repugnant or the gold of our personality—that we simply will not accept.

Inflated spouses represent themselves as much larger than they actually are. They enjoy bringing attention to their accomplishments, their stories, and in some cases, their needs. They don't hesitate to place themselves in the limelight, where they believe they can control how they are perceived by others. The goal is to impress people or at least hold their attention, steering people away from shadows. The inflation process is so insidious that some partners actually see their spouses as confident. Even worse, the inflated may very well see themselves as confident!

Deflated spouses represent themselves as much smaller than they are. Their hope is to keep their shadow material discrete and under wraps. Like their inflated counterparts, they run the risk of their partners treating them as they present themselves—in this case, as small and insignificant. They also face the danger of actually seeing themselves as inadequate, being unable to appreciate their innate gifts and talents.

Most couples divide the pie evenly, with one spouse taking on the inflated posture while the other occupies the deflated position. Inflated spouses work hard at distracting themselves and others away from their shadows. Their grand gestures, aimed at portraying them as larger than life, drag them away from their essential humanity. Deflated spouses seldom take their rightful place with genuine demonstrations of their talents and strengths.

It very well may be that inflated spouses tend to fear shadow elements deemed socially unacceptable, while deflated spouses are challenged to accept the gold they placed in shadow. Neither spouse lives life as right-sized, where they might accept themselves for who they really are.

Shadow marriage requires couples to call in their beauty and their darkness. As we commit to our authenticity, we can begin to slowly dismantle these defenses that divide us from ourselves and make a genuine flow of love almost impossible.

If we are choosing to act much larger or smaller than we are, it makes it impossible for us to be loved, because who we really are has not yet arrived in the relationship.

The dilemma is that inflation and deflation are themselves in shadow; consequently, spouses are unaware of their tendency to aggrandize or shrivel. Our spouses can be a valuable resource if we want to nudge one of these defenses into the light of awareness.

We can ask our partners if they see us as inflated or deflated. How do you see me inflate or deflate? Are there particular situations where I am prone to employ my defense? How does my inflation or deflation affect my partner?

Once we have gathered some feedback from our partners, we can begin to consciously track our particular defense. We can gradually slide this shadow into sight. We can find out how we are really feeling during our inflated or deflated experiences, and find out if there is something that is difficult for us to accept about ourselves.

## Shadow Work

The first step toward deepening a capacity for a shadow marriage is to be willing to identify and learn to embrace the traits that sit in one's own shadow. The ego is an excellent sentry; it does not allow shadow to drift into consciousness, where it can tarnish our image. Consequently, it is not an easy task to identify personal shadows. Also, the tendency to shame shadow characteristics causes us to relegate these traits to the unconscious.

The more we need to deny our experience of shame, the more we condemn parts of our personality to shadow. This condemnation usually means we deny whatever characteristics stimulate shame in us; we live psychically amputated. A commitment to our own wholeness involves some dedication to making peace with shame.

The more we allow ourselves to feel shame, the greater the opportunity to work with the shame and diminish our need to sequester major parts of our personality into shadow. Facing shame calls for a great deal of courage. It means allowing ourselves to feel what it is like to temporarily lose any measure of personal worth.

The gift of shame is that with a minimum amount of awareness, we can become clear about the parts of us that we are refusing to accept. Of course, the prevailing question is: Why should I accept what I deem repugnant about me?

There are several reasons to be motivated about doing shadow work. The more we accept what we have decided is deplorable about us, the less likely those traits will explode into our relationships as if shadow has gone autonomous. What we resist persists. What we accept eases into the fabric of our personality; and, as it does, we usually have more control over it.

What we have decided is socially unacceptable about us is almost never only a liability. It is too easy to view traits like intolerance, selfishness, and jealousy as simply unfortunate and deserving of being banished from our psychological house. Many spouses relate to their partners with extreme tolerance, irrespective of how deplorable their behavior may be. Their excessive tolerance goes a long way toward enabling destructive behaviors and attitudes exhibited by their spouses.

Some spouses insist upon remaining focused upon their partner's needs, in the name of being thoughtful, sensitive, and loving; they do whatever they can to avoid self-centeredness. Although they are the first to define themselves as kind and generally good people, they inevitably develop a great deal of self-neglect, leading to resentment and cynicism as they continually feel let down by their partners.

Jealousy is often viewed as simply an unfortunate attribute that is better left denied in shadow, yet jealousy can often tell an important story. Jealous spouses may be alerted to some act of duplicity on behalf of their partners, or they may track their jealousy to better understand their own insecurity. In either case, jealousy can bring us closer to what is going on in our relationship or within ourselves.

A commitment to shadow work will customarily deepen our capacity for compassion. The more we accept about ourselves, the more we can accept about our partners. Our spouses will inevitably benefit from the compassion we extend to ourselves.

Lastly, shadow work generates an authentic confidence. Instead of pseudo-confidence, where we present ourselves as appropriate by denying both our unacceptable traits and our splendor, shadow work allows us to continue to make peace with our genuine selves. We are able to live close to our real selves and create the opportunity for our partners to love us for who we are.

My favorite way to track my shadows is to simply observe my reactions to people. "You wouldn't catch me doing that!" "I can't believe he's doing that!" "What the hell is wrong with her?" These reactions are great indicators that one of my shadows has been spotted in someone else's behavior. Of course, at first I'm convinced that there is no way I would ever exhibit such unacceptable behavior; but upon closer examination, it is highly likely that one of my shadows is lurking about.

Another simple way to identify shadow is to interview our spouses, asking what they see in the dark corners of our personalities. As long as our spouses are not overly zealous about their feedback, they can be valuable resources for information about our shadow traits.

Tracking projection is another effective method for identifying shadow. Like Peter's judgment of Carol's intensity, we can notice what judgments we carry of our spouses. The greater the charge accompanying our judgment, the greater the likelihood that we have projected some shadow element to our spouse. We can then begin to explore the objects of our judgment as they pertain to ourselves.

We can track our projections everywhere in our lives, noting what we judge in others, and begin considering the possibility that we may be seeing something about ourselves. Noticing our reactions to characters in films is another way to ferret out our projections. I recently attended the movie *Troy*. About midway into the film, I noticed that I was having a very intense adverse reaction to the pride exhibited by the character Agamemnon. I was at the edge of my seat in disgust and anger until I began to realize that I was projecting the shadow of my pride onto that particular character in the film.

Johnson explains that it is customary to also find auspicious characteristics in shadow:

> *It is also astonishing to find that some very good characteristics turn up in shadow. Generally, the ordinary, mundane characteristics are the norm. Anything less than this goes into shadow. But anything better also goes into shadow! Some of the pure gold of our personality is relegated to the shadow, because it can find no place in that great leveling process that is culture.*

Shadow is composed of the worst and the best in us. In a shadow marriage, spouses commit to themselves to identify and take ownership for their darkness and their gold. They understand that the goal is to integrate these qualities that live in the dark corners of the personality and welcome them back to the hearth. Each spouse accepts this responsibility, knowing that the price of exiling shadow is eventual self-sabotage and hurting those we most love.

A wonderful way for spouses to begin welcoming shadow is to sit facing one another in a space where there will be no distraction. It may be helpful to play some desired music and to light incense or a candle. Spouse *A* sits, focused upon his or her breath, while maintaining eye contact with spouse *B*. Spouse *B* begins to acknowledge the gold of Spouse *A* by very slowly listing the positive attributes of spouse *A*. When Spouse *B* has finished, they change roles, with *A* giving a voice to the gold of spouse *B*.

When the entire process is complete, it may be helpful to sit in silence and appreciate what has just transpired. Following the silence, each spouse might respond to questions such as: How did it feel to hear me acknowledge what I see as your gold? How difficult or easy was it to take in the acknowledgment? Which traits listed are you prepared to own? Which traits do you resist owning?

This exercise is not about exchanging pleasantries. It's about offering our spouses an opportunity to hear how we experience the gold of their shadow.

Couples can also help to identify the more distasteful traits that lie in shadow. The setting can be designed in a similar manner as the previous exercise. Spouse *A* says, "Are you open to hearing two darker traits that I experience in your shadow?" (Limit this process to two.) If spouse *B* agrees, then *A* continues by saying, "One darker element that I see in your shadow is ___, and I experience it when you ___." Spouse *A* goes on to ask, "How does it feel to hear me reference this darker aspect of your shadow? Have you ever thought about the possibility that this darker element might lie in your shadow? If you see this darker trait as part of you, can you imagine accepting it? What judgments prevent you from accepting this particular trait?" *A* continues by identifying a second displeasing aspect of spouse *B*'s shadow. Following the questions, the spouses switch roles.

The purpose of this exercise is not to attack or berate our spouses. We are offering ourselves as shadow resources for our spouses. The exercise should not be attempted while a couple is dealing with some heavy unresolved issue.

Shadow and marriage may go together like a horse and carriage. When we deny our shadow, we practically guarantee those traits will be acted out in some unconscious way, having a damaging impact upon our marriages. The other injurious path involves spouses projecting shadow onto their partners, resulting in responses from harsh criticism to severe avoidance.

The third unconscious treatment of shadow is denial of the shadow gold, where spouses refuse to claim the uniquely wondrous parts of themselves. When this occurs, a marriage is reduced to a liaison driven by mediocrity and the maintenance of a generic expression of nuptial intimacy.

These three unmindful ways of approaching shadow grind down the very foundation of a marriage, leaving it vulnerable to the winds and erosion of alienation. A couple that has been battered by shadow denial and projection will ultimately experience a deep and immobilizing impotency that will have them welcoming the relief of separation and divorce.

## Shadow Prowess

I once heard it said that aging is not for babies; neither is shadow work, nor is marriage. It is the essential business of the soul to make peace with what has been discarded and shunned. Soul appears to long for itself, endlessly welcoming all its many faces.

Nothing calls for a capacity to endure shame more than shadow work. As we glimpse what is socially unacceptable about ourselves, we are naturally thrust into shame. What kind of strength allows us to experience the bite of shame without having to deny it or be swallowed by it? It may be, in part, a fortitude that deepens as we accept that no one is coming to save us, nor are we here to "get life right."

Giving up the wait to be delivered from the chains of shame is one of the great milestones of genuine adulthood. It is the choice to be the saved and the savior. It is the willingness to let go of childhood fantasies that suggest we might be able to go through life without claiming responsibility for safeguarding our essential goodness. We would prefer to wait for the Benevolent Father, whose blessing will make all well with us. Once we accept that opening to shadow will rain shame down upon us, and when we accept the responsibility to breathe life back into our goodness, we will have gone a long way toward deepening our capacity to engage shadow.

Efforts toward "getting it right" reek of perfectionism and induce us to move away from shadow work. "Getting it right" implies several anti-shadow postures. Of course, there is the obvious illusion that we can actually get life right. Such an attitude is characteristic of modernity, and I believe it is insulting to the Great Mystery. We attempt to comfort ourselves by attaching to the illusion that we can overcome the Mystery and its accompanying insecurity, only to fall prey to our human limitations over and over again.

"Getting it right" also implies that the restraints of our humanity somehow make us flawed and defective. The suggestion seems to be that we should be transcending the human condition, rather than making peace with it. Strides toward "getting it right" are often clever ways to distract us away from just how much is already right. As we have discussed, owning our gold can be just as challenging as claiming what we decide is objectionable about ourselves. Those of us who fear being inflated will normally be seriously challenged when it comes to owning our talents.

My suggestion is to see the honoring of our gifts as a simple celebration of ourselves and of life. There is no need to take the celebration so seriously! It's a party—time to dance and sing. We can welcome our gifts with joy and lightness.

During graduate school, I was about to begin a new semester, and I felt anxious about studying with a professor who had gained international notoriety. I asked my adviser what he thought about this man of stature. He paused briefly and said, "Ken truly knows how to enjoy his popularity."

I knew I was hearing something that might help my own gold. My adviser sounded like he was talking about a man's relationship to playing golf or sailing. He enjoyed his popularity. Shouldn't it be more complicated than that? It was the first time I thought that maybe we are simply supposed to enjoy our gifts and their expression.

The capacity to enjoy our finer attributes may be one of the greatest gifts we can offer our marriages. We can define our marriages as a place to identify and enjoy our natural endowments. The voice of love can define marriage as a place where gifts are witnessed and celebrated, a place where we are encouraged to be as much of ourselves as we dare.

Herman Hesse's great novel *Siddhartha* depicts vividly this theme of needing to "get it right." Siddhartha is a young man determined to "get it right," and in order to do so, he joins an ascetic community, where holy men teach him the spiritual practices that will enable him to "get it right." He begins to question the legitimacy of this training and wonders whether it will afford true enlightenment. Siddhartha decides to leave the erudite confines of this spiritual community. As he walks down the road away from this edifice of enlightenment, he begins to loosen his grip upon his need to "get it right." As he does so, a significant shadow dislodges from his unconscious and breaks into the light. He becomes aware of his own being when he utters, "I'm afraid of myself."

Siddhartha's awareness may be what holds many of us to the enslavement of trying to "get it right." We're afraid we won't forgive what we find in our shadow. We're afraid we will judge ourselves mercilessly. And yet the very thing we fear, we produce. We strive to "get it right" again and again, only to fall prey to our own shameful lashings.

When we remain in waiting for the promised one or continue to strive to "get it right," we engage in thanatophilia—love of death. Our choices become rigid, constricting, stripping us of vitality and depressing our passions. The more we claim the responsibility to save ourselves by restoring our own goodness and letting go of trying to "get it right," the more we allow ourselves "biophilia." Fear of life is replaced by love of life. We are grateful for the opportunity to allow life to touch us; we create who we are; we gladly make choices that bring us to a meeting with our destiny, and forgive ourselves again and again.

When we are not attempting to "get it right," we are loving life and forgiving ourselves. The strength of our loving and our forgiving affords us the chance to wander down into shadow, unearthing what we have banished about ourselves, so that we might see the diamond emerging from a piece of petrified coal.

## Nuptial Gifts

The willingness to open to shadow work may be one of the greatest gifts we can give to and receive from our spouses. The more comfortable we are working with our own shadow material, the less likely we will position ourselves as victims of our partners. A diminished perception of victimization greatly contributes to our ability to deepen intimacy with our partners. We are less likely to attempt to protect ourselves by either attacking with blame and ridicule or being predisposed to emotionally walling off our partners.

Shadow work enables us to be more intimate with ourselves and to reclaim ourselves, allowing us to bring more of who we are to a relationship. Our level of authenticity deepens as we are less concerned about how we present, and more interested in offering our partners our gifts along with what is less than laudable. The more we reclaim what is abrasive and untoward, the less probable it is that it will exist in the relationship as if it has a mind of its own, hurting those we most love.

Shadow work deepens the capacity for self-empowerment; when we find ourselves locked in conflict with our partners, we may be less likely to attempt to influence our partners, let them influence us, or need to withdraw from them. We can begin to feel some ease about looking inward and discovering how we might be contributing to an impasse. Looking inward brings with it some control that we do not have when we hold our spouses responsible for our predicaments.

The best way to access power and control is simply to ask: What does this dilemma say about me? It won't be helpful to respond to this question shamefully or in a way that is belittling; those kinds of responses are not creative. Rather, we need to answer the question by describing concrete choices or attitudes that may have contributed to the quagmire.

It takes practice and time to take responsibility for the stuck places in our relationships without adding an indictment. Slowly, we begin to witness ourselves as very personal expressions of the human condition, rather than as people who do not "get marriage right."

Shadow work inevitably makes us better equipped to deal with darkness. I am defining darkness as the challenges presented to us by life and by our destinies. Darkness is not about our souls. It is about the crisis and the hardships which are a necessary part of life—the loss of jobs, the loss of loved ones, illness, accidents, and all the other ways that life decides to disrupt the harmony of our lives.

Seth came to see me about one year after an automobile accident that left him without the use of his left arm; his left leg was amputated. Luckily, he was no stranger to shadow work which helped him to get honest about how he felt about God and himself. Many of our sessions involved Seth raging at God and voicing his self-loathing as a reflection of his damaged body.

He was willing to surrender to the power of this darkness that had mutilated him and left him feeling like half a man. Seth soon realized that he would need to find something other than a strong agile body in order to support his personal worth. Like a shadow trait, his disability challenged him to find his value in what was real about him, rather than what should be or could be.

Seth was willing to grieve his losses and turn his attention toward deepening his capacity to love himself and others. He faced his darkness, surrendered to it, and allowed it to initiate him. Seth died several years after we met. His wife's words remain with me: "Seth knew darkness. He knew how to protest it with all of his heart and he knew how to surrender to it, learn from it, and eventually accept his destiny and rekindle his love of life."

Contrary to popular belief, faith does not arise in us like a geyser streaming forth as the result of some fortuitous epiphany. Many of us experience a temporary renewal of faith as we watch scenes from films like *It's A Wonderful Life,* or when we witness our children receiving diplomas and degrees on graduation day. These experiences simply offer a momentary inspiration that suggests that our stay on earth is not completely meaningless; however, these beautifully touching moments will not forge an enduring faith in ourselves and in life.

Shadow work is by its very nature redemptive. It is not meant to make us better people; it is meant to have us make peace with ourselves and with our humanity, over and over again. We dare look for what we have exiled within ourselves, and welcome it back. We are both the prodigal son and the forgiving father. We accept that we will lose our way, acting without integrity, violating what we value and cherish; and we continue to extend a compassionate hand to ourselves. As we do, we continue to witness the innate goodness of our partners.

As we try to balance our need to be connected to our partners while remaining loyal to ourselves, we will act abusively, neglectfully, and irresponsibly either toward our partners or toward ourselves. These conditions set the stage for impasse, irreconcilable differences, and unresolved conflict. Shadow work offers a way to turn, a way to access some dimension of power in the midst of chaos and confusion.

The faith of childhood is based upon someone outside of ourselves who will care for us, treat us well, and remember that we are deserving of love. In adulthood, this person can easily become our spouse. Shadow work replaces this naive faith with a deeper belief in the creative process of marriage.

Marriage calls us to what has been shunned and denied within ourselves. Letting go of blaming our partners and turning our attention toward what we have forgotten about ourselves enable us to remember who we are, and on a good day, to reclaim who we are. Marriage offers us the opportunity to believe in our ability to stop running from ourselves no matter how scared we are of what we might find within.

Shadow work is a profound way to renew our faith in love and its power to set us right with ourselves. We can begin to see marriage as life's way of making us more capable of holding the far reaches of our experience. Shadow work calls us to the inner frontier, where we can embrace life more fully. We learn to believe in the dance of our wills with our destinies. We experience a faith in our partnership with life, letting creativity and discovery replace constriction and mediocrity. Our marriages become a way to wed life.

## Shadow of Shadow Work

I am often asked if shadow work itself has a shadow. Where there is light, there will be shadow. The shadow of this work shows up as unconscious attempts either to influence or to be excessively accommodating. Spouses can use their personal shadow work as a way to cajole their partners into submitting to their own shadow work. We can hear attempts at influence in exclamations such as: "I'm willing to work on myself—what about you?" "I wish you would examine your own behavior as much as I do; I'm the only one willing to take responsibility for what goes wrong around here."

Generally, spouses who are the objects of influence retreat more from their shadow work. Also, attempts at influence may reflect fear on behalf of the spouse who attempts to exercise influence. Rather than indulging in strategies of influence, it may serve us well to uncover the nature of the fear driving our need to influence our partners.

Accommodation is the other shadow of shadow work. Spouses committed to shadow work can over-romanticize the process, imbuing it with magical powers. We can excessively tolerate our spouses' resistance to get on with their own work, in the hope that our continued dedication will on its own, transform our marriages. We may be greatly disillusioned as we begin to accept that we cannot create a marriage alone. Accommodators would do well to attend to the shadow material of uncovering their resistance to accepting their limits.

If spouses are willing to unearth their more repugnant shadow traits and hold them with some measure of acceptance and compassion, they inevitably lose their caustic impact upon the marriage. And if each partner is willing to claim his or her own gold, the marriage becomes a breeding ground for celebration and the stewardship of personal gifts. The capacity to do shadow work will become necessary, as considerable tension is created by attempting to be connected to our partners while supporting our individual autonomy. This pressure is a reflection of the potency of a marriage to initiate us to our depths.

# 3

## *Nuptial Initiation*

Initiation rites in indigenous cultures are often formidable, exposing the initiate to the possibility of the loss of a body part, or even life itself. Initiations are, by their nature, potentially hazardous, and marriage is no different. Marriage is a dangerous initiation, and not designed for the meek of heart.

The root of the word "initiation" is "beginning" or "birth," and every new beginning is accompanied by some ending or death. In the film *The Emerald Forest*, the elders of an indigenous tribe, adorned in their ritual garb, approach a teenage boy and declare, "It's time for you to die, boy!" Their pronouncement heralds the upcoming ritual that will mark the teenager's death as a boy and his birth as a man. What makes marriage such a rich container for initiation is both the quantity and depth of the beginnings and endings that will surely take place.

Spouses will undergo numerous challenges, which will lead them to their individual depths as well as to their collective acuity. A couple's beliefs about an ideal marriage will die and give birth to new, more realistic views, which hopefully will not be unduly contaminated by cynicism and diminished faith. Other initiatory areas include betrayal, trust, giving and receiving love, exercising power, negotiating, maintaining personal freedom, the roles of responsibility and accountability, sex, money, and parenting. Marriage may very well be the most powerful container for initiation on the planet.

Some years ago, a client of mine was approaching his fiftieth birthday. He came to his session and declared that he was prepared to offer himself a rite of passage in honor of his fiftieth birthday. He explained that he was contemplating a monastic trek in Tibet. When I asked what he hoped to gain from his initiation, he explained that he was seeking new emotional and soulful depths within himself. I pointed out that his Tibetan plan would probably produce some desired results, but if he really wanted a profound rite of passage, then falling in love and getting himself into a committed relationship was definitely the way to go.

At first, my client thought I was simply being playful. I reassured him of my seriousness and went on to explain how a committed relationship has the power to thrust us into the most exuberant parts of ourselves as well as the darkest corners of our souls.

Nothing boggles the human mind more than the sanctity and the curse of falling in love. Normally, after getting a whiff of the fragrance of falling in love, we either rush forward or run away. Once touched by the enchantment, we know that something big may happen to us. Of course, the lure usually jolts the romantic initiate into grandiose fantasies of everlasting love and happiness.

We are bewitched by the possibility of uniting with our soul mate, the one with whom the gods deemed we should spend eternity. We may also be frightened to step into the vulnerable realm of romance, where we may be hurt and rejected. It is the willingness to favorably respond to the invitation of enchantment that makes us ready for a nuptial initiation. In the words of Joseph Campbell, we simply need to make the decision to "follow our bliss."

## Initiatory Preparation

If the first step of preparing for initiation is allowing ourselves to be touched by the enchantment of falling in love, then the second piece of the preparation is getting both feet in the relationship. This business of having two feet in the relationship typically goes unspoken in many marriages. In fact, if being married means having two feet in the relationship, then almost no one gets married on the day of their wedding.

Being married, or having two feet in, can be depicted using the following images: closing our hearts to others as possible life partners; closing the exits; choosing the relationship as the place where we decide to deepen ourselves; holding a vision of a future with our partners. These phrases suggest a level of commitment, devotion, and, above all, a readiness to embark upon one of the most challenging initiations: marriage. Although this idea of "having two feet in" is a metaphor and somewhat vague, I am always amazed how clear people are about the status of their feet when they decide to get honest.

The readiness to experience a nuptial initiation is a leap of faith, since there is no actual preparation. There is only some level of enchantment and then, for whatever reason, the choice to place both feet in. There is no way of making ourselves stronger, more enlightened, better-equipped, or more skillfully ready to deal with the initiation. In his book, *Passionate Marriage,* David Schnarch describes marriage as a "people-making machine." The very purpose of marriage is to help the initiate's adolescent attitudes and behaviors die and to birth deeper aspects of adulthood. The purpose of marriage is to help people grow up.

The work of Mircea Eliade and Joseph Campbell suggests that initiations have three separate stages: separation, trial and resolution, and the return. We can track these three stages of initiation within a marriage, showing how each unfolds and the challenges facing the initiate at each stage, and identify resources that may serve the initiate along the way.

Spouses experience a reprieve from the bite of initiation during the honeymoon of the relationship. This euphoric period normally lasts four to ten months. During this time, a couple continues to ride the wave of enchantment characterized by idealizations of one another and a preoccupation with how much they have in common. Harmony is the order of the day.

The honeymoon period usually ends when diverse values and choices begin to indicate just how different one person is from the other. Discord and conflict begin to show up, signaling the end of the honeymoon and the start of nuptial initiation. A typical response to the contention is to doubt the worth of the relationship. Such a reaction reflects the belief that an intimate relationship should be an endless experience of enchantment.

## Separation

Separation, the first stage of a nuptial initiation, occurs as three distinct fears become aroused in the relationship. The fear of losing our partners and the fear of losing ourselves can be viewed as death fears. Our bodies experience the fear of abandonment and the fear of being consumed as an experience of dying. The third fear is a fear of experiencing too much life. We can experience one fear or all three; normally, one fear is dominant.

The fear of losing our partners is probably self-explanatory. However, it may be worth noting that the fear of losing our partners can occur on several different levels. The most obvious loss is where they simply walk out of our lives and want nothing further to do with us. For many of us, this is the abandonment that we have feared for most of our lives. However, we can lose our partners in many subtle ways. They can emotionally withdraw from us, physically distance themselves, remove support, and withhold sex and affection.

When we fear losing our partners, the typical reaction is to become more accommodating, more yielding, and more apt to acquiesce to the needs and wishes of our partners. This tendency toward compliance pulls and tugs us away from our own desires and needs, causing us to separate from ourselves. Another common reaction when we fear losing our partners is to attempt to influence them. The more we badger our spouses, the more they normally withdraw. Our coercion takes us out of our own hearts and separates us from our best wisdom and from ourselves.

When we fear losing ourselves, we push away from our partners, prioritizing our own personal agendas, focusing upon our wishes, and viewing our partners as a potential threat to our individuality and independence. We eagerly attempt to protect ourselves while separating from our partners.

Our culture is inclined to see the fear of losing our partners as codependent, desperate, and often genderized as female; while the fear of losing ourselves is viewed as fear of commitment, fear of intimacy, neurosis, and genderized as male. My clinical experience strongly suggests that neither fear can be conveniently attributed to a particular gender. I have worked with many women who fear losing themselves, and many men who are afraid of losing their partners.

Both fears reflect a resistance to seeing ourselves for who we are and an unwillingness to accept what we see. Nothing has the power to bring us face to face with ourselves like a marriage. We say we are afraid of losing ourselves, when the truth is that what we see is our propensity to give ourselves away, or some other shadow quality that is difficult for us to accept about ourselves. We may be losing ourselves or our ability to value ourselves, but it is likely that it has nothing to do with our partners.

We claim we are afraid of losing our partners, but we are either afraid of being alone or we hold our partners responsible for loving and valuing us when we don't feel up to the task. In either case, we have personal business to attend to, which is mostly about our relationship to ourselves and not our partners.

Our fear of experiencing too much life often results in either emotional or physical withdrawal from the relationship. Nothing arouses more energy in our bodies than an intimate relationship. Nothing demands more of our attention than tender, abiding love coming right at us.

We all learn to cope with the neglect and deprivation of our childhoods by learning how to adapt to these holes and find ways to make peace with our want. We grow accustomed to and even comfortable with emotional morsels, learning to make do, rather than to endure the tension of dissatisfaction. Then it happens. Love and attention come to us in waves, and we are literally swept off our feet, not knowing how to allow ourselves to be bathed in amorous waters.

Our culture teaches us to be ashamed of our fears; therefore, in order to avoid the sting of shame, we deny our fear and get a temporary reprieve from feeling shamed. But because we are denying our fear of losing our partners, our fear of losing ourselves, or our fear of too much life, the fear finds other creative expressions. We find ourselves abusing our partners, abusing ourselves, or withdrawing from the relationship. We can't escape our fear, or the abuse and sabotage that our fear brings down upon our relationships.

Don and Helen, a middle-aged couple, were in the middle of their first session with me when it became clear to me that they each had both feet in their relationship and had entered into the separation stage of an initiation.

"I love Don and I enjoy being with him. It's just that he never seems satisfied. He always wants more of me. I don't have time for myself," explained Helen, as her fear of losing herself wove its way through her words.

"I hear that you're concerned about losing yourself to Don's expectations and not having time for yourself," I reflected.

"Yes, he doesn't seem to get enough of me. I love him and all, but I think that he is overly possessive or maybe even codependent," Helen suggested, willing to blame Don for her dilemma and pathologize him.

"You seem to be blaming Don for what's happening to you," I said.

"Well, he's always pressuring me. He pressures me for sex, to take more vacations, to play tennis more often. He's constantly in my face!" she exclaimed.

"Tell me how you handle all this pressure. I'm assuming that Don goes to work, at which time you get a temporary reprieve from the pressure," I offered, with tongue in cheek.

"I'm not handling it well! I tell you, it's too much! Something has got to change!" explained Helen, her eyes filling with tears.

"I hear it's overwhelming for you, and I'm interested in how you've been dealing with it," I said, hoping Helen would stay focused on how she was coping.

"I tell him *no* a lot and try to stay busy," she responded.

"How do you feel about saying *no* so much?" I asked.

"Guilty! I feel very guilty," she responded, her voice cracking.

"If Don would only stop hounding you, you might get a reprieve from your guilt," I suggested.

"Exactly!" exclaimed Helen.

"Unfortunately, you have no control over the degree of hounding that Don decides to exercise," I pointed out. Helen looked a bit surprised at my comment.

Helen was separating from her own goodness, and she was ready to blame her husband for her dilemma. This is a good example of the potency of the separation stage.

Helen was being called by her initiation to become more accountable for her emotions. We spent several sessions examining how she not only held Don responsible for her guilt but also held him responsible for any unpleasant emotion she experienced in her marriage. Helen began to understand how her guilt sometimes inhibited her from saying *no* to Don and from resenting him for her acquiescence. On other occasions, she would deliver her *no* harshly, punishing Don for even asking for her attention.

On a very basic level, Helen needed to learn how to identify and express her fear of losing herself in her marriage. She discovered that whenever she had felt scared as a child, her father would shame her by calling her names and belittling her. She had gradually learned to hide her fear from others, and eventually, from herself. She was being summoned by her initiation to reclaim her fear and restore forgotten parts of herself. Her challenge was to identify her fear, without shame, and learn to express it to her husband.

Helen began to notice that the more she made peace with her fear, the less time she spent analyzing and assessing Don's behavior. She gradually let go of Don's behavior as a distraction from her fear, allowing herself to become clearer about her role in the marriage, her strengths, and her shortcomings. The case she incessantly had been building against Don gradually lost its ferocity as her indictment of him was put to rest.

Helen's explorations of how she had lost herself in her marriage gradually led her to discover she was lost in a deeper way than simply her role as spouse. She had received numerous awards for creative writing as a college student and did not pursue her craft following school. Her fear of losing herself in her marriage was likely accentuated by the loss of her creativity. It was as if she were yelling out, "You can't take any more of me! I've already lost too much!"

Unlike Helen, who was afraid of losing herself and subsequently moving further away from Don, Don was afraid of losing Helen. The more he feared losing her, the more he would defer to Helen, becoming excessively accommodating of her wishes and generally taking on an acquiescing posture in the marriage. Don operated under the illusion that he could keep Helen in the marriage by being more yielding. In one session, Helen admitted that the only impact Don's deference had upon her was that she was losing respect for him. Don was confronting the fantasy that his strategies could control his wife's love and attention.

Don's initiation was not only calling him to see how helpless he was in regard to making Helen love him, but he was also willing to take a larger view of his life and the role of control. Don began to see how ineffective he was at discerning what was in his control and what was not. His introspection also led him to see that Helen was really his only source of emotional support. He better understood why he had such a strong investment in being connected to her. He also grasped that generating friends and a workable support system was in his control, and that to rely solely upon Helen placed a great deal of burden on her and set him up for disappointment.

Our therapeutic work helped Don to see that his fear of losing Helen was separating him from himself, and Helen understood that her fear of losing herself was separating her from her husband. Their separate initiations took them into regions of themselves where old attitudes and patterns of relatedness were dying, giving rise to the birth of new ways of seeing themselves and one another. They were beginning to move into the second stage of their initiation: trial and resolution.

## Trial and Resolution

During the trial, each spouse may be severely tested. This is a time when demons are aroused. The initiate will suffer, fears will be stirred, loathing will awaken, and anguish and emptiness may persist.

The initiate's response to the test constitutes the resolution. Broadly speaking, initiates will either move more deeply toward infantile and adolescent patterns of thinking and acting, or descend into greater depths of self and greater depths of intimacy. Either is possible. The psyche abhors the status quo.

Resolution often resembles resignation. When the initiate meets some demon and decides to postpone the demonic engagement, the creative forces guiding the marriage are also postponed. The result is a choice to live in emptiness or to get emotional needs met through the children, an affair, or work. There is also a regressive tendency to move into parent-child roles, where one spouse acts as a parent and the other a child.

All marriages slip in and out of parent-child dynamics. If one spouse is ill or despondent, then that spouse may temporarily be cared for by the other spouse in a way that may look and feel parental. A marriage can be debilitating when spouses lock into these roles over extended periods of time. The spouse playing the parental role can feel burdened by excessive responsibility, resentful, bitter, and lonely. The spouse in the child role feels inadequate, helpless, resentful, and excessively dependent. The common experience of both spouses is resentment.

When resolution translates into resentment, there is usually a heavy price being paid by both partners, and mutual blame is the order of the day. Resentment allows each spouse to stay focused upon the other, delaying a rendezvous with his or her own particular demon.

When the trial and resolution stage is characterized by deep resentment, it becomes extremely easy for both partners to move into resignation, with separation and divorce being popular alternatives. One common response to the challenges of the trial is simply to run.

If the initiate gets scared enough, running away can become quite attractive. The key is to find enough support, resiliency, courage, and heart to see the trial through to a resolution that feels life-affirming and genuine. If a couple has difficulty clarifying what resolution might work for them, then they might ask what they would advocate for their children or for friends experiencing a similar trial.

There are several reasons why the stage of trial and resolution often ends up being so destructive for most marriages. The primary reason is that during this time, initiates are facing the mystery and the darkness of themselves and their marriage. They also enter the trial having been contaminated by cultural illusions of nuptial bliss. Consequently, the trial can stimulate a great deal of disillusionment. However, the depth of a trial can be measured by the degree to which initiates are willing to allow the disillusionment to be about their beliefs rather than the moral integrity of their partners or the inherent value of their marriage.

## The Gift of Disillusionment

Disillusionment, although painful and often disheartening, is the decomposition of illusions. Childhood is a time to dream and create idyllic visions of life's opportunities. The trial erodes these quixotic images, replacing them with more genuine accounts of life and what it means to participate fully in a marriage. The experience of disillusionment is a death of quintessential perspectives of the human condition. Beliefs that once comforted us break down, no longer able to offer us the reassurance and amenity they once afforded us.

The trials experienced by most spouses pummel some of our most sanctimonious beliefs and ideals. Our convictions about love, trust, integrity, commitment, and loyalty are commonly called into question during the trial, leaving the initiate deeply disillusioned and grief-stricken. As old beliefs unwind, so does our security and our hold upon a future that held promises of happiness and joy. We are now grieving and we are lost.

Our culture finds grieving and being lost to be repugnant. The problem is that there is no way to grow up unless we learn to grieve and learn how to be lost. Our childhood visions of life and of ourselves must die. Before they are replaced with more reliable accounts, we will be lost. The most common reactions during the trial are to deny the grief, blame our spouses, and allow ourselves to be beguiled by a myriad of distractions aimed at helping us pretend we are not lost.

This combination of denial and pretense almost guarantees that initiates will not benefit from the potential transformative power of the trial. What dies must be grieved or it takes up residence in the psyche, accompanied by rationalization and delusion, determined to give initiates some temporary relief from the heartache of the trial. Who is lost must authentically be lost or else cling to old beliefs that have outlived their credibility which leaves initiates with the constricted and limited vision of childhood.

The human psyche abhors immobility. It will either move forward or eagerly regress. If we cannot find the faith and the fortitude to endure grief and be lost, we will retreat to the confines of childhood, even less equipped to have meaningful relationships than we were prior to our trial. We are either undoing childhood attitudes or strengthening them.

Our culture invites us to sabotage our trials and do whatever is required to maintain the diminished maturity of childhood. Our principal cultural myth is that life is basically understandable, and that with the right education, job, financial investments, spouse, and neighborhood, life can be secure and predictable.

This pipe dream flies in the face of all ancient wisdom, which instructs us that life is essentially mysterious, insecure, and highly unpredictable. Very powerful marketing is driven by the suggestion that some product or service will help demystify life and restore security.

I was recently speaking with a publicist about representing my first book. He explained how he was planning to present me as an expert in my field. I responded by suggesting that it appeared to me that the world was inundated with experts. I further pointed out that to think of myself as an expert on life's mystery seemed both arrogant and absurd. At best, we all get an opportunity to be students.

Following the conversation, it became apparent to me that the entire hullabaloo about experts is mostly about the search for a parent who will demystify life and make our way more secure. The thinking is that if we can surround ourselves with enough experts, we won't have to feel the anxiety associated with a perilous journey. No expert is going to be able to make life more secure and predictable for us. The quest for an expert is another tactic aimed at resisting our own maturation. It only keeps us in the confines of adolescence as we defer responsibility and power to some purported expert.

I witnessed how far-reaching our craving for experts can take us while I was a member of a reputable public-speaking organization. The driving philosophy of the group was that you should begin promoting yourself as an expert. There was little or no emphasis placed upon the professional development of genuine competencies. The protocol was simply this: by hook or by crook, represent yourself as an expert and gear up for success.

We are willing to sacrifice the acquisition of authentic skills in order to attain financial success. We are willing to affiliate ourselves with alleged experts in order to temporarily reduce the tension of life's mystery and insecurity. However, the price is high when we turn in the direction of the expert and away from the wisdom that our trials are meant to unearth.

Marriage is an immense initiation into the mystery of our own souls and into the mystery of life. There are no marriage experts! There are some very good students of marriage, and it may serve us to periodically listen to what they are learning.

It is easy for us to blame the inevitable pain of our trials on the neurotic tendencies of our spouses. After all, Hollywood has made it clear that all would be well if we were in a relationship with our soul mates rather than the imbeciles who somehow maneuvered into our lives. The most popular belief is that life will be significantly enhanced by the acquisition of a new and improved partner. This also allows the exiting spouse to renew an attachment to the cultural myth that life can be understandable and secure as long as you have the right stuff and the right spouse.

Don and Helen learned much about the separation stage of their nuptial initiation and were about to enter into the depths of their trial. The three of us were working in a session when Don became visibly sullen and withdrawn.

"Don, you seem unusually quiet this evening," I suggested.

"I guess I'm pretty tired," he responded. This was followed by a heavy silence that weighed down on all three of us.

"You seem distant and pensive," I said, watching his eyes moisten and his bottom lip quiver.

"I don't know how to say this. I've been having an affair with Theresa from work," he confessed, looking shocked, as if his words surprised even him.

"You've been doing what?" cried Helen, jumping out of her chair.

"Helen, I'd like you to sit back down," I instructed.

"You've been screwing another woman while you've been pestering me for sex? I can't believe this! But I sure as hell want some explanation!" Helen demanded.

"I don't know what to say. I never meant for it to go so far. I mean, I don't know if I love her, and I certainly didn't want to hurt you," explained Don.

Don and Helen were now in the grips of the trial that potentially could open them to unexplored places in themselves. But before any meaningful exploration could take place, they would both need to grieve and allow themselves to be lost. I asked them both if they would be willing to remain in couples therapy. They agreed, and Don agreed to stop seeing Theresa during our work together.

## Resources for the Trial

Don's initial attempts at negotiating his trial were aimed at flogging himself for his behavior, in the hope that Helen might show mercy and also decide to stay in the marriage. Helen, on the other hand, was determined to make Don pay, no matter how obsequious Don insisted upon being. It would be several sessions before Don was willing to let go of abdicating his power, while Helen was coming to terms with her reluctance to stop abusing power. As they both began to settle into our work, I explained that a nuptial trial stimulates deep and challenging emotions, to which many couples respond by making each other wrong or castigating their relationship. I also pointed out that there were some important ways that they could support themselves during their trial:

*Learn to identify and express emotions rather than blame or accuse the other in order to explain or justify emotions.*

*Remain radically self-responsible during the trial.* Because of the anger and fear accompanying most trials, it's easy to blame one another rather than take responsibility for what is happening. Self-responsibility can be guided by several key questions: How did I contribute to the creation of the ordeal I now find myself in? How do I feel about my contribution? What does this experience remind me of from my past? What is this trial calling me to within myself?

*Nothing serves an initiate more during a trial than remaining a student of the trial.* A common way to deal with anxiety and stress is to puff up by pretending not to be lost and making quick decisions. Claims to knowledge and decisiveness have a way of temporarily making the initiate feel back in control. It's an illusion. The trial is in control, and it serves the initiate to learn about surrendering to the terms of the trial. The ordeal is working on the initiate so something within can die and something else can be born. The trial is a kind of labor room. I don't recommend attempting to take control or running off. It's a time to surrender to the contractions of the psyche and allow the birthing process to take place. Like a fetus that is ceasing to be a symbiotic being floating in fluid, the initiate will experience the trauma of departing from the familiar and descending into the unknown.

*Resist the lure of victimhood.* Helplessness and hopelessness are inevitable feelings during a trial, and they easily seduce initiates into identifying themselves as victims of their ordeal. Deepening self-responsibility usually will restore some sense of personal empowerment. Surrendering to the dying process helps remind us that we are participating in something larger than ourselves that is aimed at deepening our capacity to engage life.

*Get a mentor.* A person who truly studies the terrain can be helpful. I recommend an interview with a prospective mentor, to help to clarify the person's suitability. Like securing the services of a particular guide who has climbed our mountain of choice, we want a guide well-acquainted with the trial stage of a nuptial initiation. The mentor's knowledge needs to be the result of firsthand experience, rather than information gathered by way of some academic pursuit. Doesn't the idea of hiring a guide who has only read about the mountain seem a bit strange?

*Create a viable same-gender support system.* I once recommended to a couple that they each generate a support system that works for them. In the following session, they explained that they were reluctant to get support from friends who would take sides and "bad-mouth" their partner. I understood immediately that we needed to talk about the nature of viable same-gender support. I explained that it was certainly beneficial to have friends who had also accessed same-gender support that really worked; however, regardless of the kinds of experiences their friends had, they could explain to their friends what kind of support would best serve them. I explained that it was okay to ask them not to take sides or to verbally assault their partner. I pointed out that they could suggest that their friends witness the challenges they faced in their trials. They could also ask questions that helped to deepen the support they offered: What can I do to be most helpful to you? What do you want from me? Is there anything I'm doing that is not helpful?

Each person approaches these supportive strategies differently.

Don and Helen initially were both resistant to being self-responsible. Helen wanted to blame Don for his unforgivable infidelity, while Don disabled himself with endless bouts of shame.

Helen's need to blame Don kept her a victim of Don and prevented her from being a student of her trial. Helen had great resistance to the self-responsible question: How have I contributed to the ordeal I now face? It took several sessions before Helen was willing to move beyond her blame and anger, and embrace her hurt and pain. She sat before me with her face in her hands, weeping uncontrollably and allowing her tears to erode the foundation of her self-righteousness and open her to a new way to understand her ordeal, a way that would include the choices she had made to get to where she was.

She gradually accepted that she had participated in her own betrayal by pushing Don away. It wasn't that she had magically created it; she had simply participated. She also began to deepen her ability to learn from her trial by becoming curious about the role of betrayal in her life.

Helen spoke of her mother's overbearing presence in her life. She described how her mother took her emotionally hostage, dictating everything from the way she should dress to how she should think. Her mother's tentacles found their way into almost every aspect of Helen's life, leaving very little space for her individuality to take root and flower.

The resolution of Helen's ordeal became clearer as she acknowledged how frightened she remained of her mother and how challenging it was to employ the kind of boundaries that would prevent her mother from usurping the heart of her spirit. Helen also began to grasp the intensity of the anger and rage she felt toward her mother but had directed toward her husband. Helen was allowing her trial to bring her closer to where she came from and closer to the truth of who she was. She had surrendered to an initiation by betrayal.

Don beat himself up regularly in the hope that Helen would call off her indictment. He had been feeling extremely angry at Helen because she had distanced herself from him. Rather than confront her, he acted it out by having an affair. Don preferred to be a victim of his own self-attack rather than to get honest about the anger and rage toward Helen that he carried.

## Resolution

Don had been significantly isolated and heavily dependent upon Helen. I encouraged him to join a men's group, where he might shed his need to punish himself and his wife. Don's trial was making him feel quite desperate, which was helping him to let go of his isolation and access more support.

Don joined the men's group, and the men encouraged him to get honest about his anger in all aspects of his life. The whole idea of being deeply angry frightened Don, and his fear became the cauldron for his resolution. He gradually became willing to see how much fear and anger defined his life.

Don began to recall how frightened his father was of his mother, and how his dad had abdicated his power, finding covert ways to express his hostility, which included several affairs. Slowly, his self-flagellation subsided as he grasped how ineffective it was as a tool for engendering sympathy and forgiveness from Helen. He began to pay attention to the serious aspects of his trial. He explored the role of anger in his life and how his tendency toward abdicating power actually intensified his anger. Don began to accept that he was a very angry man, which was his way of allowing his trial to do its work.

Don's resolution generated more meaning for him as he understood that as long as he stayed in denial of his anger, he could not be trusted by either Helen or by himself. His old self-image as a man who was gentle, sensitive, and completely trustworthy was disintegrating. He experienced grief and relief as his unthreatening and compliant persona began to die. His resolution was giving rise to a dangerous and evocative man who understood that the acceptance of his anger made him less dangerous to those he loved.

## The Return

The final stage of an initiation is the return, in which the initiates return to themselves, their partners, and their communities more equipped and more ready to be who they were meant to be. Helen and Don understood that they needed to be more honest about the anger and fear within themselves, and to be more honest with one another.

Helen understood that she had participated in her mother's betrayal of her by refusing to confront her mother. She understood her reluctance to tell the truth to her mother as self-betrayal. She also took responsibility for distancing Don with anger that was more fittingly directed at her mother.

Don knew that he had been perpetuating a male legacy of abdication that included covert expressions of anger and rage. He understood that this had set him up to be the scapegoat in his marriage—the betrayer, deserving of shame and ridicule. Don's self-betrayal was very clear to him. The experience of an authentic return in an initiation will inevitably be characterized by a deeper consciousness of the role of self-betrayal in the initiate's life, and the birth of a deeper experience of self-loyalty.

Don and Helen supported themselves through their trial and surrendered to it. They both grieved the loss of particular beliefs and dreams, the loss of old personas and ways of connecting to one another that no longer accommodated their deepened sense of self and their renewed intimacy. They strengthened their capacity to endure the tension of their grief and of being lost as they explored the unknown territory of their individual and collective souls.

Every marriage provides an opportunity for a nuptial initiation, a chance to die and to be reborn. In fact, marriage may offer more opportunity for initiation than any other human endeavor. It may be important that we approach marriage with a large collection of naive and idyllic beliefs.

How many of us would say the words "I will" if we knew that those words were going to bring us to initiations characterized by betrayal, abuse, deception, and emptiness? How many of us would willingly step into an initiatory cauldron containing forces that relentlessly knead and push us toward depths that are frightening and bewildering, and yet move us closer to who we were truly meant to be?

# 4

# *The Shame Shadow*

The shadow of shame is potentially highly corrosive of marital bonds and can severely inhibit the deepening of a couple's intimacy. Shame is most harmful to a marriage when it is denied and placed into shadow. There are a number of questions to address regarding the shame shadow: What is it? Where does it come from? How do we protect ourselves from getting close to our shame? How does it impact a marriage? How can it ultimately serve a marriage?

The shame shadow is similar to all shadows in that we deny its existence and relegate it to the unconscious, where we hope it will eventually die. Unfortunately, this is not the way of shadows. The greater the denial, the more prominently the shame shows up in our lives, in a myriad of unconscious ways aimed at helping us defend against experiencing it.

## What Is Shame and Where Does It Come From?

Shame is an attitude. It often has an emotional component, with accompanying thoughts and behaviors. Most of us become acquainted with shame in childhood. There are countless opportunities to become acquainted with shame throughout childhood.

Erik Erikson first pointed out that shame is a natural reaction in children who are developing autonomy by exploring their limits. Shame becomes a natural reaction to discovering that we can't do as much as we anticipated. The situation can be compounded when children do not receive parental permission to remain investigative or are penalized for failing to achieve some intended goal.

Shame is induced when parents shame themselves and therefore model shame as a way to cope. Shame is promoted when parents act shamefully but do not take responsibility for their behavior. Children often overcompensate for shameless parents by taking on the shame for the parent. When a child experiences their trust being violated, they often respond by shaming themselves, especially, if the person violating the child's trust is loved by the child. Parental expectations with pressure to excel can be shame producing.

Our parents might have shamed us when they felt overwhelmed by the demands of parenthood, or when they felt afraid of losing control of us. Unless parents were themselves raised in a shameless home, where they learned to be responsible for their feelings, they likely will not address their fear, but simply shame their children in an attempt to modify the child's behavior and regain control.

Children are particularly susceptible to being deleteriously impacted by the shaming voices of parents. Children base much of their identity on how they are treated. If they are affirmed and loved, they quite often experience themselves as lovable. If they are shamed, then they often view themselves as lacking any real value or importance.

When a parent shames a child, the message is that there is something inherently wrong with the child–the child is "damaged goods." Nothing erodes a child's positive self-concept more than shame. If parents believe they can subdue their fear of losing control of their children by the use of shame, then shame becomes a norm in the family.

There is a double edge regarding the use of shame as a parenting strategy. Are there any benefits to using shame as a way to modify a child's behavior? Shaming children can produce immediate results, as children avoid enacting certain behaviors in order to avoid the sting of being shamed. However, as the shame wraps a stranglehold around children's personal worth, convincing them that they are not good people, they are more likely to act out rage and revenge, demonstrating the validity of their parents' perception. The suffocation of personal worth happens when the shaming experience is not an isolated incident by rather a pattern of behavior exercised by the parent.

## Defending Against Shame

In his seminal work, *Shame* by Gershen Kaufman, the author describes a series of strategies we employ in order not to feel shame. One such strategy is *rage* which helps to distance others and hopefully give a reprieve from being witnessed in our shame or from being further shamed. Another strategy is *contempt.* The contemptuous individual gets to reject before being rejected. It is another form of distancing others before our shame can be exposed.

Kaufman points out that *striving for power or control is another defense employed in an attempt to compensate for the defectiveness which underlies internalized shame.*

Staying on top allows the individual to avoid feeling the vulnerability and "undeservedness" of shame. *Blaming* is another insulating strategy against shame. It is a way of distancing others in the hope of preventing continued feelings of shame. It is also a technique aimed at freeing ourselves from culpability and making others responsible for the mistakes and mishaps of daily life.

Another defense against shame is *internal withdrawal*. Children can easily retreat to the confines of their own inner worlds where they create a refuge from shame often crafted by their imaginations. As adults, we can emotionally "wall" people off in order to get a much needed barrier from the possibility of further shaming. *Perfectionism* is another strategy aimed at protecting us against the sting of shame. Unfortunately, perfectionism guarantees the very flawed person we were attempting to avoid. It sends us into a spiral of constant striving and failing.

# Defending Against Shame–Defending Against Marriage

Kaufman points out that *Rigid defending strategies will in turn produce distorted relationships with others creating new pressures*. Those of us who take the defending strategy of perfectionism strive to prove the shaming voices wrong or to ascend to heights where it is easier to stay in denial of the driving force of our shame. It is analogous to Sisyphus pushing the rock up the hill only to see it roll back down, giving rise to an eternal act of labor.

Perfectionists are attempting to attain personal worth through the ever illusive process of achievements. Their rock always rolls down the other side and they must start all over again, striving to achieve the unattainable. Many go to their death bewildered why it is that their accomplishments never gave them the personal worth they so longed for and allegedly deserved.

Perfectionists know how to succeed at school and at work. They know how to read the rules and play by them. They carry their shame just beneath the surface, seething with a deep sense of inadequacy. They know how to have a fleeting sense of personal value because of their achievements. However, they have no idea how to give themselves an enduring sense of worth based upon whom they are.

Perfectionists cannot love themselves for who they are and consequently cannot be loved by others for who they are. They commonly know how to be admired and needed, but almost incapable of being truly loved by a spouse. They are too busy proving their worthiness.

Perfectionists often have a great amount of difficulty appreciating and loving their spouses for who they really are. They often are strongly attached to a vision of who their partners could be in an ideal world.

*Rage* commonly creates a marriage based on fear and avoidance. Spouses who are recipients of *rage* become excessively vigilant, not allowing for spontaneity, joy, play or relaxation. These spouses either become extremely isolated or they turn to others in order to get their emotional needs met.

Raging partners can have the power to throw their spouses into a kind of emotional spasm which is similar to getting the wind knocked out of them. Spouses hit by the energetic force of *rage* shiver as if getting knocked out of their bodies. Receiving *rage* can literally feel like being hit physically.

*Rage* is meant to be a distancing strategy and it is usually successful. A marriage where rage is a common commodity will lack warmth, passion and emotional intimacy.

*Blame* is another prevailing defense against shame. It is another distancing strategy meant to transfer shame to another and reducing the likelihood that our own behavior will be called into question. *Blame* is highly corrosive to a marriage. Spouses who are the object of *blame* begin to see their partner and their relationship as an ongoing threat to their personal worth.

A marriage based on *blame* will define personal accountability as dangerous. That is, spouses are not simply responsible for their mistakes, they are the bad people who make mistakes. When responsibility becomes defined as *blame*, spouses begin to find ways to avoid being responsible. The consequence is that it becomes nearly impossible to make agreements, resolve conflicts, solve problems and hold a vision of a future.

Similar to the impact *rage* has upon a marriage, when *blame* is rampant in a marriage spouses begin to indulge in avoidance, getting their emotional and possibly their sexual needs met elsewhere. Avoidance also becomes a way to protect feelings of self-esteem.

Kaufman points out that when *contempt* is modeled by a parent, it becomes a likely candidate for strategy employed later in adulthood to defend against feeling shame. *Contempt* is a potent strategy since it totally rejects whomever it is directed at. When spouses protect themselves against shame through the use of contempt, the dynamics in a marriage are riddled with fault-finding, condescension and judgment.

*Contempt* is an aggressive way to wall ourselves off from our spouses. It makes us nearly completely unapproachable and guarantees the elimination of intimacy.

*Striving for power* is an attempt to compensate for the feelings of inferiority and inadequacy that inevitably accompany shame. A preoccupation with securing power has serious adverse consequences in a marriage. Power begets power. When spouses attempt to control their partners, their partners entrench themselves in their own need for power and control as a way of preventing themselves from being steamrolled.

As power dynamics become a norm in a marriage, strong competitive agendas are established where spouses are locked into a win-lose mentality leaving little or no room for genuine collaboration. The climate of the relationship becomes inundated with a tension that incapacitates creativity and growth. The marriage is reduced to a constant round adversarial jousting.

If one spouse *strives for power* while the other remains more passive and submissive, then there is a fertile breeding ground for resentment on behalf of the passive spouse. It is common for the submissive spouse to either withdraw or act out in some vindictive manner in order to retaliate.

*Striving for power* inevitably communicates a need to define our partners. It tells our partners that we know best and we will decide who they are and how they should live. *Striving for power* sends the message that we do not believe in our spouses' ability to define who they are and craft a life that is vital and meaningful.

Kaufman identifies the last coping strategy aimed at defending against shame as *internal withdrawal*. This particular defense is often described with some euphemism such as *he's withdrawing to his cave*, or *this is simply her process, her way of moving into deep reflection*. On occasion, I have even heard it described in spiritual terms, *this is her way of connecting with her guides or angels*. I have also heard withdrawers claim that they were simply taking care of themselves, with no regard for the impact that their withdrawal has upon their spouses.

*Internal withdrawal* like so many of the other defenses is a distancer. Instead of pushing the other away, individuals simply go away themselves. The strategy is to prevent any further shaming by simply not being available for form of contact.

*Internal withdrawal* walls-off a spouse. The withdrawer is not available for any form of engagement. *Internal withdrawal* literally puts a marriage on hold. The withdrawer has the power to shut down a marriage, bringing partners to their knees in helplessness.

In his seminal work, *Healing the Shame That Binds You* by John Bradshaw cites other defensive strategies against shame, with the most noteworthy being *people pleasing and being nice*. Smiling people pleasers live a veneer of niceness and pleasantry suggesting that they are surely without shame. Over time, even they begin to believe in their masquerade.

The goals of excessive conviviality are to avoid authentic contact which is intended to prevent others from noticing how flawed we feel and to take people hostage. The strategy is to make others captive to our niceness in the hope that they would not dare attempt to shame such a nice person.

*People pleasing* in a marriage creates diminished authenticity which guarantees the loss of intimacy. It also places severe restrictions upon any personal growth since it entails the elimination of truth. *People pleasers* often find their congeniality evolving into deep resentment since they spend so much time betraying what they really think and feel.

Defending against shame guarantees that shame remains denied in shadow, and as we shall see, the feeling of shame does not have to be damaging to a marriage but the strategies employed to defend against shame can be devastating to a relationship as is internalized shame.

John Bradshaw cites the injurious impact that our defenses against shame have upon a marriage: *Shame-based people find other shame-based people and get married. As a couple each carries the shame from his or her own family system. Their marriage will be grounded in their shame-core. The major outcome of this will be a lack of intimacy. It's difficult to let someone get close to you if you feel defective and flawed as a human being. Shame-base couples maintain non-intimacy through poor communication, nonproductive circular fighting, games, manipulation, vying for control, withdrawal, blaming and confluence. Confluence is the agreement never to disagree. Confluence creates pseudo-intimacy.*

## Tracking Denied Shame

In order to get more conscious of shame we will need to be able to track its comings and goings, and a marriage is a great place to do the tracking. We will also want to exercise compassion for ourselves as we unearth the shame which is devouring our personal value. My hope is that it's becoming increasingly obvious just how much compassion is needed when doing this kind of shadow work.

Besides the defensive strategies of *perfectionism, striving for power, internal withdrawal, blame, rage, contempt* and *being a nice person;* there are a number of other indicators of internalized shame lying in shadow within a marriage.

> *\*Little or no tolerance to hearing no as a response to a request.* Spouses carrying denied shame hear a negative response to their requests as either a statement about the inappropriateness of their request or the inappropriateness of themselves for asking. The intolerance to hearing a negative reaction establishes a tension in the relationship. The requesting spouse sends the nonverbal message that negative responses are simply unacceptable. Spouses live with the

anxiety of expecting an intense reaction from the requesting spouse when they don't hear a favorable response.

*A compulsive need to evaluate a spouse's request as irrational or inappropriate.* With internalized shame running the show, it may be almost impossible to say *no* to our partners. Our shame makes it very challenging to simply allow our partners to feel dissatisfaction. We translate their dissatisfaction into our inadequacy and our shame. We protect ourselves from feeling shame by going on the attack, judging our partners' requests as irrational or absurd. The role of requests, giving them and receiving them, can go a long way toward flushing out denied shame. Many couples experience such pain and turmoil in regard to requests that they choose not to tell their spouses what they need and want, deepening the chasm separating them.

*Resistance to being accountable, making amends, and apologizing for mistakes and violations of agreements.* Spouses carrying internalized shame often find it very challenging to be accountable for their behavior. Any mistake or shortcoming throws them into a downward spiral of shame. Their response to a personal blunder is either denial or to blame someone else.

*A compulsive need to apologize.* Some spouses respond to their mistakes by incessantly expressing regret. Their denied shame prevents them from getting to any genuine acceptance of forgiveness of themselves.

*High resistance to taking risks.* Shame-based spouses are not open to new behaviors, where all the possible hazards have not been duly assessed. They find it extremely difficult to accept faltering in some unforeseen fashion. They prefer a rigid life-style, pretending it gives them greater control over possible mishaps.

*Employing isolation as a way to cope with problems and conflicts.* Shame desires isolation. Spouses carrying denied shame will tend to isolate themselves when encountering personal problems. Husbands often show up in my office feeling shame about being there. They hold some cultural dictum that real men can effectively attend to any problem in their marriages–they don't need help. When spouses are carrying denied shame, they commonly withdraw from their partners during a conflict, in order to avoid activating their shame by feeling ill-equipped to address the problem.

*Being paralyzed by the need to make the right decision.* Internalized shame establishes the illusionary rulebook of right and wrong decisions, with the need to avoid wrong ones. This is perfectionism at its best. The thinking is that right decisions do not have any of the unfortunate consequences associated with wrong decisions. When I hear spouses tell me they can't make a decision, I normally respond by suggesting that the issue is not that they are unable to make a decision; rather, they are unwilling to tolerate any negative consequences, which will inevitability arouse their shame. What they know is that they will be ashamed of any decision that is less than pristine.

*Intolerance of diversity.* Internalized shame often leaves us resistant to accommodating diverse beliefs and values. Spouses carrying denied shame often believe there is a right way and a wrong way, and they cannot tolerate the thought that their way might not be without blemish. If their partners' views are different from their own, they will defend themselves from feeling shame by making their partners' views wrong. I often hear spouses reporting that they constantly experience their preferences and beliefs as being under attack. They often describe their spouses as consistently attempting to convert them to an ideology they resist ascribing to.

*A high need for anonymity.* Spouses choosing to remain anonymous do not want to be seen. They hold the belief that if they are witnessed for who they are, they will be shamed by their partners in the same way they shame themselves.

*A feeling of utter worthlessness as a response to trivial mistakes.* This is the feeling we are attempting to deny, distract from, and make go away. We will do almost anything to avoid the caustic feeling of shame. It may be that on a cellular level, we carry an ancestral terror of being deemed worthless and therefore ostracized and left for dead. In any case, let's note the potency with which we deny shame.

## Dismantling Defensive Strategies

Before we can begin to transform internalize shame into simply feeling ashamed, we will need to dismantle our defensive strategies. This dismantling process is not about eradicating our defense of shame. Rather, the goal is to diminish the strategy enough to gain access to our shame and to minimize the injurious impact the strategy has upon our marriages.

Part of the challenge is that the ways we defend against shame are usually cloaked in denial. Spouses who are perfectionists either tell themselves that their perfectionism is a good thing and/or that it does not have a negative impact upon their own lives or the life of their marriage. Once there is a crack in the denial, spouses can begin to learn how perfectionism sets them up to ultimately experience their defectiveness since the perfect version of oneself is unattainable.

It is helpful for perfectionists to learn how they have been living with an adversarial relationship with their humanity. As we expect a deified status, we violate our humanity. Recovering perfectionists can support themselves by learning more about the value of humility and what it means to have a gracious relationship with their own limits.

*Contempt* can be more challenging to deal with than perfectionism. The intensity of the contempt will reflect the degree of fear and terror the individual experiences in regard to visiting shame. If spouses living from contempt allow themselves to disengage from the contempt, they will inevitably drop into the depths of self-loathing. Our denial is customarily inexorably fixed.

The most likely path to great mindfulness will be the feedback from a loved one who is feeling overwhelmed by the toxicity of the contempt. If recipients of the feedback are willing to work with the idea that our contempt is having a significant adverse impact upon someone whom we allegedly love, they can begin to track our choice to live contemptuously.

The next step will be the willingness to feel the fear which sits right behind the contempt. We will need to learn how to allow ourselves to feel fear, talk about it and support ourselves through it. Developing a viable support system can be very important. A place where we can feel safe to express our fear. A significant identity shift from disdain to fear occurs when we live outside the grip of contempt.

Dismantling *rage* means being willing to identify, feel and talk about our hurt and fear. Addressing rage entails learning how to allow ourselves to feel vulnerable. It is very helpful to learn the difference between feeling vulnerable and being vulnerable. Feeling vulnerable means feeling scared and being safe. Being vulnerable means feeling scared and being unsafe. When we feel vulnerable we are actually safe, when we are vulnerable we are likely in some sort of danger.

It can be very beneficial for men who are learning to dismantle their rage to do so in the context of other men who are addressing the same lesson. Deconstructing rage often leads to deep feelings of hurt that are best identified and experienced in a supportive environment.

Dismantling our *strivings for power* also entails learning how to identify, feel and talk about fear. It also means learning how to distinguish what is in our control and what is not. As we become more efficient with this distinction, we can learn how to let go of what is not in our control. Learning to let go inevitably involves uncertainty and fear.

Taking down the strategy of *blame* involves a willingness to get responsible for our lives and getting responsible means being willing to be self-focused. It calls for a commitment to the daily practice of explaining our experience by citing our own choices. Inevitably, when we attempt to stop blaming others, we begin blaming ourselves. It will be important to learn how to have compassion accompany our new founded self-responsibility.

Undoing *internal withdrawal* will call for willingness and courage to reach out to others. Internal withdrawal normally carries with it a propensity for compulsive self-reliance. Spouses withdrawing tend to believe that they really do not need any one. They are typically confused about the distinction between solitude and isolation. Solitude is a genuine comfort gained by spending time alone. While isolation is obsessive need to be alone because of the belief that contact with others would be either harmful or useless.

In order to let go of a need to withdraw, we need to be willing to feel our fear as we reach out and employ boundaries that will take the place of our withdrawal. We might have to say *no* to a friend or ask for a modification of the support they are offering.

Dismantling *people-pleasing and being nice* can be a great welcoming back to ourselves. The challenge will be to support ourselves through the fear of being authentic. There may be grave concerns about being rejected or abandoned. It can be helpful to understand that our people-pleasing has been a huge act of self-abandonment. It will be helpful to enact our authenticity in small increments and observe the consequences. Inevitably, our genuineness will not mean the end of the world.

As we dismantle our defensive strategies, we will begin to feel our internalized shame. It now becomes important to develop a concrete plan to transform the belief that we are shameful to simply a feeling of shame. We begin to move away from feeling we are essentially defective to experiencing a passing feeling of self-loathing.

## Internalized Shame

Certainly, the denial of shame and the way we defend against it diminishes our essential life force, and so does internalized shame. *Internalized shame is not simply a feeling of self-loathing that grips us temporarily: it is a static state of being where we feel essentially damaged.*

Bradshaw suggests there are three ways that the feeling of shame translates into a state of being. The first is the identification with shame-based models. Essentially, this is the map of "personhood" we acquire from parents who have a shame-based identity themselves. Secondly, the trauma of being sexually, physically or emotionally abused translates into a feeling of abandonment. When children's needs and feelings are neglected they respond by devaluing their own emotional lives. Thirdly, current experiences of feeling shame are connected to childhood shame until a kind of identity loop is created whereby we see ourselves now as the same shameful person we always have been.

Internalized shame will surface in a variety of ways that abate our ability to relate to ourselves and to our partners. Internalized shame makes it extremely challenging to effectively communicate requests in a marriage, to remain accountable for personal behavior, to actively engage in reasonable risk-taking, to remain physically and emotionally accessible to our spouses, to participate in creative and decisive decision-making and to exercise the ability to accommodate the diversity of beliefs and values existing between us and our partners. Internalized shame also has a dire impact upon our capacity to receive and give love.

Spouses carrying internalized shame are often quite effective at the art of giving but significantly impaired in regard to receiving. Their shame grinds down a sense of deservedness, making it difficult, and in some cases, nearly impossible to receive. As deservedness continues to erode, it can be easy to let go of a desire to be loved and settle for being needed. Being needed interferes less with low deservedness driven by internalized shame.

Receiving is as essential as giving to the building of intimacy; each has the power of igniting the life of the other. The giving of love can only be manifested as much as a receiver allows. And obviously, receiving cannot occur without active engagement with a giver. Giving and receiving are in a powerful dance, capable of unfolding into a crescendo of intimacy, or being sabotaged by internalized shame.

It is important to be clear that indicators of internalized shame are not a forewarning of shame in need of being identified and eradicated by the end of the day. The goal is not to evolve into a state of complete shamelessness. We can feel shame and let it go just as we do any other feeling.

We live in a culture that delights in the idea of an antiseptic personality. It invites us to take seriously the idea of a sanitized self, removed of all neurosis and any other psychological blemishes.

The very idea there is some pristine paradigm of human nature is an insidious call to shame. We are invited by the self-help genre to focus upon the improved self we can become, rather than encouraged to hold the self we are, with compassion and grace.

Our work with internalized shame is work about witnessing how we deny who we are. Our hope is simply to allow ourselves a glimpse of the person beneath the cover of denial and permit ourselves to learn from what we see. We have more opportunity to do this kind of work in a marriage since internalized shame will express itself in a myriad of ways on nuptial terrain. Addressing our defensive strategies is prerequisite to effectively attending to internalized shame.

## Transforming Internalized Shame

*Letting ourselves be conscious of our shame and allowing ourselves to feel the shame are great first steps in the transformative process.* Learning to allow ourselves to feel our shame and to acknowledge the feeling will afford us some valuable objectification and detachment from the feeling. From this vantage point, we are not damaged goods, we simply feel like damaged goods. We can begin to notice the difference between being our shame and feeling it. We also can see that the feeling of shame begins and ends. We begin to accumulate evidence that we can actually bear our shame. As we discover that we can endure beyond shame, the need for denial is less compelling.

*We can further move out of internalized shame by calling it into the light and telling our shame stories to trusted others.* As we give a voice to our shame and receive the understanding and empathy of others, we further separate the feeling of shame from who we actually are. We can feel it and acknowledge that it is not us. Some of the wisdom behind the original idea of the confessional in the Catholic Church was probably about making peace with shame. Unfortunately, the Church has been more skilled at generating shame than it has been at helping to purge it. A great deal of the power of Twelve Step Meetings is due to the opportunity its members have to tell their shame stories. It came be helpful to relate shame stories to our spouses, as long as we believe the disclosure would not unduly hurt them or ourselves in the process.

*Further movement with internalized shame happens by identifying feelings that were shamed and unacceptable in our families of origin.* As children, we only tolerate our emotional lives being shamed by others so long, before we grab the control and shame ourselves. If expressing sadness or fear was shamed by our parents, then we probably will prefer shaming ourselves before we allow the expression of sadness or fear.

Many females will shame themselves before they give themselves permission to express anger. The cultural injunction is that women jeopardize their gender identity if they are angry. They are no longer real women, but have become bitches. However, men are not immune to denied anger. Men who tend to be more culturally sophisticated, academic or drawn to a spiritual path, are more likely to deny their anger, since anger is not compatible with their desired persona.

In his seminal work, *Emotional Intelligence*, Daniel Goleman sites Zillmann's research which argues against catharsis as a way to cope with anger. The argument being that catharsis does not dispel anger but merely incites it. Of course, the thinking here is that anger is something to diffuse. It is extremely difficult to be a sophisticated, educated gentleman and not be compelled to think of anger as something to abate.

Goleman's recommendation in regard to working with anger is to use your awareness to cool yourself down. I would agree that the use of awareness can often avert unnecessary and regrettable flare-ups of anger and rage. However, Goleman is keeping with the prevailing thinking, which suggests that the priority needs to be the control of anger and not allowing anger to teach us. We do a great injustice to ourselves, to our marriages and to our children when we emphasize control and not learning.

We want to be able to manage our anger such that it does not have an injurious affect upon our relationships with others. As we have seen, clear, robust anger may not be anywhere near as destructive as covert and passive anger which slowly eats away at a relationships.

We also want to manage our anger such that it does not have a deleterious impact upon ourselves, resulting in conversion reactions, which often show up in the body as headaches, neck, jaw and back pain. Above all, we want our anger to maintain its ability to teach us more about who we are.

Ritualizing the energy of anger is one of the most creative ways to contain, express and learn from our anger. The key is to find a class, group or training that is committed to developing ways to physically act out anger and rage. Classes in Reevaluation Counseling, sometimes referred to as Co-counseling, are highly recommended because they teach skills that people can reproduce on their own without professional assistance. Some aids in the physical expression of anger include hitting pillows, yelling and screaming, biting down on a towel, ringing a towel, punching a bag. We want to find the way that serves us best and do it initially in a social setting where we can receive support before trying it on our own.

It is extremely important to remember that the energy of anger possesses a great capacity to teach and when we construct a safe environment to act it out, we will inevitably allow ourselves to learn from it. We may learn about the grief we often carry just beneath the anger; or the shame we have about our fear and cover up with anger. Many people learn about areas where they have been unwilling to forgive themselves or others.

Other lessons include the depth of hurt and its accompanying shame or the powerlessness that was masquerading as bravado. There is also much to learn about our relationship to our passion and how we honor or sabotage our desire. Anger can also teach us a great deal about our sexuality since it comes from the same internal fire.

The suppression of anger often occurs because we experienced our parent's anger as a declaration that we are bad. We begin to take responsibility for how our partners might feel when we are angry at them. We do not want them feeling ashamed of themselves in the presence of our anger, as we did with our parents.

Bradshaw points out that internalized shame can be viewed as rage directed inwardly. All the more reason to explore discharging anger and rage has a way of unwrapping the tentacles of internalized shamed from the core of our being.

We also withhold our anger in the way of making a deal, I won't make you feel bad by being mad and you won't make me feel bad by being mad. As we shall see, these kinds of deals can be quite popular in fused relationships.

*When we are willing to identify and express the truth of our sadness, fear and anger, the grip of shame starts to loosen.* I am suggesting that our expression not be limited to verbal utterances; even at the risk of jeopardizing our femininity or sophistication, as in the case with anger, or masculinity as it may pertain to the expression fear. Emotions are mostly about physical energy and we do ourselves well to learn how to identify and express these energies.

We can further transform internalized shame by giving expression to its energy and the weight of its encumbrance. Our shame stories often include anger, rage, hurt and fear. I recommend writing poems, short stories, letters (not necessarily to send), drawing pictures, working with clay and designing rituals aimed at depicting a life impacted by shame. Any form of narration will help dispel the power of denial and create accord with our shame.

Our desire is an essential element of our emotional lives. *The more we think, feel and act from our desire, the more we loosen the grip of internalized shame.* Reclaiming our desire is one of the most authentic acts we can perform. Internalized shame decomposes under the light of our desire and with it, adaptive postures such as obligation, excessive responsibility and acting in compliance with the expectations of others.

*Committing to self-compassion has the power to erode internalized shame.* Compassion cannot win the battle against internalized shame unless it is brought to the highest level possible. As long as we believe we have more important purposes that self-compassion, internalized shame will have a field day. Being compassionate with ourselves must be our highest personal or spiritual commitment. We must be willing to take it extremely seriously a day at a time.

There may be feelings of betrayal toward those who treated us without compassion. There may be thoughts of a lack of deservedness or selfishness. The key is to notice these feeling and thoughts and make the decision to hold ourselves with compassion the best we know how, simply because there is no other way to get home, home to our essential self-worth.

*Learning to be self-trusting helps to dislodge internalized shame.* When we trust another we hold the belief that that person will tell us the truth and treat us compassionately. When we trust ourselves we hold the belief that we will allow ourselves to know our own truth and we will treat ourselves compassionately. Getting closer to our own truths means bringing our attention regularly to what we believe, what we want, what we feel and what we value.

Again, we see the value of self-compassion. It's critical to not get hung up with wonderings and reflections of who we are or what we are. It is simply a decision. We extend compassion to ourselves or not. The idea is not to get caught up in attempting to extend compassion to ourselves perfectly but rather maintain the focus of making the decision to do so the best we can.

I witnessed a friend recently struggling with an important decision of whether to allow his adult son to remain living with him or ask him to leave. My friend pondered the decision endlessly, refusing to accept himself as the person who would offer housing to his son nor would he accept himself as the person who would ask his son to leave. He did not have an ounce of compassion for either man and subsequently remained a hostage to his own unwillingness to extend himself compassion.

The employment of the kind of boundaries that do not allow us to be shamed by others is also a valuable expression of the kind of compassion that engenders self-trust.

I am a strong adherent *of welcoming the one who is wounded and the one who is gifted as immense opportunities for reducing internalized shame.* Being raised in a family guarantees that we will be wounded and gifted. The inevitability of being abused or neglected is an essential element of family life. We instinctively wall off the parts of us that were wounded, because we believe that those parts caused our parents to withdraw love. We live with the delusion that we are protected from further wounding by banishing the part of ourselves that caused the retraction of parental love.

It may not be our wounds that we find to be worrisome, it may be our gifts. Our gifts or talents make us shine, make us more visible; parents can react to them by feeling envious or even inadequate. We may very well decide to sequester the parts of us that carry gifts in order to become less visible and therefore less prone to be shamed, or in order to love our parents by not allowing our gifts to make them feel less than.

*There is great opportunity to transform internalized shame by learning to make mistakes.* Nothing calls us to shame more than making a mistake. It is not helpful to wait for all internalized shame to be vaporized before we learn how to make mistakes, if for no other reason, all internalized shame is not simply going to disappear. Learning how to make mistakes is a counterculture phenomenon. Our culture does not want us to learn how to make mistakes, it only wants us to know how to avoid them. The culture fosters perfectionism, shame and ignorance about how to make mistakes.

There are several significant skills to making mistakes. The first and foremost is the ability to notice the defensive strategies that arise when we make a mistake. For example, rage and blame can by typical mistake-making responses.

The next skill involves allowing ourselves to feel the shame that comes as we let go of the defensive strategy. Next, we learn to be accountable by identifying to ourselves and to invested others the nature of the mistake. If the mistake involves a violation of one of our values, we make an amends to the injured party, which is a sentiment of regret with a commitment not to reproduce the adverse behavior. If our behavior was the result of ignorance, we may need to acquire new skills in order to fulfill our commitment.

As we become less guarded regarding making mistakes by dismantling our defensive strategies, learning to feel our shame and reclaim our personal worth; we take more risks and inevitably become more creative.

Lastly, we go a long way toward moving out of internalized shame *by remaining a student of shame.* The real disability of internalized shame is staying entwined in the defensive strategies we created against it. Those strategies maintain denial of our shame and keep shame in shadow.

As denial subsides with the calming of our defensive strategies, we are able to call our shame out of the shadows, enabling us to be more directly in relationship to our shame. We are now well-positioned to begin shifting the role of shame from one of an unfortunate nemesis to one of an emotion we feel and let go of. Shame can teach us where we come from and how we struggle in holding our essential goodness.

## Shame, the Teacher

David and Marie, a couple in their early forties, came in for couples therapy, reporting that they wanted to work on their sexual relationship.

"Marie is constantly suggesting that we should be sexual. She wants it when we go to bed, when we wake and sometimes in the middle of the afternoon! She doesn't let up! I think she's a sex addict or something!" declared David, sounding exasperated and overwhelmed.

"I'm wondering which of these times works best for you," I asked.

"None. When do I get a chance to initiate?" David exclaimed, that blaming his over-sexed wife who was allegedly not allowing him to fully express his sexual prowess.

"You sound like you're blaming Marie for what's going on. Have you ever asked Marie to back off and give you a chance to initiate?"

"Yes, several months ago I suggested that she give me some breathing room," said David, becoming more composed.

"How did that work out?" I asked.

"Well, we didn't have sex for several weeks," said David, his gaze lowering along with his voice.

"Okay, so let me see if I understand this. Marie obliged you by backing off for several weeks and it sounds like you didn't capitalize upon her passivity," I pointed out, hoping David would be curious about his lack of initiative, remain self-focused and let go of his need to blame.

"Yes, that's what happened. I just don't understand it. I love Marie and I'm very attracted to her. I don't get why I didn't do something," David explained, sounding angry at himself.

"You seem puzzled about your lack of action, especially in the light of your love and attraction to Marie," I said.

"Yes, I just don't get it," he admitted.

"Why don't you start by telling me something about where you learned about sex?" I suggested.

"I guess I really didn't learn anywhere. I went to Catholic school right up through the twelfth grade."

"I'll bet you learned a lot about sex in those twelve years," I said.

David was being invited to look at the denied shame he carried in regard to his sexuality. The little or nothing his family and teachers said about sex effectively communicated that there was nothing more sinful than sex. With some reluctance, David began telling his shame story. He described how dirty he felt when he masturbated, and how he had waited until he was married to Marie at twenty-two, before engaging in sexual intercourse.

I pointed out to him that Christianity leaves men with two precarious options for sexual partners. We either have sex with Mary Magdalene which reduces sex to something lecherous or with the Blessed Virgin, which by definition is a con-tamination. Christianity simply does not offer us a third option in which the erotic and the sacred can find an amiable interface.

I suggested that David and Marie design some simple rituals whereby they would bless one another's bodies—merging the carnal with the sacred. They both enjoyed ritual as part of their spiritual lives, so they were open to the possibility of ritualizing their sexual lives. A month later, they reported how they began their love-making with a blessing.

David was creating peace with the shame that had been generated by his religious affiliation; however, he stumbled into another kind of shame, one I call gender shame.

David, like most men, had been acculturated to believe that men, real men, are always ready to have sex. David had been viewing his reluctance to be sexual as an aberration. We spoke about the cultural myth that men are primed and eager to be sexual at a moment's notice. I went on to explain that much of the research on human sexuality suggests that men and women are quite similar in regard to their propensity to be sexual.

David was learning a great deal about the religious and cultural influences that had affected his sexual identity. David was starting to develop a creative rapport with his shame. The closer he moved toward his shame, the more he understood that his sexuality was not inherently sinful. He realized that the shaming forces of the past were powerful, but with his denial lifted, he could claim his sexuality, feel his shame and fear, and continue to own his erotic life. Marie was more than willing to work with him by, listening to his shame stories and blessing his passion.

Shame teaches us where there have been breaches in our relationship to ourselves. One of the most prominent teachings in all mystical traditions is the importance of sustaining and renewing a relationship with our essential goodness. Shame shows us how that relationship has been ruptured and reveals the variety of defenses we employ as we attempt to salvage some semblance of "okayness" in lieu of a solid relationship with our innate value. We blame, we run, we hide, we attack—all in the name of attempting to squeeze out a drop of personal repute, while denied shame consumes our entitlement to feel good about ourselves.

Ultimately, shame can be an enormous invitation to our humanity. Shame calls us to the frailty and vulnerability of the human condition. There are no for-mulas for creating a viable marriage which means we will make mistake after mis-take, falling into inadequacy and confusion with the accompanying shame.

# Conscious Shame and Marriage

There are a number of areas where conscious shame stimulates a creative marriage and helps the relationship become more life-affirming. It is important to remember that no marriage will be completely void of denied shame. That's not the goal! Our objective is to remain receptive to subtle shifts in the way we carry shame, so we can get closer to ourselves and those we love.

A couple may become more engaging as they dismantle defensive strategies and become more conscious of internalized shame. Increased engagement is the result of a willingness to see and hear as well as to be seen and be heard. Our capacity to share our perceptions of the world and of one another deepens. We are more likely to fight without demeaning one another's characters. We will offer compliments, encouragement and support more freely. Mindfulness of shame encourages engagement because mindfulness itself diminishes shame, leaving us more willing to be seen.

A couple's interest in sex normally rises with conscious shame. An active sex life usually reflects the degree of emotional intimacy experienced by a couple. Emotional intimacy greatly depends upon the level of accountability exercised by each member of the relationship. As awareness of shame is heightened, there is less of a need to avoid being accountable. Couples begin to acknowledge their own mistakes and ways they may have mistreated one another, and make amends for acting counter to their own values and expectations. Essentially, the couple learns to be accountable without shame.

Creative problem-solving is enhanced as a couple becomes more conscious of shame. As the need for perfectionism diminishes, the creative spirit of a couple flourishes. There is less dedication to being right, and more freedom to generate unique approaches to a problem. A couple begins exploring life more and lets go of a need to "get life right."

The same can be said of decision-making. As conscious shame replaces denial, acceptance of a couple's humanity replaces perfectionism. Spouses carrying denied shame tend to defer to their partners, finding it difficult to feel entitled and be clear about what option they feel comfortable with. They are inclined to remain voiceless, and eventually become resentful. A couple becomes less invested in making the right decision and more capable of taking risks, and forgiving themselves when things do not work out according to plans. They become more decisive as they hold themselves in compassion regardless of the outcome.

A couple's conflicts become lighter. Instead of a showdown to prove who's right and who's wrong, a conflict becomes an expression of diversity, a chance to view the true uniqueness of each spouse. The need to convert our spouses to our own views begins to diminish, and the need to be right loses its intensity. Curiously enough, the more one spouse lets go of a need to be right, so does the other. It also gets considerably easier to witness the needs and idiosyncrasies that give rise to the other's position.

A relationship that calls in shame and allows it to be seen for what it is is a relationship that is in the process of releasing shame. I almost hesitate to say it, in fear that readers will see the process of becoming conscious of shame as a way to exterminate it. Let me say again that both denied shame and conscious shame are here to stay. And it is true that there is no better antidote for the toxic bite of shame than to welcome and accept it.

We have discussed the impact of denied or internalized shame upon individuals and their marriages. We have described ways to identify how internalized shame is moving through our lives, become more conscious of it, transform it, and eventually learn from it. Like all shadows, shame lurks somewhere behind our denial, gathering strength from our need to banish it, yet is ready to bring us greater life and depth, if we are willing to invite it forward.

# 5

## *Dark Night of Marriage*

Couples enter into the "dark night of marriage" when either or both partners descend into an experience called regression. At least ninety percent of the couples coming to my office over the past twenty years entered in a state of regression, and if it hadn't been my office, than it probably would have been the office of an attorney, where one of them would be seeking a divorce. Unless this powerful shadow known as regression is addressed, couples either live out their marriages in daunting mediocrity, or they separate.

Almost every couple I have seen reports their problem as being one of communication. It is as if there is a bad-communication epidemic. "We just don't know how to talk to each other anymore." "Every discussion ends up in fight." "She doesn't listen to me." "He doesn't tell me what he is really feeling." And the list goes on.

My understanding is that poor communication is almost never the problem, but rather a symptom of the problem: a deterioration of their rapport. And nothing undermines a couples' rapport more than unattended regression.

## What Is Regression?

Regression is a response to an experience in which we retreat back to childlike ways of thinking, feeling, and behaving. Sometimes it is simply a reaction to some external stimulus, like a smell or a song that can send us back, like a time machine, to some period during the first ten or twelve years of our lives.

Regression often happens to me when I smell honeysuckle. Some of my first adventures were on my bike with my friends, heading to a local swimming hole along a road bordered with lots of honeysuckle. One whiff and I lose forty-five years. I am back on my bike, traveling all of two miles away from home, on a quest with my comrades.

Regression happens in a marriage because spouses are either experiencing a threat to their safety, or there is something being said or done that feels challenging to their personal self-worth. When either our physical safety or our personal value are at risk, we can quickly return to more primitive ways of taking care of ourselves, called regression.

James and Linda, a couple in their late thirties, came to see me, saying they wanted to improve their communication by eliminating their constant bickering. I didn't need to ask any questions about the status of their communication, since they obliged me by offering a vivid demonstration.

"Whenever I help out around the house, Linda criticizes what I've done. It's never good enough for her! She never appreciates anything that I do!" explained James.

"You mostly take care of yourself! The only thing you see is the kickoff time of the afternoon game! Everyone knows that sports come before me and the kids!" charged Linda.

Holding his breath and beginning to perspire, James said, "You only care about spending money, and I'm supposed to make sure there's enough of it in the checking account for you to satisfy your every wish!"

I decided to interrupt at this juncture, pointing out that they had clearly showed me an example of the problems they were having in their communication. What I didn't say was how regressed they sounded. They spoke to each other like two six-year-olds whose ability to cope was quickly deteriorating. Before their communication could be remedied, they would need to learn how to bring themselves back to adult size.

In the case of James and Linda, one accusation was enough to drive both of them into the depths of regression. Quite often a look, a gesture, or an innocuous comment can easily bring an adult ego-structure tumbling down. All it takes is something said or done by one spouse to remind the other spouse of some painful childhood experience of abuse or neglect, returning them to their childhood in an instant.

## Why Do We Regress?

Is it some aberration of the human psyche indicating a need for extended treatment? Regression can help to deepen our life experience and aid our development, and it should not be viewed as a pathological condition. Whenever I am on Block Island, Rhode Island, engaged in one of my favorite summertime activities, boogieboarding, it takes only one wave for regression to completely wash over me, and I start giggling, splashing, and carrying on like a ten-year-old. Regression can allow us to tap into the spontaneity, joy, and the uninhibited playfulness of childhood.

Regression is a collapse of sophisticated defenses. Normal adult ways of negotiating the complexities of worldly affairs are temporarily suspended. Regression is the psyche's way of revealing unfinished business from the past. In the case of James and Linda, they later learned that they were both commonly shamed as children, making them extremely sensitive to any remark sounding less than completely flattering.

Not only does the psyche abhor unfinished business from the past, it also has a less than favorable reaction to coping mechanisms that can't accommodate an evolving maturity. What better way to let us know that the ways we have been buttressing ourselves are really built on sand? A single look or utterance can send a forty-year-old adult reeling in juvenile actions and attitudes. There is a rich opportunity here to reexamine our beliefs, our values, and our choices, and ask if there might not be a more resolute way of responding to life's tension.

The collapse that accompanies regression can be a great time to get honest and understand ourselves on levels simply not available to us during our "more adult" states. Ego collapse can reveal the cutting edges of our emotional maturation, or lack thereof. It is especially good at showing us where we struggle to hold our personal worth. We may be called to these edges when we hear our spouses holding views quite different from our own, or when our spouses decide to confront us.

We often wonder why we get the same results in a relationship, or even in different relationships. If we have not interrupted regressive ways of responding to our spouses, then we simply recreate old patterns that are severely inadequate when it comes to guiding the course of a marriage. These patterns include black-and-white thinking, histrionic emotions, and behavior locked into fight-or-flight.

The ego is not especially fond of seeing itself out in full plumage, strutting about, and assured of its prowess in every human endeavor. Consequently, the popular reaction to regression is to remain unconscious of it, while blaming someone for the accompanying discomfort.

Ego collapse reveals weaknesses we possess, especially those pertaining to being in the presence of diverse beliefs and attitudes, or simply being confronted. However, these areas of diminished strength run deeper than solely the inability to effectively handle diversity and confrontation. They commonly suggest an interior injury that causes us to struggle to protect and defend our essential goodness.

Most of us experience our goodness as tentative and subject to change, depending upon conditions like our achievements and the reactions others have to our choices. Our hold on our essential goodness may be so fragile that we have little or no tolerance for failure, or being in the presence of diverse views and opinions. Failure gets defined as personal inadequacy, and diversity simply stimulates the need to prove we are right and others are wrong.

The human psyche remains faithful to its sacred mission: to reveal where we struggle to maintain our essential goodness. Our choice is either to surrender to the process and collaborate with the psyche, or to fight its attempts to illuminate our fragility. If we choose to fight, then we will experience our collapse as simply an unfortunate occurrence in the human condition. If we see our regression only as a hapless event, then several consequences will ensue.

The most obvious result is that we remain unconscious of our regression, thus denying it and keeping it in shadow. When it remains in shadow, it defines us. I like to say that it means placing a kid in the driver's seat of the bus and looking the other way. The metaphor is rich, suggesting the intensity of the drama and levels of calamity that are inevitable when a child is in the driver's seat of a life.

Unconscious regression places us at odds with the psyche's attempt to reveal inner weaknesses so that we can strengthen our interior support. Remaining unconscious disallows for the dismantling of regressive patterns and replacing them with an abutment that can hold our essential goodness. However, the psyche is formidable and unyielding in its mission to reveal what needs attention. It will persist in generating collapse after collapse irrespective of our refusal to cooperate. The psyche is so determined in its mission that it's possible to actually have an inverse relationship between one's chronological age and one's psychological age.

## Unconscious Regression and Aging

It is very common to encounter people in their seventies and eighties living in daily regression as a result of staying unconscious about their regressive states. Octogenarians talking and acting like kids are simply the likely outcome of denying regression and not attending to the needs and vulnerabilities contained in every ego collapse. The result is a pseudo-eldership, lived virtually from being constantly in collapse, characterized by narrowness of thinking and exaggerated emotions coupled with primitive coping mechanisms. It becomes only too easy to forget about the sacredness of authentic eldership.

Some folks do pay attention to their collapses, learn from them, age with grace, and deepen their capacity for genuine wisdom. Many cultures view such people as their richest resource. Unfortunately, our culture has wandered a long way from understanding the gifts inherent in conscious aging. Paying attention to the role of regression would go a long way toward supporting the reclamation of the dignity of the aging process.

# The Impact of Unconscious Regression upon Marriage

Unconscious regression can be devastating to a marriage. If a couple lets their regressive selves drive the marriage bus, then recklessness and possibly a fatal accident may result. The psyche depends upon emotional investments to trigger a collapse; hence, regression will appear at work and in our marriages more than any other place in our lives, especially if we are effective at maintaining superficial friendships, which will almost guarantee that our social lives will remain immune to regression and to any depth. It seems like a cruel trick that relationships with the greatest amount of meaning and care run more likelihood of stimulating regression.

But it does explain why so many of us are satisfied with perfunctory relationships, and why so many spouses report that people have no idea who their partner really is.

Unconscious regression erodes individual strengths, and eventually erodes the strength of a marriage. Characteristic of such marriages is a prevalent theme of abusing and abdicating power, alienation, hopelessness, diminished sexuality, and a reduced capacity for creative problem-solving. Children of such marriages either rigidly achieve in an effort to soothe the pain of their parents, or act out.

The issue is not whether couples will regress or not; that is a given. The question is about whether or not couples are willing to become conscious of their regression and learn from the accompanying collapse. I call this kind of learning "deep shadow work." There is not much joy in being willing to notice that our adulthood was just yanked away and we are operating as eight-year-olds. It takes courage, fortitude, humility, and the ability to hold ourselves lightly, not allowing our egos to shatter because of a temporary loss of adult mettle.

Living in a marriage where there is a commitment to remain conscious of regression and learn from the endless throes of collapse is tough business. It is certainly not meant for the faint of heart. A colleague of mine calls it "the roughest game in town." It is a profound initiation into personal and collective depths. Those willing and bold enough to become conscious of their regressive experiences will benefit by being able to identify when they are losing adult ground and slipping swiftly into childhood.

# Indicators of Regression

Once we are willing to track our regressive states, we must develop the ability to determine if we have lost a grip on adulthood. This can be a challenging task, and it calls for practice. Spouses who were "parentified children" usually have great difficulty accepting the idea that they become regressed. A parentified child, often the oldest sibling, is encouraged to leave childhood early, act like an adult, and either help parent their younger siblings or help their parents manage the challenges of daily living. Essentially, they were not given permission to be children, so they find the idea that they can become childlike as adults repugnant, and often feel shame about the temporary loss of adulthood.

I want to note something my friend and colleague Henri Nouwen said: "There is no truth without compassion." Nouwen reminds us that we will stop searching for the truth about ourselves unless we hold our truths with compassion. It's just too painful to continue to look at ourselves if we insist upon beating ourselves up when we find something unfavorable, and we just might find something unfavorable when we are becoming more aware of regression in ourselves.

Here are some indicators of regression that can go a long way toward helping us identify when we are becoming regressed:

> *Verbosity or dead silence.* Regressed states often leave us feeling out of control. Children often feel out of control of their worlds, and a common reaction is either the excessive use of language or no language at all. The deep silence is usually accompanied by shallow breathing.

> *Almost a complete inability to identify what we want or need.* Children don't have the introspective capacity to accurately identify what they need, especially under stress. Clients who are regressed often respond with a blank stare to my question, "What do you want from him/her?" If they have enough "adult" available to them during their regression, then they can figure out that the need to badger their spouse probably reflects some unfilled desire. They are just regressed enough not to have any idea what it might be. If they are fully regressed, they might respond with something like: "I don't want anything from him; he's just always mean to me."

> *Extreme thinking.* A regressed spouse will think and talk in absolutes. Common terms include "everyone," "no one," "always," "never," and "every time." Children do not have the cognitive ability to hold the subtleties of human experience that inevitably move out of black and white into gray.

*Fear is not experienced as simply an emotion but rather a lack of safety.* As adults, we can experience fear, and with the exception of situations posing immediate danger, we are safe. For children, their fear often announces the presence of something they have no control over and therefore is a potential threat to their safety. I often intervene with clients who are feeling fear, reminding them that although they feel scared, they are safe. If clients have any foothold in adulthood, they begin to have a higher tolerance for feeling fear as they remind themselves they are safe. If they are much regressed, they look at me like I am speaking nonsense.

*Loss of options.* Seriously regressed clients will often report that they have no options. Moderate regression will generate one or two alternatives at best. Fear of a loss of safety stimulates rigidity of thought and behavior, significantly stifling creativity. Many a divorce is decided upon from a state of regression, where partners see only one choice.

*A need to become unusually aggressive or deeply withdrawn.* This is essentially a fight-or-flight reaction to a potential loss of safety. My assessment of domestic violence is that it typically occurs during highly regressed times. Techniques aimed at anger management are meant to alter immediate behavior and do little or nothing to deepen the perpetrator's maturation. Perpetrators of physical abuse would be more effectively served if they underwent training aimed at heightening awareness of regression and what to do in order to reclaim some adulthood. It should be noted that verbal aggression can also be regressive and significantly abusive.

Physical and emotional withdrawal that walls off a spouse for days or weeks at a time is no less regressive and abusive. What is noteworthy is that both the aggressive spouse and the withdrawing spouse would describe their behavior as an attempt at protecting themselves. If the regressing spouse is unconscious of his or her regression, then he or she will describe the acting out as motivated by a need for protection. What goes unrealized is that the need for protection is being assessed from a child's point of view, making it highly unlikely that there is a need for extreme protection, and likely that the behavior employed for protection is not very effective.

*The tendency to decide that interpretations of reality are accurate depictions of reality.* This resembles the magical thinking of childhood, when children believe their thoughts to be clear representations of reality. If I believe there is a monster in the closet, then there is a monster in the closet. There probably is at least a hint of magical thinking in most of our daily thought patterns; however, it becomes accentuated in regression, and we are convinced that reality is as we conceive of it.

James and Linda, the couple mentioned earlier, slipped into magical thinking when they were regressed.

"I know you are not coming right home after work and you are hanging around with that sleazy waitress down at the bar-and-grill across from your office," Linda declared, with complete certainty.

"I'm not hanging out with some waitress, but I do know you are having an affair with that new trainer at the gym," James countered, with an equal amount of confidence.

I am not suggesting that we should completely doubt our intuitions, but rather that we should treat them as possible accounts of reality. In the midst of regression, our interpretations and intuitions gain full credence, in accordance with a child's magical thinking.

*Spontaneous perspiration, cold hands, dry mouth, and shallow breathing.* These symptoms are indicative of the fear accompanying regression. If these physical reactions occur with two or more of the other indicators, it may be a reliable sign of regression.

*The belief that we must go it alone—there are no allies.* The more regressed we become, the more we believe that there is no viable support.

## Remaining Students of Regression

I strongly encourage spouses to use these indicators in order to become conscious of their own regression. Each of us has our hands full in becoming students of our own regressive states. The goal is not to analyze our partners, pointing out to them that they have obviously regressed and are no longer acting appropriately as adults. Having knowledge of regression gives us a kind of power, and we would do well to use the power wisely, rather than abusing it in order to express anger at our partners.

The more effective we become at identifying regression within ourselves, the easier it is to spot it in our partners. The temptation is great, but I strongly recommend refraining from accusing spouses of regression.

If we truly believe that our partners are significantly regressed, it makes sense to gently detach by suggesting we would rather continue the discussion later, or by letting our partners know that we would prefer to pick up the topic at another time. It is important to remember that it is our perception that our partner is regressed, and our judgment that now is not the best time to talk. We want to detach without blaming our partners for obstructing the course of the discussion. It is also recommended that the detaching spouse take the responsibility of initiating the discussion at a time soon after the original exchange.

When one or both spouses is regressed, it is not an appropriate time to make important decisions or initiate attempts at creative problem-solving. Whenever possible, don't let kids drive the marriage bus!

Regression begets regression. When one partner becomes regressed, it is extremely likely that the other partner will become regressed within minutes. This probably occurs because the initial regressed spouse typically makes hurtful or insulting statements, reminding the second spouse of painful events of the past, plunging them quickly into their own regression. It doesn't take long before two kids are in the kitchen attempting to address issues they know little or nothing about and treating each other very unkindly.

## Respect the Demon

Sandra and Curtis had been working with me for some time and had gotten quite savvy about their regression. They were able to identify when each of them was moving into regression, and they were becoming quite skilled at getting the support they needed when they were regressed. In fact, they began feeling quite confident as they noticed how effectively they intervened in their own regression and how infrequently each of them seemed to actually become regressed.

They came to their session and began describing an incident that took place several days prior to the session.

"I had called Curtis to find out what his plans were for lunch. He explained that he was going to eat lunch in at his office. When I drove by a local restaurant, I noticed him and his blond twenty-four-year-old secretary getting into the car in the restaurant parking lot. I decided to follow them back to the office. As I drove, I kept telling myself that following them to the office in order to confront my husband was not a good idea. I didn't care. I was going to do it anyway." Sandra detailed the experience, shaking her head from left to right, visibly angry at herself.

"I politely got out of my vehicle and asked Curtis to take a ride with me. He agreed, and added that he had an important meeting in thirty minutes. Once he was in my car, I proceeded to rip him a new asshole. I decided he was cheating on me, and I would accept no other interpretation of the lunch with the cute blonde. Both of our energies escalated, and finally Curtis grabbed me by the throat. I lost control of the car, and we hit the guard rail. Fortunately, we were not going very fast, and there was only minor damage to the vehicle. However, it was not enough to snap me out of my regression. I asked Curtis if he would get out of the car and assess the damage. When he did, I drove away, leaving him some ten miles away from his office," Sandra concluded, her voice dropping off.

I knew how disappointed Sandra and Curtis were about their behavior. I too enjoy indulging in the illusion that I have moved beyond the grips of regression, only to periodically be reminded that under the right conditions, my six-year-old self is but a half a step away. On many occasions, I have bet on my maturity to hold steadfast in the presence of my wife's regression, only to consistently lose the bet.

Regression is powerful. It not only wobbles the adult legs of the spouse initially regressing, but within minutes, anyone close by is going down too. Respect regression by gently and swiftly detaching. Detachment will go a long way toward eliminating unnecessary drama. Besides, your own regression is just around the corner, so there is no need to participate in your partner's regression.

I reminded Sandra and Curtis that the issue is not whether or not we become regressed, but rather our capacity to be both accountable for and compassionate about our regression. They were able to summon enough fortitude to get back in the game and forgive themselves and one another for acting out.

## "Reparenting" Ourselves through Regression

Just as children need a clear and loving parent, so do we, when we are in the midst of regression. As adults, we are the ultimately the best parental resource we can muster. Unfortunately, the days when some allegedly more capable individual was in charge of our care are over.

The first step is to gain some competency at identifying when we are regressed, and then to deepen our acceptance of ourselves as regressed. Identification of our regressive states will usually generate enough objectification to allow us to parent ourselves while we are regressed. Practice will generate a greater ability to be regressed while taking care of ourselves through the regression.

Regression comes in all sizes. Some last only a few minutes and call for minimum parental backup. Other regressions may go on for hours or days, calling for greater parental resolve. The sooner the regressive state can be identified and a "reparenting" intervention introduced, the quicker the return to adulthood.

There are four basic parental competencies that can be employed in reparenting. They can help to move us through regression, restoring us back to adulthood and helping us learn from the regressive experience. I call the composite of these skills the "BEND reparenting model." The letter *B* stands for boundaries, *E* for encouragement, *N* for nurturing, and *D* for discipline.

Often a regressive experience indicates that some needed parental intervention was absent during childhood. Our present situation is somehow restimulating that unmet need. We are actually getting the chance to offer ourselves the kind of parental support and guidance we missed as children. It is a great opportunity to pull ourselves from the clutches of simply being victims of our own childhoods. We can actually replace parental abuse and neglect with love, clarity, and effective guidance; that is, of course, if we are willing to be conscious of the very humbling experience of regression.

**Boundaries** are the choices we make that separate us from others and keep us focused upon our own intentions and our own needs. Employing effective boundaries while regressed is both critical and challenging. Regression is not a good time to explore novel ventures, make important decisions, or attempt new and challenging enterprises in general. It's a time to pull in, get support, and focus on getting our "adult legs" back and learning from our regression.

Boundaries help to diminish unnecessary drama and serve to create a container where our regressive experience can take place, while minimizing negative fallout. Of course, the key to utilizing boundaries effectively is the ability to employ some adult thought and action. If there is little or no "interior parent" available, then it is important to seek support from friends, a mentor, or a counselor who can help with the employment of workable boundaries.

If we know we are regressed, it can be extremely helpful to let our spouses know and suggest a boundary aimed at terminating a discussion until later. We can explain to our partners that we know we don't have our best thinking available to us, and that postponing a discussion about our sexual relationship is probably advisable.

*E* stands for **encouragement**. For many of us, there was a shortage of this valuable parental commodity during childhood. We can offer ourselves encouragement by reminding ourselves that we have what it takes to reclaim our adulthood, and that being in a regressive place is natural. Encouragement brings some ease to our challenge, and reassurance that we are okay. Again, if we cannot find enough inner strength to advocate for ourselves, we can turn to a support system and request encouragement.

I don't recommend turning to spouses for encouragement, especially while we are regressed. From a regressive posture, we will usually find whatever support a spouse offers insufficient, and we won't hesitate to let them know.

*N* represents **nurturing**. Being able to nurture ourselves, or to successfully access nurturing from a supportive person, can be difficult during a regression. A strong regression throws us into survival mode, where we are ready to either fight or run. What we really need is love, but in an intense regression, it will feel dangerous or too vulnerable to allow in love. Our defenses are up; convinced that no one is to be trusted, we are prepared to do or die on our own.

It may be useful to make a list of what we consider nurturing when we are not in a regressive state. Items on the list might include some favorite music, walking in the woods, meditating, reading poetry, talking to a particular friend, or sitting and holding a favorite pet. If we experienced severe neglect or deprivation in childhood, there will be a tendency to see nurturing as corny. Those of us who were neglected learn to go without, and we are attached to a self-image of being able to "make it" with little or nothing.

It can be helpful to jot down the name of a person or two whom we might be willing to contact when we are regressed. Ask your support folks if they would be open to being contacted when you slide into a regression. It is a great advantage to have a support structure in place long before we move into a moderate or severe regression. Once again, those of us familiar with being neglected will have the tendency to remain in deprivation and to see the need for a support structure as somewhat silly.

A number of years ago, I was in a fairly heavy regression. It was late in the evening, and I had just enough "adult" available to acknowledge that I needed to reach out for help. For all practical purposes, I was seven years old, having almost forfeited all of my forty-four years. It is not all that easy for a seven-year-old to dial the phone and be clear about what he needs.

I managed to reach a good friend and began to describe what I was experiencing, although it was challenging to call a male, since my father had been considerably unavailable. My friend understood the nature of regression and knew that the person on the other end of the line was mostly a kid.

He told me, "I think you need to be held." The second I heard it, I knew he was right, although I felt embarrassed and ashamed about being so needy, which was the way I monitored my needs as a child. Before my parents could reject my needs, I did it first, protecting myself from their dismissal. I knew it was what I needed—and what I had gone without through most of my childhood. I somehow mustered enough "interior parent" to say, "I'll be right over."

I immediately drove twenty-five minutes to my friend's house, although I do not recommend putting a seven-year-old behind the wheel of any vehicle. When I arrived, my friend greeted me, and we proceeded to a quiet and private area in his home, where we sat on the floor and he held me for about thirty minutes. I continued to weep the entire time, allowing current as well as old tears to leave my body. As I drove home, more my rightful age, I knew I had provided myself with several important gifts.

I had given myself an element of parenting that I had needed my entire life. On many occasions as a child I had come into the house hurt or humiliated, needing to be held and given some temporary comfort in order to let go of my pain. The protocol for my parents was to attempt to talk me out of my feelings or to shame me. Driving home that evening, I knew I had gone a long way toward letting go of my compulsive self-reliance and blaming my distress on my parents' unavailability.

Although reaching out for help when I'm regressed is somewhat easier now, it still calls for a great deal of inner strength to punch in the telephone number of a good friend. I can still hear old voices summoning me back to deprivation: "What are you, a big baby? Get over it and grow up! Come on, dig in! Don't be so needy and dependent! Be a real man!"

*D* stands for **discipline**. Contrary to our modern notion of discipline, which suggests independence, self-reliance, and a tenacity to hold the course alone, the root of the word comes from "discipleship." The ancient connotation suggests the mastery of utilizing others as valuable resources. I have already alluded to the significance of enlisting others in our support when we ask if they are willing to be available for us during our regressive periods.

I was once interviewed by a television talk-show host who asked about the topic of men being intimate with women. She asked what I believed to be the single most important factor for men developing intimacy with women. I responded by saying, "A good male support system." She looked stunned. I explained how men can diminish their isolation and take the burden off of their partners by developing viable same-gender support.

Again, I am defining discipline as the mastery of human resources, knowing how to best use disciples. Imagine what it would have been like for us as children if our parents accessed viable help and support when they were regressed or when they felt overwhelmed in their parenting efforts!

Achieving mastery of our human resources calls for discernment and focus. We need to discern who is capable of offering the support we need when we are regressed, which includes knowing who we trust. Friends who practice getting support during their regressions might be great allies during our own regressions.

Focusing on where and when are also valuable considerations when seeking support. The "when" is easy to identify: as soon as possible! As soon as it is clear that regression is happening, it is a great time to get support. Why wait until the damage incurred by your childlike state is severe or even irreversible? As I stated earlier, decisions to separate or divorce are quite often made from a regressed place, as are most homicides and suicides. The consequences of regression vary from being innocuous to absolutely devastating.

We can identify quiet, private places to receive our support, places where we are unlikely to be interrupted. Whenever possible, don't drive. Ask your ally to meet you at your residence or to drive you to the desired destination. If you are not satisfied with the place you have chosen, give your dissatisfaction a voice and do what you can to modify the environment in order to meet your needs.

The "how" of mastering our human resources can be difficult to accurately identify. When in doubt about how you want to be supported, it may be enough to just have your friend be with you until you find your way back to adulthood. Often it will serve us just to be witnessed by friends as we express our feelings. We can also request encouragement or some form of nurturance, as in my personal example.

Another approach is to ask your ally to actively help you move through and learn from your regression. This can be done by utilizing a model for addressing regression recommended by John Lee in his book *Growing Yourself Back-Up*.

The regressed individual takes a comfortable physical position, paying attention to an easy rhythmic breath and deciding whether some gentle contact might be appropriate. The ally asks a set of questions aimed at facilitating the person through their regression. The following dialogue is an example of this process: "RP" is the abbreviation for the regressed person and "A" stands for the ally.

> **A:** Would you be willing to describe how you feel right now?
> **RP:** I'm really angry and sad.
> **A:** Would you describe the situation that gave rise to these feelings?
> **RP:** Yes. I asked my husband to talk about an incident that occurred last night between us, and he said he was sick of talking, and stormed out of the house.
> **A:** What does this situation remind you of from your past?
> **RP:** It reminds me of my mother refusing to talk about anything that made her uncomfortable. She never would take any responsibility for her goddamn behavior! *(Yelling and shaking her fists.)*
> **A:** What would you like to have said to your mother?
> **RP:** You stupid bitch! Grow up! What's wrong with you? You make me responsible for everything that goes wrong! I hate you!
> **A:** What would you like your mother to have said to you?
> **RP:** Catherine, I want to make amends to you for my behavior. From now on, I won't blame you, and I will take responsibility for my mistakes and shortcomings.

The model is most useful when the ally sticks to the suggested script without analyzing or becoming attached to a specific outcome. The goal is simply to create an opportunity to identify and emotionally experience the original situation calling us to our regression. In our example, Catherine goes a long way toward "growing herself back up" when she is able to separate her husband's behavior from her mother's and experience the emotions and the needs associated with her mother's behavior.

As we embark upon the quest of "reparenting" ourselves, it will do us well to remember that we are inclined to parent ourselves the way we were parented. Whatever level of boundary employment, encouragement, nurturance, and discipline our parents brought to parenting us is probably what we will bring to ourselves. It takes commitment, courage, and practice to move beyond the limitations and legacies of our parents and give ourselves a greater resolve in our self-parenting.

Our culture has a fetish-like attachment to the directions of up and forward, making it all the more challenging to face regression, a movement down and back. But before we can free our souls and open our hearts to the work and intimacy of marriage, we need to become mindful of the small, wounded part of ourselves that still attempts to get our compassionate attention. It may be that any meaningful marital progression depends upon conscious regression.

# 6

## *The Shadow of Power*

In an ancient initiation taking place along a crocodile-infested river somewhere in central New Guinea, initiates risk the actual loss of body parts. Committing to marriage brings spouses to the heights of empowerment and the depths of helplessness. Once the words "I will" are pronounced, two powerful forces within the human psyche are aroused and proceed to drive an individual toward the unknown depths within.

The first drive is the need for affiliation, love, togetherness, intimacy, and unity. The second force is driven by the need for independence, autonomy, self-reliance, and individuality. Following the honeymoon period of a marriage, when couples are enveloped in euphoria, the needs for unity and separateness begin to constellate and collide. The need for unity is often accompanied by a fear of abandonment; and the need for separateness is usually ushered in by a fear of being consumed, swept away into the needs and expectations of the other.

These fears create a variety of predicaments that call couples toward the fear of losing the partner and the fear of losing oneself. The essential power of marriage to deepen maturation comes from the alchemical interaction of these fears, which force couples to examine their beliefs, values, and choices in ways that would be unnecessary outside of marriage.

Hank and Julie came in for couples counseling. Hank initiated the discussion by explaining that he found his wife's willingness to financially support a friend (who was experiencing economic woes) unacceptable and intolerable. What made the situation so challenging for Hank was that Julie expressed no willingness to stop subsidizing her friend's bank account. He did not want to lose Julie, but he wanted to remain faithful to his own values and beliefs. Once Hank was able to stop morally judging Julie and acknowledge his fear, the tension created by these two needs drove him closer and closer to himself.

I prompted Hank to examine his relationship to money, his family's view of freeloading, his fear of being exploited, the role of boundaries in his relationship, and his need to control his wife. His psychological inventory was created by his fear of losing Julie and his fear of losing himself. If he had attempted to diminish the tension by either immediately accommodating Julie's need or writing her off, he would have lost a valuable opportunity for self-discovery.

The fear of either losing our partners or losing ourselves drives us to abuse and abdicate power. I am defining power as "the ability to influence a desired end." An abuse of power occurs when the influence exercised actually diminishes or violates the partner in some way. An abdication of power occurs when we decide we are either unable or unwilling to execute influence over a desired end, often resulting in a violation of the partner.

The act of abdicating power drips with irony. Those of us engaging in abdication are not simply throwing in the towel and settling for complete helplessness; rather, we are taking a circuitous route toward some desired end. Our abdication can be seen as a covert attempt at securing influence.

John and Barbara had been seeing me in marriage counseling for a month when Barbara spoke of her resentment.

"John, I just can't take it anymore! I've always gone along with whatever you wanted. I've gone boating, fishing…even hunted with you! You don't appreciate anything I've done for you!" Barbara exclaimed, with a volcanic energy that sounded as if it had been boiling in a hot lava pit for years.

"Barbara, it sounds to me that you've sacrificed yourself for a very long time," I said.

"Fifteen years! And now it's my turn!" she responded.

"Barbara, how did you come to decide to wait fifteen years to get your needs met?" I asked.

"Well, I don't know. I was trying to be a good wife," she said, sounding ambivalent.

"I'm sure that you were trying to be a good wife. What I hear is that you sacrificed your own needs in order to secure the perception that you were a good wife, and I can't help but wonder if you didn't really feel entitled to have your needs met. Maybe you didn't feel as if you had the right," I suggested.

"It's starting to feel like a pretty high price for 'good wife' status," she said, with an air of confidence.

Barbara's fifteen-year abdication of power was due to her own inability to legitimize her needs and confirm herself as a good wife. Barbara's abdication placed her in a long, tedious struggle with power.

Why do we abuse and abdicate power in the most significant relationships in our lives? It is an important question, and I don't want to suggest that there is only one answer; however, there are at least several driving forces. The first is the belief that we don't have any ability to influence some desired end; *i.e.,* we believe that we are helpless. The more we believe that we are powerless, the more frightened we become and consequently less mindful and discerning about how we are wielding power. At times we simply act sadistically, wanting to punish our partners; this is often motivated by feelings of deprivation or neglect.

The overriding issue is that power is not talked about in most marriages. We simply do not have an adequate vocabulary to address issues surrounding the abuse and abdication of power. Power agendas remain a constant in all marriages, which means that couples are regularly attempting to secure the ability to influence some desired end.

## Abuses of Power

Most of us abhor the idea that we might be abusing power, so it can be quite challenging to identify when it happens and take responsibility for it. It may be helpful to cite abuses of power that take place in most marriages.

Shaming is a standard expression of abuse and can be expressed through such utterances as: "What's wrong with you?" "I thought you were a responsible and upright human being!" "You're so selfish; can't you ever think of others?" and "You're not a very thoughtful person." Shaming calls a person's goodness into question based upon who the person is.

A first cousin to shaming is blaming. The only difference is that blaming attacks a person's goodness based upon what he or she has done. Examples of blaming include: "The party would have been a success if you hadn't gone on and on with your jokes," "The dishes need to be done again, because you obviously didn't do them with care," and "The only reason we lost is that you played like a moron."

Analyzing is another popular expression of abuse, in which we explain our partners' behavior by identifying some key psychological deficiencies: "You don't seem to possess the kind of maturity that would afford us a healthy and happy marriage," or "You and your mother are both inclined to attempt to exercise control over the lives of others as a distraction from focusing upon your own issues."

Teaching is another form of abuse that takes on a condescending flavor as one partner attempts to teach the other about the fundamental truths of life: "You can't go around trusting everyone," "You really need to stand up to your boss if you want him to respect you," and "Did you really think that you were going to get her to see your point of view without being assertive?" are some examples.

Breaking agreements without renegotiating is a prevailing abuse of power among married couples. One partner makes an agreement with the other and proceeds to change his or her mind without approaching the spouse with an intention to redefine the terms of their agreement.

Deception is another common abuse of power enacted within the confines of most marriages. Deception occurs when we hold secrets whose content our spouses would be readily interested in. Lying, by either misrepresenting the facts or omitting valuable information, constitutes an abuse of power through deception. The betrayal experienced in the case of marital affairs is often the result of the injured party feeling deceived, rather than the affair itself.

Bullying is another form of abuse often found in marriages. It is carried out by antagonizing, dominating, or intimidating our spouses. It's done physically when we use our physical stature to impose influence on our partners. It is enacted emotionally when we threaten our partners with the withdrawal of cooperation, love, sex, or attention. Stereotypically, the six-foot-five, 250-pound husband is characterized as the bully; however, a petite wife may be quite effective at bullying her husband.

Sarcasm is another ordinary expression of marital abuse of power. Sarcasm is an indirect expression of anger in which disparaging and contemptuous remarks are made, aimed at belittling the other. Sadly, the recipients of sarcasm often do not actively confront the sarcastic spouse, which results in sarcasm becoming the norm in a marriage. Such passivity allows the toxic elements of sarcasm to become corrosive of trust and intimacy.

A popular abuse of power is the use of ultimatums. An ultimatum is a statement by one spouse declaring the beliefs or choices of the other spouse unacceptable. The explicit suggestion is that if the spouse continues with these beliefs or choices, he or she runs the risk of losing their relationship with the giver of the ultimatum. An ultimatum essentially communicates that your spouse cannot have both his or her own decision and a relationship with you.

Ultimatums are an attempt to exploit the understanding that our partners want both to be with us and with themselves. Ultimatums are usually issued when a spouse is regressed. The message of an ultimatum is usually: *I'm scared and I don't know how to take care of myself, so you need to sacrifice yourself so I'll feel more secure.*

In his book *Passionate Marriage*, David Schnarch discusses ultimatums. "Ultimatums are only binding on the person who issues them. If you don't follow through on your ultimatum when your partner doesn't comply, you violate your integrity—and your partner knows you're not serious. People who issue frequent ultimatums have little integrity."

The most obvious abuses of power are threats of violence and actual physical violence. Such mistreatment is more common in marriages than in any other relationship. There seems to be some correlation between the degree of closeness in a relationship and the propensity to abuse the other's physical boundaries. Domestic violence rates continue to rise.

There may be no such thing as a marriage that is immune to power abuse, because there is no such thing as a marriage that is immune to regression. The goal is not to sanitize marriage of all its abuse, but rather to become accountable for whatever abuses we are prone to enact. Becoming accountable means that we commit ourselves to identifying whatever abuse we are perpetrating, taking action that curtails the particular abuse, and being open to discussing with our spouses the effectiveness of our accountability. Before we can become accountable for our abuses of power, we need to become effective at identifying when we are regressed and learn to reclaim our rightful psychological age.

## Abdication of Power

Abdication of power is as debilitating to a marriage as abuse of power. Spouses abdicate when they relinquish their capacity to directly influence a desired end. As mentioned earlier, it is unlikely that spouses who abdicate power are actually abandoning all attachment to some desired end; rather, they have learned to engage in self-sacrifice as a way to procure their desires. Their propensity to be excessively yielding often results in cynicism and resentment rather than fulfillment.

Abdicating spouses are often attempting to secure the approval and acceptance of their spouses. They believe their self-sacrifice can readily demonstrate that they are deserving of love. The willingness to relinquish abdication comes when they realize that unnecessary self-sacrifice neither confirms their righteousness nor guarantees the appreciation of others.

There are a number of common expressions of marital abdication. The most popular is the refusal to support personal needs and desires. Abdicating spouses either defer to the needs of their partners or indulge in unusual levels of confusion about what they want and need.

The deferring spouses are eager to know and prioritize what their partners want and need. They represent themselves as either wanting what their partners want or simply having no strong preference. Their deferential posturing can be very seductive for their partners, especially if the partner is accustomed to having his or her own way.

Another example of abdicating power is the employment of ineffectual boundaries. Abdicating spouses are reluctant to say *no*. They erroneously believe that they will get their needs met through excessive compliance and adaptation.

I was working with Maryann and Jack, a middle-aged couple, when Maryann's tendency to abdicate power by employing ineffectual boundaries became the focus of our session.

"I don't understand why Jack doesn't cooperate when I make requests of him," Maryann pointed out.

"It sounds like you have a hard time getting Jack to respond positively when you want something from him," I responded.

"Yeah, he never does what I want to do," she agreed.

"And you—how do you react when Jack makes requests of you?" I asked.

"Oh, I always go along with Jack's plans," she said matter-of-factly.

"Always?" I asked.

"Well, yeah, I always agree to join him."

"Are you telling me that every request Jack makes piques your interest and you feel highly motivated to comply?" I pushed.

"No, not at all. Much of the time I have no interest in Jack's ideas."

"How does it happen that you come to agree so often?" I wondered.

"Oh, I don't know. I don't want to disappoint Jack or create an unnecessary problem," she answered, her face looking more girlish than womanly.

"So you don't want to disappoint Jack," I reflected.

"Yeah, that's right. But he doesn't seem to have a problem disappointing me! You'd think that he might be a bit more supportive after all that I've given," she said, her jaw increasingly tightening.

"Maybe you've been responding favorably to Jack's requests as a way of gaining some leverage toward influencing Jack to support your needs," I suggested.

"Well, maybe so," she responded, her voice meekly dropping off.

Maryann's abdication of power is a good example of employing ineffectual boundaries in the hope of being able to influence some desired end. Maryann began to discover that there was *no* relationship between her reluctance to say *no* to her husband and her husband's receptiveness to her needs.

One of the most potent methods of abdicating power is through addiction. An addiction will arrest a person's creative energies, abate their capacity for intimacy, thwart the ability to engage in cogent thought, and nearly extinguish their ability to remain accountable. People can be addicted to street drugs, prescription drugs, alcohol, gambling, sex, food, and work. The goal of addiction is to distance addicts from their emotional lives, leaving them dependent upon their substance or their addictive activity in order to cope with the everyday challenges of life. When one spouse is addicted, there is only one person attempting to have a marriage, which is obviously a great burden—and, considering the definition of a marriage, an oxymoron.

Confusion and ignorance can be ways of abdicating power. Abdicating spouses explain why they don't meet their partner's needs by claiming not to understand the process of doing so. Confusion and ignorance are often meant to disguise the abdicating spouse's need to punish and act passive-aggressively. A dead giveaway of this dynamic is that the abdicating spouse is neither curious about how to meet the partner's needs, nor do they commit to any process that would lead to acquiring the appropriate interpersonal skills. The stronger the claim of ignorance, the stronger the need to punish.

As we saw earlier, the threat of withdrawing support, sex, attention, and affection is a form of bullying. The actual withdrawal of sex and affection may constitute an abdication of power. This form of abdication is usually punitive and driven by the spouse's anger or need for revenge, but spouses almost never admit their need to punish; rather, they explain their behavior by describing themselves as busy or tired.

The most subtle and yet extremely influential form of abdication is a partner's refusal to develop personal gifts. For a variety of reasons, people often resist taking the responsibility to identify and develop their innate skills and competencies. These spouses are minimizing themselves by inhibiting their development. Inhibited development leads to unnecessary dependency and resentment.

Marriages are renewed as couples willingly take accountability for abusing and abdicating their power. Accountability happens when spouses not only identify how they abuse and abdicate power, but are also willing to intervene when abusive and abdicative behavior occurs.

## Creative Empowerment

There are more creative approaches to power that afford us the opportunity not only to diminish unnecessary tension, but to deepen our capacity to learn about how we hold and exercise power. The first step toward creative empowerment is to make the idea of power "talkable." So many couples don't talk about the role of power in their relationship. The more power receives the amount of attention commensurate with its role in a marriage, the more resilient a couple can become when working with power issues. There are a number of ways that a couple can begin to focus their discussion about power. Some questions might be: "How do you see me exercise power in our marriage?" "How do I see you exercise power in our marriage?" "What impact does our employment of power have upon one another?"

As well as speaking to one another about the role of power, it is extremely beneficial for each spouse to have a support system where they can further explore their relationship to power. It is very helpful to hear friends talk about the ways they abuse and abdicate power. Being able to talk about power diminishes the likelihood that an abusive act will erupt out of the unconscious, creating hurt and havoc.

Many spouses approach the issue of power as if it is mostly an issue between themselves and their partners; certainly power often gets played out as a struggle of wills. We replay childhood scripts and scenarios, which are mostly about bigger and stronger people obstructing our wills and frustrating our attempts at influencing some desired end. We readily reproduce these scripts with our spouses, seeing them as major interferences with our power. Once we are holding the perception that our spouses are hindrances to getting what we want, it's natural to abuse or abdicate power in order to deal with such a formidable foe. Unfortunately, we almost never have much control over the choices our partners are going to make.

Whether we are attempting to influence our partners or allowing our wishes to get swept away by the desires of our spouses, we are giving up responsibility for our own lives. We try controlling our partners because we are afraid to stand alone amidst the diversity of our differing desires. We need the endorsement of our spouse's affiliation in order to help us hold the legitimacy of our intentions. Or we can surrender responsibility for ourselves by being accommodating and allowing our spouse's intentions to define who we are.

We talk about creative empowerment because in a marriage, there is constant variability in how we move toward some desired end. Our moods, our attachments, and how we feel about ourselves all contribute to our efficacy, as well as the resoluteness we can summon in response to the willfulness of our spouses. Actually, it may be accurate to say that we do not empower ourselves twice in exactly the same way. Our personal histories and present life situations all contribute to make the process of self-empowerment a very creative challenge.

Power is an essential dynamic in all marriages, and often remains so even in divorce. Consequently, nuptial power struggles are inevitable, and most of us do not want our marriages to be one endless power grind; hence the need to become creative in the endeavor of supporting our desires while remaining an ally to our marriages. One essential key is to do whatever is in our control to avoid being a victim of our partner's choices while encouraging our spouses to avoid becoming our victims.

It's not easy to negotiate our way around victimization. It will call for practice and resolve like we have never known before. We will be called to back ourselves up, refusing to succumb to the way of the victim. The following skills allow us to creatively stand up for ourselves without abusing our partners.

> *Remaining self-focused.* Staying focused on ourselves is a critical starting point. Unless we are willing to bring our attention to what we feel and want, we will do a serious disservice to ourselves and our relationships. Our desire consti- tutes fifty percent of the overall power of our relationship. If we ignore our desire, we put the eight-cylinder engine of our marriages on four cylinders.
>
> Spouses who tend to abdicate their power often respond to this suggestion by defining it as selfish. What is noteworthy is that abdicators are often inclined to place themselves in deprivation and feel victimized by their part- ners. They are usually willing to suffer just so much loss, in the name of not being selfish, before they begin berating their partners for their pain. Soon, those who claim not to be self-focused (in order to avoid being selfish) are demanding that their partners give them more time and energy.
>
> *Employing effective problem ownership.* We will revisit this skill several times throughout the book, since it is a significant prerequisite for building inti- macy. Effective problem ownership defines the problem and identifies the per- son who has the problem. The problem is simply some unmet need, and the person with the problem is the spouse with the unmet need.
>
> Most of us grew up in families where it was not in our best interest to be clear about our unmet needs. We soon learned that we would be ridiculed, shamed, or "guilted" out of bringing a voice to what we needed; however, the tension of holding our unmet needs silently would soon give rise to getting good at being unconscious about what we needed, thereby diminishing the tension.
>
> Another coping mechanism is to become blameful. In this case, we give ourselves permission to be aware of the unmet needs, but we hold others responsible for our frustration. This propensity is a setup for viewing our part- ners as the perpetrators of our deprivation and seeing ourselves as their vic- tims.
>
> Effective problem ownership moves us into the power to address our unmet needs while freeing us from being our partners' victims. If your partner is the one with the unmet need, then you can posture yourself as their ally. We can listen as they clarify what it is that they actually need. We can negotiate as

they make requests of us. We can brainstorm, helping them access a resolution that best meets their need.

*Employing effective boundaries.* Without effective boundaries, it is literally impossible to get creative about working with power in our marriages. We will say more about boundaries in the next chapter. But for now, let's say that a boundary is something we put in place, allowing a lot, some, or nothing at all to pass through.

What are the dynamics in a marriage that we can allow to pass or not pass through our boundaries? The first is emotion. We can have three levels of responses to our spouses' emotions, each indicating a specific kind of boundary. If we experience their sadness as our own or hold ourselves responsible for their sadness (and therefore responsible for doing something about it), then we are employing a boundary that is allowing a great deal to come through.

It is worth noting that if couples employ boundaries regularly that allow much to come through, then the individuality of each spouse runs some risk of being lost. Instead of having "your sadness" and "my sadness," there is only "our sadness."

The second option is a boundary that allows almost nothing to pass. In this case, one spouse's sadness is definitely that person's sadness. In this case, the partner feels none of the spouse's emotion, and feels no responsibility for it or to fix it. The benefit of this boundary is that the spouse who is sad gets to experience his or her sadness as a unique expression of who he or she is. The tradeoff here is that the other spouse's boundary may result in him or her being viewed as distant or uncaring.

The third alternative is a boundary that allows some of the spouse's sadness to pass through. In this case, the spouse who isn't sad may get the benefit of not being responsible for the other's emotion, while also appearing to be empathic and available.

The idea that there are three kinds of boundaries is simply a benchmark, allowing us to get a working idea of the options available to us. The key is to become effective at identifying how much of our partner's identity we want flowing through to us and defining us.

What has been said about emotions is also true for beliefs and values. Our partners will inevitably hold a host of beliefs, from religious ideals to where to go on vacation. And their values will span across an endless array of topics, from child-rearing to same-sex marriages.

We can execute strong boundaries aimed at preventing ourselves from being influenced in any way whatsoever by the beliefs and values held by our spouses. Or we can employ very weak boundaries, resulting in our consistent conversion to the beliefs of our partners. The third alternative is to exercise a partial boundary, whereby we allow ourselves to be somewhat influenced without completely surrendering our own position—that is, of course, if we truly believe it is in our best interest to change.

Behaviors constitute another transaction that occurs between spouses. The range of behaviors varies wildly, from very abusive to extremely loving. And again, our choice of boundary varies, from allowing ourselves to be fully affected or somewhat affected to not being affected at all. Ironically, my work with couples suggests that the weakest of boundaries are often in place when abuse is headed our way, while our strongest boundaries may be warding off our spouse's best efforts to love us.

Holding power creatively in a marriage calls for a great deal of mindfulness regarding the status of our boundaries. Creative empowerment is driven by asking questions about boundaries: What kinds of boundaries have I been employing? What do the situations where I feel victimized by my spouse suggest about the status of my boundaries? Where are my boundaries serving me in my marriage, and where do they not serve me? Are my boundaries supporting my desired outcomes? Of course, the creative edge will continue to be infused by the challenge of supporting what we want while remaining an ally to our spouses' desires.

*Power through surrender.* Nothing boggles our western minds more than the idea of generating power through surrender. We westerners understand power to be an act of will. Our cultural bias promotes a skewed view of power, in which someone's will dominates or influences the will of another. The only paradigm we know results in some form of subjugation; hence, marriage is easily transformed into an arena for endless jousting, with spouses striving to knock one another to the ground. Entrenched in this battleground, spouses lose any perspective of one another as allies.

Surrender is not abdication. Unlike capitulation, surrender is an acknowledgement of what is not in our control and entails a redirection of our attention and energies to what is in our control. The "Serenity Prayer" says it well: "God grant me the serenity to accept the things I cannot change, the courage to change the things I can, and the wisdom to know the difference." Spouses who expend tireless efforts at attempting to influence their partners are in a self-defeating pattern. Our partners either choose to be or not to be receptive to our influence; it is their choice, and it serves us to perceive the dynamic of influence as their choice.

In order to live the power of surrender, we will need to find the strength to endure those moments when we acknowledge our powerlessness and choose surrender. It is only too easy to be ashamed for being powerless, since the willfulness paradigm does not tolerate such quintessential expressions of the human condition.

The story of surrender does not end with accepting what we cannot change. Surrender and willfulness were meant to dance together. Before the dance can continue, we may need to experience the feelings that accompany our powerlessness, including the likelihood of some grief. Once we realize that our best efforts are not enough to effectively influence our partners, we may feel angry, sad, and inadequate.

It may take some work to get clear about what we really want. It may also be challenging to find the entitlement that allows us to feel deserving enough to pursue our desires. It can be only too easy to take some solace in our heroic efforts to do the impossible, irrespective of guaranteed failure. We may need to discover that sainthood does not normally result from endless struggle. It may be that we are being called to make peace with our own limitations before we can exercise the wisdom to effectively discern what is in our control and what is not.

Once we have some level of acceptance of our powerlessness, it is critical to return our attention to what is in our control. As we do so, we need to remain focused upon what we want and the best way to employ our wills toward manifesting our desires. Too much surrender or too much will makes us victims of our partners and victims of life.

Either power through surrender or power through willfulness alone is seriously inadequate to facing the challenges of power in a marriage. Creative empowerment means using both expressions of power and deepening the wisdom to know when and how. Toward this end, marriage remains a potent initiatory container, inviting spouses to explore the depths of their own relationship to power.

*Remaining responsible for our own self-worth.* It is tremendously disempowering to wait for our spouses to declare that we are worthwhile human beings, plus it is simply not their responsibility. But it can be only too easy to get caught in a childhood pattern of attempting to attain the approval of our parents, and casting our marriages into a parent-child dynamic that precludes any hope for true intimacy.

The more responsibility we take for our own goodness, the more power we have over making sure that it happens. We are not supposed to assess our deservedness or the appropriateness of feeling good about ourselves. Our responsibility is to make sure that we remain vigilant about acknowledging our essential goodness while protecting it from outside sources of ridicule and shame. We then have more power and energy to devote to our personal and professional development. We are also freed from the unnecessary burden of feeling resentful and vengeful because our spouses did not deliver an appropriate amount of validation.

*Remaining students of power.* An intimate relationship requires that the participants remain students of power. It would be silly to suggest that if a couple follows the six suggested steps of creative empowerment, then their marriage will be immune to abuses and abdications of power. The goal is not to sterilize a marriage of its toxic expressions of power! Marriage is actually the place where we all can become more familiar with the many ways we maneuver in order to influence or avoid being influenced. At best, we can become more cognizant of how we abuse and abdicate power, and continue to learn how to become more creative with our expressions of power.

There are a number of questions that lend themselves toward clarifying how we hold power in our marriages. How do I abuse power? How do I abdicate power? What do I understand about how abuse and abdication affect my spouse? Which two elements of creative empowerment would be helpful for me to focus on? Which component of creative empowerment is most challenging for me?

In summary, we have discussed six conditions that can help us to carry power creatively in our marriages:

*Remaining self-focused
*Employing effective boundaries
*Employing effective problem ownership
*Surrendering
*Remaining responsible for our own self-worth
*Remaining students of power

# Radical Self-Responsibility

A marriage is one of the most powerful containers for learning how to be responsible for our own lives. There are constant invitations to either control or be controlled. One way to move out of the control/controlled dynamic is to remain self-focused and aware that each of us is the primary facilitator of our own disempowerment and emancipation.

Learning to be radically self-responsible may be one of the most challenging aspects of growing up, and marriage offers constant opportunities, if we want them. One of the Latin roots of the word "responsibility" is *curaae,* meaning "concern, care, and under the management of." When we are radically self-responsible, we exercise care and concern for our own lives and see our lives as under our own management.

There are several demons to be faced in the quest for radical self-responsibility, making it significant shadow work. If we are willing to flirt with radical self-responsibility, it becomes quickly clear that we are alone. We were born alone, we die alone, and we ultimately manage our own lives alone. The greatest disillusionment at a divorce is the end of the dream that someone would always be there for us. I am not suggesting that our partners cannot love us, collaborate with us, support us, and join us on numerous adventures and projects. The point is that each of us must ultimately manage our own emotions and see ourselves as the creators of our happiness, our sorrow, our fears, and our anger. Most importantly, the depths of radical self-responsibility will take us to the management of our own goodness and lovability.

We will persist in sabotaging our personal empowerment unless we are willing to remain students of power, specifically learning about what is in our control and what is not. Many spouses expend much time and energy abusing and abdicating power because they are attempting to control the uncontrollable. At the top of the list of things out of our control should be items like our spouse's choices, whether or not our partners love us, and whether or not they will choose to stay with us. We cannot control our partners. We can control how we respond to our partners.

Our partners have the right to have a full emotional life; that is, they can respond to our choices by feeling glad, angry, disappointed, scared, etc. We also have a myriad of ways to respond to their emotions; we can defend, justify, explain, protest, attack, or withdraw, or we can allow them to have their emotions without deciding that their emotions somehow define us.

Another nemesis to being radically self-responsible is the shame and guilt that often accompany making a mistake. We attempt to avoid feeling ashamed or guilty by blaming others for our situation. Consequently, if we want to deepen our capacity for self-responsibility, we need to be ready to face our shame and our guilt. Unless we are predisposed to the experience of these dark forces, we will abuse power by blaming our partners and seeing ourselves as the victim of their choices.

## Remaining Students of Power

As we remain students of creative empowerment, some important questions arise: What really is my desired end? How might I be obstructing progress toward that end? What support or resources can I access in order to help me generate a more creative relationship with my obstruction? What one choice am I willing to make that will help me access this support?

Once we are self-focused, we can expand our inquiry into our relationship with power. The obvious understanding of power is that our desired end is to invigorate our relationship to life. Sometimes this is true. We want to make choices that open us to life and allow us to experience the adventure and depth of life.

However, creating a dynamic relationship with life is not always the desired end. Often we are directing our influence toward protecting ourselves from life. When sheltering ourselves from life is the desired end, we exercise our power in the direction of closing ourselves off and avoiding opportunities for adventure and depth. This need to have an adversarial relationship with life often generates tension and conflict when our spouse is attempting to have a dynamic relationship with life.

Pete and Maureen, a couple in their mid-fifties with a great deal of tension in their relationship, came in to see me. It became clear that Maureen was eagerly attempting to open herself up to life. Her children were grown, and she had returned to school to study literature. She had recently joined a women's support group and wanted to go on adventures with her husband. Pete, on the other hand, was very content in front of the television, watching a variety of sporting events.

"Pete, I want you to come to class with me sometime," she told him.

"Your class is on Monday nights, and I won't be able to get home in time for the kickoff of the Monday night football game," he responded.

"How do you feel about Pete's rejection of your invitation?" I asked.

"I'm getting used to it. But I guess I'm also pretty angry," she admitted.

"Have you told Pete about your anger?" I inquired.

"Yes, I have, and I get nowhere! I extend invitation after invitation to him, and he doesn't seem to be at all interested," she declared.

"Well, I'm wondering how you plan to take care of yourself in regard to all these rejections you have been receiving."

"I guess I will continue to explore life alone. It's not what I want, but what other option do I have?"

Maureen was learning to surrender and accept that she had no power over Pete's handling of her invitations; however, she was also willing to allow her will to bring her closer to life.

I reminded Pete that Maureen was planning to continue to open up to life but to discontinue her invitations to him. Pete appeared indifferent. Maureen explored life alone for years and eventually met a man who was also interested in opening to life. Pete and Maureen were soon in divorce proceedings.

Pete could have benefited significantly from Maureen's invitations to join her life explorations. He could have allowed her passion to bring him more creatively in touch with his fear of life, with his wife, and with himself. Instead, he chose to employ his power toward protecting himself from life, in the end losing his wife, and most likely losing himself.

It is important to engage in some honest introspection regarding the nature of the ends that we are attempting to influence; that is, to be clear about how we want to employ our power. The topic of power is like sex, in that almost everybody wants it, but no one wants to talk about it.

Another important way to relate to power is to see our partner's choices and their willfulness not simply as an impediment to our personal empowerment. We can view our partner's exercise of power as the context—the place where we have decided to learn about power. Learning about power cannot happen in seclusion. It must have a container where power becomes a real-life issue, where some particular end is desired, where choices need to be made, often in the presence of fear, confusion, and anger. Learning about power anywhere is hard work. It's important not to view a marriage as troubled or dysfunctional because a couple has decided that their relationship is the place they have chosen to learn about power.

Power is the ability to influence a desired end. As long as married couples have desires and become regressed, they will abuse and abdicate power as ways of acquiring those desired ends. Consequently, there is no way to sanitize a marriage, purifying it from all abuses and abdications. If couples want to strengthen their individual integrity and deepen their connection to one another, they must be willing to be accountable for abuse and abdication in an ongoing way.

Couples can commit to being clear about their desires with themselves and with their partners. They can also clarify how they intend to pursue those desired ends. Accountability also includes being honest about how we feel about our partner's desires and how they affect us. Accountability involves taking care of ourselves if we feel obstructed by our partners' pursuit of their desires. And of course, accountability happens when we actively attend to our regressive experiences.

The more we hold ourselves responsible for what we get or don't get in our marriages, the greater the opportunity to deepen our individuality and our connection to our partners. Nothing is more beneficial to a marriage than the willingness to let go of seeing ourselves as the victim of our partner's willfulness and begin defining our lives as the creation of our own empowerment.

# 7

## *The Soul of Intimacy*

One of the greatest promises of marriage is intimacy; however, we are constantly reminded of the fact that many marriages are plagued by isolation, hostility, and estrangement. It appears that our expectations of a blossoming intimacy have somehow eluded our best nuptial efforts.

We naively believe that although intimacy may have never truly been in our lives, we need only fall in love with the right person and make the appropriate vows and presto—intimacy at its best. Most of the couples with whom I have worked have not asked themselves what intimacy means for them, nor have they asked how much of it they want, if any at all. When I ask couples if they experience any intimacy in their relationship, they either think I am asking them if they have regular sex, or they understand what I am asking and they are relatively sure they don't have any.

The couples who report little or no intimacy in their lives suggest that there are two indicators of lost intimacy. First, they don't feel good about themselves when engaging with their partners. Secondly, they don't feel heard or understood when communicating with their partners.

When I ask couples to describe the presence of intimacy in their marriages, they usually tell me that it is a warm, positive feeling. They understand intimacy to be a feeling of pleasure or joy.

We are a culture that worships the god of feeling good, experiencing pleasure, or at least the absence of tension and pain. We measure the value of our decisions, and the actions of others, based upon whether or not they make us feel good.

Harmony and tranquility in a marriage are almost never viable barometers of the level of intimacy. What they typically indicate is one of two powerful shadows: either the presence of a great deal of fusion or a great deal of avoidance. Nothing can dry up a marriage more quickly than harmony; in fact, it is normally more deadly than ongoing friction. A harmonious marriage is usually one stripped of each person's uniqueness and soulfulness. The dark side of marital serenity is the likelihood that at least one spouse is no longer fully participating in the relationship.

We are a culture that has significantly stepped away from living the authentic life. We settle for looking good. Authenticity doesn't feel good. It is often challenging, tension-provoking, and frightening.

I was reminded recently of our fondness for imitations when I was ordering lunch with a friend at a local restaurant. I ordered a chicken Caesar wrap and my friend ordered the same, but before he ordered, he asked if the wrap came with real chicken. I thought he was kidding and that the waitress would naturally get a chuckle from his quip. To the contrary, he was quite serious, and the waitress reassured him that the chicken in his sandwich would be real. We are now willing to settle for imitations in almost every aspect of our lives—in our food, in our business practices, in our politics, in our education, and in our marriages.

We choose fusion or avoidance as imitations of intimacy. We naively think that the imitations are easier. Nothing could be further from the truth. Imitations temporarily soothe us and offer a momentary reprieve from the tension inherent in the authentic life. Imitations like fusion and avoidance inevitably turn the human psyche into caricatures of humanity, lacking depth and soul.

## Fusion Feels and Looks Like Intimacy

Nothing can quite create the illusion of intimacy like fusion and avoidance. Both of these imitations are capable of casting a deep, rich aroma of intimacy. As we shall see, intimacy is an ongoing initiation into individual and collective depths, and such initiations are both painful and frightening. In a culture dedicated to immediate gratification and the avoidance of pain, fusion and avoidance become attractive options in lieu of authentic intimacy.

The attraction to these illusions is based upon the fantasy that intimacy is mostly about generating a tranquil marital atmosphere. Of course, the longing for harmony is about the need to avoid the ferocity of initiation, as if the power of initiation won't ultimately have its way.

We are looking for a way to express our individuality while finding a way to satisfy our need for human connection. Fusion pushes for the need for affiliation, while avoidance aims at satisfying the need for individuation. The gift of fusion is that sooner or later, one or both spouses will get sick of being joined at the hip, and begin longing for the experience of being a separate and unique individual. The gift of avoidance is that one of the spouses may begin to yearn for togetherness. Each dissatisfaction has the power to hurl a marriage into crisis, offering a couple the opportunity to confront their fusion or avoidance, and to surrender to an initiation into intimacy.

The overriding attraction of fusion is that it can generate an aura of togetherness, while temporarily numbing the tension that is generated when we strive to maintain an individual path while being part of a relationship. The soul is eager for connection, and fusion is an attempt at creating it while eliminating the threat of aloneness. Fusion helps generate the illusion that there is an escape from our existential loneliness. Fusing couples believe they can safeguard their harmony by minimizing the role of individual needs and values. The goal is oneness at all costs.

It can be extremely misleading to suggest there is a right way to engage in intimacy. The soul is striving to find its way to itself as well as to the other. This is not a matter of "getting it right," but rather allowing the fusion to teach us about our fears and what we can learn about human connection.

Fusion is mostly a way to be in a relationship and cope with the tension of inevitable loss. Love may bring us warmth, companionship, and eroticism, but the only guarantee is loss. Eventually, one partner will either leave the other or die. Most of us play the "together forever" game, but it may be that just below the surface, we know the truth about love and loss.

There are a number of dynamics aimed at fortifying the life of a fused couple. Abdication of power is one way couples attempt to maintain the status quo of their fusion. Each spouse may believe that their togetherness is dependent upon deferring to the other. They prioritize the needs and wants of their partner in hopes of eliminating conflict and disagreement, and therefore separation. But abdication hardly ever guarantees long-lasting harmony. The more likely outcome is passive-aggression, as the partners reach their intolerance points for self-sacrifice.

Another driving element operating in a fused relationship is minimizing the value of boundaries. Since boundaries in a marriage are designed to secure the separate identities of each partner, boundaries are threatening to the fused couple, who are attempting to demonstrate they are one. Fused spouses do not say *no* authentically to one another.

Fused partners inevitably settle for being needed. In order to be loved, spouses must be willing to bring their unique selves to the relationship. Obviously, we cannot be loved if we do not bring who we are to our marriages. Consequently, being needed is the likely alternative to being loved. It is quite common for couples to switch in and out of the roles of needing and being needed, promoting dependency and successfully averting being loved.

Couples attempting to maintain their fusion will customarily seek affirmation from the other; they define their partners as responsible for making them feel good about themselves. It's a setup, since it is impossible for one adult to be responsible for generating another's personal value. This process of seeking affirmation from our partners translates into: "I will not threaten our fusion by separating enough from you in order to affirm myself."

Fused couples are "other-referented"; they refer to the other as a way to construct their own identities. In a real sense, they are borrowing their identities or appropriating good feelings about themselves from their spouses. They get their beliefs and values from their partners or they seek their partners' approval. They are attempting to avoid threatening the relationship in any way, with the goal being the prevention of any form of separation or the termination of the relationship.

Fused couples make nonverbal deals. Some examples are: "I will not do anything that upsets you, and you won't leave me," and "I won't hold a belief or value that threatens you, and you won't leave me." When one spouse behaves contrary to a nonverbal deal, there is an opportunity for the couple to confront their fusion.

Couples desiring to undo their fusion will have some challenging yet rewarding work ahead of them. Very few couples enter my office claiming they are ready to move beyond their fusion to a more authentic experience of intimacy. Fused couples do report feeling frustrated and angry about a partner's behavior, which is usually in violation of a nonverbal deal.

In some cases, one partner's personal growth is increasing a desire for greater autonomy and separateness. The partner moving into personal change can be viewed as threatening to the status quo of the relationship. Their spouse may experience a significant level of insecurity.

In order to move out of fusion, spouses must be willing to raise their consciousness about the choices that have fostered fusion. It is critical for them to hold their awareness with compassion and start to employ more effective boundaries, ones that allow for a greater expression of individuality while maintaining a connection to one another. The initial employment of boundaries may feel like the bottom is falling out of the relationship. There may be a significant period of adjustment. Spouses need to return to themselves, feeling the joy and fulfillment of their authenticity, before creating a meaningful connection to their partners.

Fused couples are often "other-referented" when they explore problems in their relationship. They each decide that the other is the source of the difficulty. Fused spouses rarely see themselves as part of the problem. Not only are they accustomed to keeping their attention on their partners, but they see any reference to themselves as part of the problem as a reason why their partners might leave them.

Raising consciousness about how we have advanced fusion in our relationships can stimulate shame, especially if we have been invested in "doing our relationships perfectly." It is important to unearth our awareness with as much compassion as possible. It is critical to be working with a therapist who is capable of advocating compassion while encouraging spouses to remain self-focused and self-responsible.

It can be very challenging to dispel the belief that we can keep our partners by becoming extensions of them. On the surface, this particular belief appears to be relatively easy to shift, once it is understood that there really is nothing we can do to keep our partners in the relationship; however, undoing the belief is itself a significant initiation.

Children have a deep resolve when dealing with abuse and neglect. The greater challenge is feeling out of control of their worlds, which they often cope with by the use of magical thinking, which gives them a feeling of control over monsters, dragons, and the love of family members. We are not simply talking about adults, who can grasp that they cannot control whether someone decides to stay with them or leave. We are rather talking about kids, who magically believe that they can control who stays or leaves, because to not have such control inevitably leads to isolation, and even death.

Within the above context, it becomes much easier to understand why spouses in their forties and fifties are arguing in support of their having control over the coming and going of their partners as if their life depended upon it, because in some emotional sense, it does. Quite often, before spouses are willing to fully accept their helplessness over whether their partners choose them or not, they must face their fear of dying. On the other side of their fear of death, they may discover the erosion of fusion.

Deconstructing fusion calls for a willingness to become and remain a student of boundaries. Relationships are organic, and as they shift and change, boundaries must also shift in ways that can best support the vitality of a marriage.

What is a boundary? A boundary is any thought or behavior that helps separate us from our spouses. As we saw in a previous chapter, boundaries can be slightly, moderately, or extremely permeable. The nature of the boundary will often be determined by how much individuality a spouse needs to reclaim, and the reclaiming is done through emotional separation.

What is an emotional separation? An emotional separation is a psychological detachment allowing spouses to define who they are as unique and different from their partners. As we shall see, this separation process through the use of boundaries is not only critical toward undoing fusion, but it is also a prerequisite for the creation of intimacy.

## Three Levels of Boundaries

There are essentially three levels of boundaries. The first level can be described as extremely permeable. Permeable boundaries allow our partners' intention, beliefs, and values to flow directly into us and define us accordingly. An analogy would be pouring water over a wire-mesh screen. The screen allows the water to flow directly through, holding none back.

Charles and Corin came in for couples counseling, with Corin complaining about Charles's drinking.

"I really don't get it. When Charles and I met six years ago, Charles had thirteen years of recovery in AA. We get married, and he begins drinking—at first a wine now and then with dinner, and then a few scotches before dinner," explained Corin.

Corin went on to describe how she had been coping with Charles's drinking, while Charles sat quietly with his chin braced against his chest.

"Charles, I'm wondering if you want to say anything about your drinking," I asked.

"I do. I get scared when Corin and I spend an excessive amount of time away from one another, or if we get into different activities," said Charles.

"I hear you, Charles, but I'm not sure what that has to do with your drinking," I said.

"It's got a lot to do with my drinking. You see, when Corin and I got married, Corin was a social drinker. She would have a glass of wine every now and then. I didn't want her having a glass of wine with some other guy," confessed Charles.

Charles's sobriety constituted too much of a boundary for him in light of his wife's drinking. He believed that if the boundary were permeable and he became more like her, he could control whether she stayed or left him. Charles soon returned to AA and began addressing the illusion he had created in regard to permeable boundaries.

A fused marriage is consistently operating with permeable boundaries. Is there a place for permeable boundaries in a marriage? Permeable boundaries may be useful in times of crisis, illness, or some kind of trauma, as well as during lovemaking. A spouse sick with the flu tells her partner what she needs from him; the husband listens and responds accordingly, without adding his own intentions, allowing her needs to define his behavior accordingly.

The second level of boundary is semipermeable. This quality of boundary allows us to be touched and influenced by our partners without sacrificing what is essential to our own characters. The analogy here is that of water poured over a piece of cheesecloth; some of the fluid is allowed to pass, and some is prevented from moving through.

Charles and Corin began crafting more semipermeable boundaries in their marriage. Corin was already relatively effective at allowing herself to be influenced without sacrificing her individuality. As Charles gave up the illusion that his permeable boundaries gave him some measure of control over Corin, he became more competent with the employment of semipermeable boundaries.

Charles's work with semipermeable boundaries included allowing himself to feel the fear he experienced when he noticed that he and Corin were different. He learned to comfort himself and ask himself over and over again just how different his preferences, beliefs, and values were from Corin's. If he wasn't sure, he let that mean that he was probably different from her, at least for the time being. Crafting semipermeable boundaries taught Charles a great deal about holding the tension created by acknowledging his uniqueness.

The third level of boundary is impermeable. This kind of boundary allows nothing to pass through. Couples living with impermeable boundaries are quite often deeply isolated from one another. They simply do not know each other. They refuse to allow themselves to be touched by the other, and as we shall see, they participate in avoidance in lieu of intimacy. Couples with intense fears of being consumed often live with impermeable boundaries. The fear of being swallowed up by a spouse can result in a defense aimed at completely keeping the spouse at a distance. The analogy is that of pouring water into a glass cup; it is an impermeable boundary, allowing nothing to pass through.

It may be quite appropriate during times of physical or emotional abuse to employ impermeable boundaries. This kind of boundary is quite helpful when spouses are in need of support and safety. Impermeable boundaries are also useful when a spouse has felt extremely dominated by a partner and wishes to reverse that process.

All three levels of boundaries operate in all marriages. Remaining a student of boundaries means staying focused on the level of boundary we typically employ in our relationship, and asking whether the boundaries we use are actually getting the job done. We can also ask what a particular level of boundary might suggest about our fears and what we need from our relationships. The key is not to attempt working with boundaries perfectly, but simply staying close to our own "learning edge."

I recently had an important lesson about how my boundaries were operating in my own marriage. I pride myself on my ability to employ semipermeable boundaries. Connie and I recently visited our son, our daughter-in-law, and our two-month-old granddaughter. One evening, while the baby slept, we decided to watch a movie containing some violence.

My wife's anxiety normally builds when she is viewing a film in which someone is being hurt or could potentially be harmed. She copes by either fidgeting in her seat or moving about the room like a gymnast, the latter being her coping mechanism of choice on this particular evening.

As I watched her from the corner of my eye, I became increasingly judgmental of the excessively permeable boundaries she employed between her and the film. I wanted to yell, "It's only a movie!"

The severity of my reaction began to get my attention, and I wondered why I was responding to her so strongly. Within moments I realized that the boundaries between me and my son and my daughter-in-law were very permeable, since I was afraid of what they might think of Connie's varied gyrations. But if I was allowing their reaction to my wife to define me, then the boundaries between Connie and me, in that moment, were also considerably permeable.

Excessively permeable boundaries have a way of sneaking up on us. Embarrassment and fear of what others might think are helpful indicators of the status of our boundaries.

## Avoidance: Another Imposter

Like fusion, avoidance can create an atmosphere of harmony and contentment. If a couple minimizes the amount of time they spend together physically and emotionally, it becomes easy to pretend that they have a good thing going. What they actually have going is the ability to stay out of one another's way.

Avoidance can be characterized as employing impermeable boundaries, since the spouses do not allow themselves to be moved or influenced by the other. The intensity of the avoidance can vary from light to severe, with the latter condition accompanied by impermeable boundaries. The avoidance can be emotional or physical.

Physical avoidance happens when spouses simply do not spend much time in one another's physical presence. Couples can indulge in numerous levels of physical distancing, everything from meeting annually to working different shifts. The most popular modality of physical avoidance is spending an inordinate amount of time at work. Excessive work is often portrayed as a good thing, guaranteeing adequate household revenue.

Emotional avoidance also occurs on different levels. The quantity of a couple's emotional avoidance is often directly proportionate to their physical avoidance. They simply do not have the opportunity to be emotionally connected. Just as important is the quality of emotional connection.

If couples seldom or never incorporate their emotional lives into their relationship, there will obviously be significant emotional distancing. The next strongest level of emotional distancing happens when couples limit their emotional lives to how they feel about other people and events. The least amount of emotional distancing happens when couples are expressing how they feel (mad, sad, glad, scared, ashamed) about themselves and one another.

It is this last level of emotional connection, where people are talking about how they authentically feel about themselves and one another, that can make intimacy an extremely challenging initiation. The first guideline is to make all feelings absolutely acceptable. A shadow marriage places no censorship on any genuine feelings, especially if the list is kept to the five mentioned above. I recommend that spouses commit to remaining responsible only for their own feelings.

The idea of remaining responsible only for our own feelings is a huge initiation. We all come out of childhood believing we are responsible for the feelings of others, and that others are responsible for ours. It's a tangled web. The way out is a commitment to be radically responsible for our own feelings, which means that although others can do and say things that have an emotional impact upon us, we are responsible for how we support and attend to ourselves. This level of responsibility is empowering, since we don't have any control over the remarks and actions of others. Our feelings belong to us, and to no one else.

Couples often respond to the notion of radical responsibility by suggesting they can say anything they want to their spouses, since they are not responsible for how their spouses feel. On the contrary, it does not make sense to act capriciously or intentionally sadistically when we love someone and we want to build a relationship based upon trust and integrity.

The absence of conflict is a common way that couples fool themselves into believing they are actually intimate. It is very difficult for disengaged couples to experience any form of discord, because they keep their lives so separate. Collision is highly unlikely if two people are traveling on significantly different paths. But the absence of collision does not equal intimacy.

## Confronting Avoidance

Couples retreating from one another are coping with the tension they experience when they get close. This tension is ordinarily the fear of losing their individuality and autonomy. They feel safe behind strong impermeable boundaries, where they believe they can maintain their power and their freedom.

A common misconception held by retreating couples is that their partners have the ability to strip them of their individuality. Spouses willing to confront their avoidance must be willing to confront this myth and come to the understanding that their autonomy cannot be taken; they can only lose it by giving it away. This process also calls for radical responsibility, in which spouses hold themselves responsible for any loss of their individuality. Once spouses can realize that the giveaway is their responsibility, it becomes important to explore the nature of the giveaway.

Quite often spouses discover that one aspect of giving themselves away is that they have polarized their boundaries. They are either employing impermeable boundaries or they are utilizing excessively permeable boundaries, ones that cannot support their individuality in the presence of outside influences, so they become extremely predisposed to the beliefs and values of the partner. With the boundary options limited to two, they will inevitably choose avoidance (impermeable boundaries) as a way to survive.

Many couples talk about guilt and taking responsibility for their partners as being the two driving forces behind an avoidant relationship. They feel guilty for not effectively meeting their partners' needs when they move closer to them, or they feel responsible for their partners' happiness. Essentially, retreating couples are claiming that if they become closer to their partners, they will become fused and lose themselves. It is what most couples know: they will either be in avoidance or fused.

In David Schnarch's *Creating the Sexual Crucible*, he alludes to the attraction of avoidance and fusion and tells how no specific gender has an edge when it comes to intimacy: "When the focus is intense intimacy, there is no consistent gender difference in intimacy tolerance: almost no one wants it."

Ray and Jean, a couple in their fifties, came to see men complaining of the avoidance Ray brought to their marriage.

"We've been married for seven years, and I'm just real sick of it. When he's home, he is either in the garage or down in the basement. And of course, he spends fifty to sixty hours at work," she complained.

"It sounds like you don't get to see your husband much. How long has this been going on?" I inquired.

"Since the beginning—all seven years! He's never been available," she answered.

"Tell me, how have you dealt with this for seven years?" I asked.

"Well, it wasn't easy. I had to make a lot of the decisions and deal with plenty of the household problems on my own," she said.

"It sounds like you were burdened by many of the household responsibilities," I reflected.

"You bet I was!"

"I don't understand how you continued to be so tolerant of the isolation and the many obligations you endured," I said.

"Oh, I don't know. I guess it just came with the territory," she responded.

"One thing I would say about the territory is that your tolerance may reflect something that you have been getting along with the hardship," I suggested, calling her away from simply being a victim of the situation.

"Well, it did give me control of almost everything that was going on in the home," she meekly speculated.

"That makes sense to me. Along with all the responsibility, you also got to control much that transpired," I concurred.

Jean was initially resistant to acknowledging and accepting her role in the creation of the avoidance with Ray. It took some time before Jean was willing to stop blaming Ray and become self-focused, which eventually led her to accept how she did enjoy the control that Ray's absence afforded her. She admitted that she wasn't sure what would happen to her preferences if Ray became a full participant in the relationship.

Jean's fear of losing control, if Ray stepped into the marriage with his desires, is a common theme in estranged marriages. It was initially difficult for Jean to see how much of herself she was losing as she and Ray buried themselves in avoidance. Jean soon appreciated how she had lost the part of herself who could learn to stand for what she wanted and negotiate with her husband. She had lost the part of herself that could participate in problem-solving and decision-making and truly collaborate with her husband. She had lost the opportunity to co-create an intimacy with Ray, which might truly feed her soul.

Ray patiently listened as Jean explored how she colluded to create the avoidance, what she feared, and what losses she had endured. It was Ray's turn to examine how he had contributed to their alienation.

"So, Ray, tell me about your time out in the garage and down in the basement," I petitioned, surprised to see him leaning forward and appear eager to explore his piece of the story.

"Well, before I get into a description of my extracurricular activities, I've got to tell you that I'm feeling relieved. I really thought I was the one screwing things up," Ray explained.

"I hear your relief. And it's just true that no one person can generate the level of avoidance the two of you have been experiencing," I said.

"I do spend quite a bit of time out in the garage. I've got an old woodstove out there, which makes the place real toasty."

"It sounds like you've really taken care of yourself out there."

"Yeah, I've got a hot plate and a pot of coffee. I'm very content out there," Ray continued.

"Tell me a bit about what you do out there."

"Woodworking. My garage is my woodworking shop. I make chairs and tables, and occasionally I take on a project like a hutch or a desk," Ray explained.

"It sounds like your creative juices get going out in that garage."

"Oh, yeah, I get a great deal of fulfillment out of woodworking. I wouldn't give it up for the world," Ray asserted.

"I'm wondering if you've considered the impact your garage time has had on your marriage," I said.

"Jean doesn't like it at all. She's always complaining about it."

"Yes, I've heard how Jean feels about it. I'm interested in how you feel about it. What do you consider to be the impact of your garage time upon your marriage, not Jean's marriage?" I pushed.

"Well, that's difficult to say. I never really thought about how I feel about it," Ray admitted, looking confused and dazed by the question.

"Ray, I've got the idea that when it comes to the marriage, you let Jean think about it and define it. In a sense, it's Jean's marriage," I suggested.

"I never thought about whose marriage it is," responded Ray, sounding angry, yet willing to consider the proposition.

"I hear you, but doesn't it make sense that in a real way, this is Jean's marriage, since you're offering very little input regarding the nature and direction of the relationship?"

"Yeah, I think that's true. I just never considered the implications of my lack of involvement," confessed Ray.

"I think you can see that the marriage does not benefit from your vision, your values, and your best wisdom. I'm wondering how you came to remove yourself from the marriage and whether you have any investment in getting back into it," I inquired.

"Oh, I don't know. I guess I'm afraid of some possible conflict," explained Ray, rubbing his forehead as if he were trying to brush the tension out of his body.

Ray went on to discover that he believed it was his responsibility to take care of Jean, even in the midst of a fight. One reason he was avoiding her was because he knew he would not defend himself while fighting with Jean. He realized there was no way for him to effectively represent his needs, if they were diverse from Jean's needs. So he had quit. He had grabbed his tools and headed for the garage.

Ray believed he could keep Jean in the marriage by simply never offering her any form of contention. He began to learn that his avoidance seriously diminished the vitality of the marriage, with his wife wondering if there was any reason to stay in the marriage.

Eventually, Ray decided to risk bringing his desire and his needs into the marriage. Initially, it meant giving himself an orientation based on what he wanted from Jean and then finding the courage to confess his desires with a clear voice. Ray's work culminated with a need to learn how to support himself in the presence of Jean's disagreement and unfavorable responses to his desires.

One of Ray's greatest challenges was to learn to detach enough from Jean's anger and pain so that he would not have to take refuge in his garage. His garage had become an impermeable boundary. He began to see that in the midst of a fight with Jean, he needed to learn to protect himself, hold a semipermeable boundary, and have faith that Jean would be fine without his assistance.

Ray was willing to become a student of boundaries so that he could learn how to take care of himself while remaining connected to Jean. He learned how to create a semipermeable boundary, one that allowed him to declare his desire and acknowledge Jean's response, without sacrificing himself because of the tension produced by their diversity.

Ray began spending less time in the garage, more time with Ray, and consequently more time with Jean.

We can see fusion and avoidance as attempts to deal with the quandary of how to be in a marriage and meet the need for connection and closeness, while also supporting the need to remain a separate and unique individual. As a rule, couples quite often fall either into the fused category or the avoidance category.

Fused couples have chosen not to risk the possibility of separation and abandonment, but in the process, they abandon themselves. Avoiding couples refuse to lose themselves, and subsequently lose their partners. Some couples enact both fusion and avoidance. They fuse and then run away from one another in order to reclaim themselves. Or they avoid one another and then run to one another for an interlude of fusion.

The most intimate and evolved of couples get themselves fused and into avoidance. The goal is not to be perfectly intimate. Couples serve their relationship well by taking a periodic inventory of the status of their relationship. The following shadow questions are meant to nudge the nuptial dynamics out of the unconscious and into the light of day.

Is one or both of us presently leaning into fusion? Is one or both of us presently choosing avoidance? How do I feel about our fusion or avoidance? Do I presently fear losing myself in our relationship, losing you, or both? If I'm into fusion, what choices can I make to take care of myself and our relationship? If I'm into avoidance, what choices can I make to take care of myself and support our relationship? Do we have a pattern of one or both of us tending to get into fusion or avoidance?

## Intimacy: What Is It?

From what has already been said, it should be obvious that intimacy is neither fusion nor avoidance, although both readily masquerade as intimacy. Intimacy is the unity of two separate and unique individuals. Fusion pushes for the unity aspect of intimacy, while avoidance champions the separate and unique individual portion of the definition. The key is to identify how we can craft a unity with our partners without depriving ourselves of our individuality.

I am often asked what it takes to get ready for intimacy; my response is that it is the willingness to get lost. Unfortunately, in our culture, it takes a great deal of courage to get lost, and getting lost catches a bad rap.

Our culture is founded upon a cosmology that is extremely misleading, one that says that that life is understandable and predictable; and that with the right education, friends, jobs, and financial investments, it's also secure. Any human experience that threatens the validity of this paradigm is disparaged. Getting lost is one of those experiences.

Our culture also frowns upon being a novice. Mystery demands noviceship. The mystery of intimacy is perpetually calling us to some "learning edge." Intimacy calls for a willingness to remain a student. If that kind of learning is not desired, then I highly recommend letting fusion or avoidance be your path.

If we dare to follow our hearts, then we will get lost and we will need to be willing to learn again and again how to get back to ourselves and back to our beloveds. We either fuse and get lost in the other or avoid and get lost in our favorite distractions. Intimacy reminds us of life's inherent mystery, unpredictability, and insecurity. Unless we have the willingness to get lost and to be novices, we aren't ready for intimacy.

Authentic intimacy possesses the power to teach and to initiate. Rather than preparing for intimacy, we surrender to it, allowing it to teach us about deepening unity with another while strengthening our own individuality. If we are willing to remain students of intimacy, then we will craft the competencies necessary to create unity while enhancing our consciousness about ourselves. However, it is important to be clear that this process is no walk in the park; it is a severe initiation and not meant for everyone.

Once we are able to shed intimacy of its idyllic tint of rose, we can view the hue of its many tones. This vast array of colors reflects the depth and mystery we will face within ourselves if we are willing to surrender to intimacy and kindle what I call "intimacy maturity."

## Intimacy Maturity

Thanks to the work of Robert Moore and Douglas Gillette, we have a way to map the maturing psyche. Their book entitled *King, Warrior, Magician, Lover* depicts four archetypal energies we can access in order to guide our efforts toward supporting our development as persons. The emphasis needs to be on the word "efforts," since maturation does not come automatically with age or by becoming formally educated. Ancient Latin meanings of maturity suggest it is about ripening at the right time. Ripening calls for the proper temperature, light, water, and rich soil. We can imagine irrigating and enriching the soil at the right time in order to support ripening, and so it is with our souls. We need to irrigate and enrich at the right time.

Fortunately, the human psyche possesses numerous right times to ripen. Right times often include times of loss, times of great challenge, times of transition, and times we are lost. Those can be very good times for our ripening and for asking poignant questions. How do we learn to carry our hearts in a way that they can be open and yet protected? How do we live our desire? How do we live our love? How do we keep our curiosity fresh and vibrant? How do we remain students of our own lives? How do we deepen our capacity for freedom?

Our culture is not interested in questions that facilitate our ripening, or our deepening. We are pretty much on our own when we try to access the kind of support we need in order to live the questions of our ripening. It will call for steadfastness and a tenacity of effort in order to stand for our maturation.

Our ripening calls for effort, and what Moore and Gillette have given us is a way to identify this effort and ways to exercise it. My colleague, Dr. Tom Daly, developed a coaching model called "Four Gateways Coaching" that further helps with the application of archetypal energies.

An archetype is an ideal pattern of skills and powers. And as an ideal, it is not something we become; rather, it is something we allow to point us in a particular direction, like a compass. For example, the Warrior archetype points toward the skill of boundary formation. The energy to set boundaries lies within us. We may need support and guidance in order to understand how we came to minimize the value of boundaries and how to arouse the energy within us in order to implement more effective boundaries.

We will explore the energy of each archetype, the shadow expression of having too much or too little of a particular energy, and how the archetypes interface to bolster our intimacy maturity.

# Warrior

The mature Warrior values action and setting boundaries. Warrior energy assesses the amount of action and boundary needed for a particular situation. This energy is essential in order to maintain engagement while safeguarding our individuality.

Warrior energy is eager to take some action, rather than succumb to passivity. When it operates in excess, its shadow boundaries include abuses of power, which often express themselves as violations of our spouses' boundaries. When Warrior energy is deficient, its shadow manifests itself as abdication of power and feeling victimized by our spouses.

Mature Warrior energy is dedicated to bringing authenticity to saying *yes* and *no*. Effective boundaries can be understood as the degree of authenticity with which we say *yes* and *no*. When our positive and negative responses are genuine, we honor our own needs and values. We go a long way toward engendering trust for ourselves.

Spouses who say *yes* too often will not trust themselves, especially within the context of marriage. They also run a high risk of not being trusted by their spouses. An inauthentic yes is often an attempt to please or a way of making a covert deal for something desired at a future date. When we say *yes* authentically, our spouses understand that we are not patronizing them but rather truly involving ourselves in the marriage. Spouses who say *no* too often are either attempting to punish their spouses or they are invested in avoidance.

An authentic *no* supports our separateness and uniqueness by confirming our individual tastes and preferences. An authentic *no* also supports our unity with our partners, since it makes us more trustworthy. An authentic *yes* supports our unity with our partners because it allows us to join them in some shared belief or activity. An authentic *yes* also supports our individuality because it reflects a genuine desire of ours.

Mature Warrior energy separates, excludes, and includes. It goes a long way toward strengthening our individuality, as well as our unity with our spouses.

The Warrior sees conflict as a way to call forth what truly matters to us and to our partners. Marriages without conflict are either severely fused or in deep avoidance, and therefore in need of some Warrior energy, if intimacy is going to be a possibility.

Mature Warrior energy does not bring a win/lose attitude to the conflict. There is a deep, abiding understanding that win/lose always translates into lose/lose. If our spouses win the fight, we lose. If we win, we also lose, because it is likely our partners will retaliate and find ways to seek retribution.

In a conflict, mature Warrior energy does two things. It directs us to be resolute about getting our own needs met, and it refuses to accept a resolution whereby our spouses don't meet their needs. This is a form of devotion that strives to craft conflict as pregnant with possibility, rather than relying upon submission or domination. The mature Warrior is much more invested in creativity than in winning.

Some of us are better at standing for our own needs and sacrificing our spouses' needs, while others are better at sacrificing themselves. It can be meaningful shadow work to identify whether we are self-sacrificing or other-sacrificing.

Michael, a college professor in his late fifties, came to see me, complaining he was unable to hold his own in his marriage. He described an adversarial relationship between his daughter and his wife that deeply troubled him.

"Have you let your wife and daughter know how the turmoil between the two of them is affecting you?" I asked.

"No. I didn't think that I would matter," Michael responded.

"Have you told your wife that you want the tension between her and your daughter to end and that you want them to work on their relationship?" I probed.

"No. I realize that I can't make my wife do something about it, so I don't bother to say anything," he said.

"I would suggest that you let her know that you expect her to attend to the problems that exist between her and your daughter, and that you have little or no tolerance for how their relationship has been playing out," I recommended.

"Yes, but I can't make her change!" he responded emphatically.

"Because you can't make her change doesn't mean that you need to sit out of the game completely!" I explained.

Michael's response is a good example of a husband carrying too little Warrior energy. He convinced himself that if he couldn't change his wife, then the only alternative was to be her victim. Michael slowly learned that he could bring his desire for reconciliation between his wife and daughter to bear upon his marriage. He understood that he was standing for something he truly believed in, and over time, his wife came to understand it too.

Mature Warrior energy does not expect intimacy to be pain-free. Through Warrior eyes, suffering is viewed as a natural ingredient in any initiation. We are able to carry pain in a way that minimizes blaming others or seeing ourselves as their victims. Suffering is viewed as a vehicle for learning. Mature Warrior energy is effective at discerning necessary suffering from unnecessary suffering.

We can summarize what the archetype of the Warrior brings to intimacy maturity:

   *Ability to remain engaged in a relationship through action
   *Ability to employ effective boundaries through authentic expressions of *yes* and *no*
   *Ability to engage in conflict with neither a need to submit nor a need to dominate
   *Ability to carry suffering creatively

Here is a series of questions that can help to focus our learning in regard to the Warrior. How do I presently protect myself in my marriage? How effective is this form of protection in regard to promoting my individuality and unity with my partner? Is there a way for me to protect myself that would serve me more effectively? Is there a risk I need to take in order to further support our intimacy? Is there some action I need to take in order to support either my individuality or unity with my spouse? How effective am I at honoring my own boundaries and those of my partner? What skill do I need to develop in order to approach conflict more creatively?

## Lover

Our culture remains relatively confused about mature Lover energy. We tend to celebrate the shadow expressions of the Lover as expressed in excess and characterized by jealousy, seduction, and compulsion. We limit ourselves to these shadow images of the Lover and then wonder why our relationships don't work. But it is often difficult to understand shadows of the Lover unless we can have some vision of the Lover in its maturity.

Mature Lover energy has the ability to honor emotion (anger, sadness, gladness, fear, shame) in ourselves and in others. To honor these emotions means to see them as essential to the human condition and certainly as fundamental to intimacy. To honor them means to be willing to develop the ability to express emotions and talk about emotion. Expression happens when we cry, shake, tremble, yell, and make a variety of emotive sounds. Mature Lover energy creates space for our emotional humanity without ridicule or the necessity for analysis.

Both the verbal and nonverbal expression of emotions support the uniqueness of our emotional lives as well as unity with our partners, as we allow them to witness who we are emotionally and accept support from them, if so desired.

The mature Warrior can supply the right boundaries for the Lover's expression of emotions. Sometimes these boundaries are aimed at protecting us from our spouses who want to fix us by talking us out of our more painful emotions. Or our boundaries might be designed to keep us from violating our partners with our anger and rage, or attempting to seduce them with our pain. Boundaries are also extremely helpful as we allow ourselves to feel our feelings without having to act or make some particular decision.

Another significant aspect of the mature Lover is the ability to play, which serves a vital role in the creation of unity. Play lightens the interaction in a marriage. It removes the heaviness that accompanies confrontation and the many subtle ways that partners get into one another's hair.

Play ignites Eros, especially as a way to hold otherwise serious issues. A frolicsome climate in a marriage goes a long way to freeing up spouses to feel and express their desire and maintain their sexuality.

Desire is the fuel of intimacy, and it is the mature Lover that allows us to actually feel our desire. Desire supports separateness and uniqueness when we express our desire regardless of our partner's level of receptivity. It also encourages unity, as desire focuses us and moves us toward our partners.

When a couple stops giving a voice to their desires, whether it includes the partner or not, their intimacy dries up. Chronic illness, workaholism, excessive worry, and depression all tend to evaporate desire. A playful attitude can revitalize desire, allowing spouses to feel the fullness of their desire and feel desired.

Desire is often experienced as attraction. I encourage couples to talk about their attraction to one another. It can be very valuable shadow work to talk about what attracts us to our partners and what does not. This exercise calls for Warrior energy to supply effective boundaries that prevent us from taking full responsibility for our spouses' attraction to us.

Issues such as body weight, hair color, clothing, the use of language, table manners, personal hygiene, and a host of other idiosyncrasies add or subtract from our attraction to our partners. As they hear what supports our attraction and what does not, they are left with the choice to make changes or maintain their present appearance and preferences.

The mature Lover views sensitivity as a form of personal empowerment, sustaining empathy and compassion. Sensitivity is a strong unity-producing aptitude. It allows for the building of a creative rapport, where spouses allow themselves to emotionally take in their partners' experiences. They can feel their spouses' grief, sorrow, and joy. Sensitivity maintains its power when accompanied by semipermeable boundaries supplied by Warrior energy. With effective boundaries in place, we can allow ourselves to feel with our spouses, without attempting to fix them or to make their pain our pain.

Another important function of the mature Lover is the ability to maintain an active relationship with experiences that are raw, natural, and uncivilized. The mature Lover engenders a trust for what is instinctual within the body and is uninterested in convention. These subtle cues from our bodies inform us of our needs for more separateness or more unity. It is curious that intimacy and hand-to-hand combat, more than any other human endeavors, call for the unbridled flow of the instinctual.

Staying in touch with what is natural and uncivilized within us can be extremely challenging. During childhood, many of us had our bodily functions shamed. Everything from belching and bowel movements to our emotions was shamed. We got good at not noticing and at separating from all the animal functions of our bodies so we could avoid being shamed.

Both my professional and my personal experience suggest that the most unnoticed and unspoken need in marriages is the need for attention. We were either shamed for our need for attention as children, or we figured out that our parents felt overwhelmed, and our need for attention would just push them over the edge. So we protected our parents and ourselves by either not speaking our need for attention, or getting good at not noticing we even had the need.

It is great shadow-work practice for couples to make it a point to speak of their need for attention at least on a weekly basis. The attention we seek may be a need to be seen, to be heard, or to be touched. A wonderful unity-building question is to ask our partners if they need some attention from us. Sometimes the opposite is true; it may be important to declare that we are not in a place to provide our spouses with attention.

When couples surrender to what is raw and natural in their souls, they step into the uniqueness of their relationship. The mature Lover delights in an instinctual arousal that becomes the signature of a marriage, which can be seen in the way a couple touches, talks, looks at one another, and makes love.

A powerful shadow of the Lover is too little of what is raw and natural. The outcome is depression, in which the instinctual is literally depressed or held down in favor of compliance with convention. When a couple experiences diminished Lover energy, they are on their way to being buddies or housemates.

We can summarize what mature Lover energy brings to an intimate relationship:

*The ability to honor emotions
*The ability to play
*The ability to view sensitivity as a form of personal empowerment
*The ability to maintain an active relationship with what is raw, natural, and uncivilized

Here are some helpful questions to focus learning on Lover energy. How do you presently feel about yourself as a spouse? What feelings (anger, sadness, gladness, fear and shame) are more difficult or easier for you to get in touch with? How do you feel about your unity with your partner? How do you feel about the status of your individuality in your marriage? When do you feel closest to your partner? What time or times in the past can you recall when you felt very positive about your marriage? How do you feel about the sexual connection to your partner? What do you want from your spouse?

# Magician

The Magician is the archetype our culture prizes, although it does not prioritize Magician energy as it pertains to self-awareness. The cultural bias reserves Magician energy to better understand the world of science and technology. We do not use the energy of this archetype to learn more about making peace with the mystery and insecurity of life, hence we limit the scope and depth of the archetype and the depth of our own maturity.

The great shadow of Magician energy is that it is directed away from self-awareness and relationship awareness. If there is a starting point for initiating intimacy maturity, it is Magician energy, which enables us to be students of ourselves and our relationships. We should note that self-inquiry is customarily the first step in most spiritual traditions, especially the mystical traditions. Intimacy is a rigorous spiritual path, one not for the faint of heart.

Unless we are willing to be students of our own interior landscape, we won't be able to identify what we bring to our relationship and what we need to learn about fully participating in a relationship. Our inner worlds are a rich vista of gifts and wounds. As we take in-depth looks at ourselves, we will inevitably fall short of the idealized version we have of ourselves. Marriage, more than any other initiation, summons our best as well as our worst.

Being students of ourselves involves not only the willingness to candidly look at who we are, but also willingness to decide how we want to be accountable for what we see. Marriage calls us to our frailty. If we so choose, our marriages will offer us opportunities to see how we are self-centered and self-neglectful, abuse power, abdicate power, blame others, and allow ourselves to be victimized or employ ineffective boundaries. A marriage creates a powerful container for the development of self-inquiry, since we can constantly receive feedback about the impact we have upon our relationship.

One of the great payoffs of nuptial learning is that we can begin to see that the characteristics we avoid in ourselves are the same ones we typically avoid in our partners. This is shadow work at its best. If we deny our own arrogance, greed, and vanity, or our gifts and talents, then we will push our partners away when they exemplify these traits in themselves.

Marriage is something we create, and something that creates us. This can only be done intimately when we remain students of ourselves and our relationships. Embracing curiosity and wondering about ourselves supports our individualizing and our unity with our spouses by confirming our willingness to join them in the co-creation of the marriage.

Magician energy also possesses the ability to maintain a vision and bring logic and creative imagination to our marriages. So often, couples get caught in the petty struggles of everyday life, unable to hold a vision of why they are together. The Magician can remind us of the bigger picture, allowing us to loosen our grip on the incidentals of the nuptial journey.

Magician energy can help us to objectify and not personalize every insensitive comment and irritating habit of our spouses. Couples are taken aback the first time they hear me say, "This isn't about your marriage; it's about marriage." A great way to take the edge off of our marital issues is to remember that what is occurring is not particular to our marriages, but rather is characteristic of the nature of an intimate marriage.

Mature Magician energy can be very helpful in supporting the diversity in the relationship. This energy wants to be creative, finding new ways to support our own individuality while not insisting that our partners be clones of us. We can tap the imaginative juices of the Magician in order to address old problems in new ways.

Mature Magician energy is able to develop, channel, and contain personal power. We develop personal power by identifying how we can actually influence some desired end and by letting go of anything that we cannot influence. We channel personal power by assessing what is needed in order to effectively influence some desired end. We contain personal power by calling upon Warrior energy to create boundaries, preventing us from attempting to change that which is out of our control, or stopping us from becoming involved in a situation that does not serve us.

These three acts of personal empowerment strongly serve the deepening of our individuality, as well as our unity with our partners. Learning about personal power sheds light upon our gifts and talents, deepens faith in our efficacy, and strengthens our autonomy. It contributes to unity with our partners by communicating that we are not attempting to be excessively controlling of them. It also tells our partners we are not into being unnecessarily dependent upon them.

Another proficiency of mature Magician energy is the ability to define a marriage as an initiation and create marital ritual space. When couples are able to understand marriage as an initiation, they are not so quick to jump ship and simply end up in another initiation with another partner. They can also better grasp the meaning of a trial and figure out how to support themselves through it.

Rituals are stories put into action. The mature Magician delights in the creation of ritual, when a couple can take the stories of their passion, their fear, their love, and their shadows and bless them in ritual.

Tantra yoga is one of the best examples of ritualizing the erotic in a marriage. Couples can transform their bedrooms into a temple of sexuality by utilizing incense, candles, sacred artifacts, costumes, perfumes, and whatever helps to create ritual space. Before engaging in touching, they might sit just out of reach, facing each other with their eyes closed, breathing from their abdomens. They continue to hold this posture until they believe they have released the clutter from their minds and are ready to welcome the partner. When they open their eyes, they can focus on allowing their gaze to offer welcome to the partner.

The above is simply an example of the possibilities. We are in a culture barren of ritual, so we must get creative with our Magician energy. As a marriage makes room for the mature Magician, more ritual can be integrated in the life of the marriage, celebrating the sacredness of the nuptial initiation.

We can summarize the gifts of the mature Magician:

*The ability to remain students of ourselves and our relationships
*The ability to employ vision, logic, and creative imagination
*The ability to develop, channel, and contain personal power
*The ability to define marriage as an initiation and create ritual space

Here are some helpful questions aimed at supporting learning in the area of the mature Magician. How do I prevent myself from maximizing my learning about myself? What do I need to do in order to hold more responsibility for my learning about intimacy? What do I identify as my strengths and weaknesses as a spouse? What do I identify as my partner's strengths and weaknesses as a spouse? What is my present perception of our relationship? What can this perception tell me about myself? What is easier for me to see: my need for individualizing, or my need for greater unity with my partner?

# Sovereign (King and Queen)

Lover energy allows us to feel our desire, while the archetype of the Magician provides us with the ability to identify and understand our desire, and Warrior energy protects and safeguards our desire. It is the energy of the Sovereign that grants us the power to live our desire.

Mature Sovereign energy affords us a life lived from desire. Spouses living their desire deepen their capacity for intimacy maturity. When spouses live their desire, each partner supports their uniqueness and provides the stuff of unity. They can unite their desires!

Most couples with whom I have worked actually believe that their primary role in the marriage is to support their partner's desire. Couples are usually in disbelief when I explain that their primary responsibility is to know, feel, protect, and live their own desire. Once they get a bit beyond the shock, they are convinced that the living of their desire within the marriage will lead to complete bedlam.

If a couple is fused, they will see the living of individual desire as creating extreme isolation, ending in the eventual demise of the marriage. It calls for considerable daring for spouses to each live their own desire. It is also a great way to renew a sex life, since rejuvenated desire in the kitchen often leads to rejuvenated desire in the bedroom.

Couples soon learn that a commitment to live personal desire (while championing the desire of our partners) diminishes abuses of power as well as abdication of power. It also makes less room for resentment to fester, since people are not being deprived.

If we regularly practice self-loyalty by living our desire, we are less likely to sabotage the desire of our partners. We can define ourselves as self-loyal while remaining allies of our partners. Intimacy gets a tremendous boost as spouses view one another as responsible for living their own desire. We are then free to focus on living our own desire. Trust is enhanced as each spouse lives with increasing integrity.

We can understand integrity as coming from the word "integration." Contrary to popular belief, integrity has no moral implications. To live with integrity means that what we desire and value can be detected in our behavior. The choices we make actually reflect our beliefs; our behavior is likely to tell the story of our inner worlds. Mature Sovereign energy thrives on integrity and has little or no interest in what is appropriate or proper.

Shadow expressions of the Sovereign show up as either too little or too much interest in our spouses' desires. When there is too little attention to a spouse's desire, fear of not getting desires met is probably driving our focus. When there is too much preoccupation with a spouse's desire, we are probably attempting to please in order to control their behavior.

Mature Sovereign energy delights in diverse expressions of creativity and generativity. This archetype knows how to support diversity in a marriage. As Sovereign energy matures, so does our capacity to welcome different beliefs, values, and tastes. We diminish the need for our spouses to be like us!

One of the great nuptial paradoxes is that the more our spouses experience us as willing to accommodate their individuality, without sacrificing our own, the stronger the likelihood of authentic unity. The more comfortable we are with our own beliefs and values, the less we need to convert our spouses to our way of thinking. Being comfortable does not simply refer to the satisfaction we feel about the soundness of our beliefs; it is also the capacity to make peace with standing alone with our convictions.

Too little willingness to accommodate diversity often reflects a Sovereign shadow. Resistance to diversity can be a great reminder to focus our attention back upon what we desire. The more we give ourselves our own desire without guilt and shame, the more we can support our spouses' diverse desires. As a rule, we only give our partners what we are capable of giving ourselves.

The ability to take marital leadership is a significant expression of mature Sovereign energy. It is leadership that is manifested by championing our own competence and confidence, as well as that of our partners. It would certainly take more than a single lifetime to become competent at intimacy. But intimacy does call for a deepening that can best be done by accessing these archetypal energies and their accompanying proficiencies. And if spouses are going to live at the "learning edge" of acquiring new skills, they will need to invigorate their confidence.

In a relationship where mature Sovereign energy is being exercised, two people will be taking the leadership necessary to live an intimate relationship. In order to address the challenges of intimacy, spouses need to identify what will support their individual and collective learning. Mature Sovereign energy is aware of the need to encourage ourselves and our partners in order to support a level of confidence that will effectively facilitate learning.

There is a powerful cultural conspiracy disabling and crippling marital leadership. This destructive scheme defines women alone as capable of taking leadership within a marriage. Most of my colleagues concur that over ninety-five percent of the phone calls we receive from people seeking marriage counseling are from women. Once in the office, it is inevitably the women who focus the direction of the therapy. Men are still relegated to the role of provider and are told by the culture to remain ignorant and powerless in regard to intimacy.

A recent nationally televised commercial for a cell phone depicts the husband as completely confused about his daughters' intentions regarding the use of their new cell phones. The wife intervenes with the appropriate comment, causing the daughters to spontaneously embrace her. The commercial ends with the father calling for a group hug, which goes ignored by the wife and daughters, who leave the husband standing alone, dumbfounded and excluded.

It appears that not much has changed since the eighties, when my children insisted that I sit with them every Thursday evening to watch *The Cosby Show*, followed by *Family Ties*, starring Michael J. Fox. The husbands in both shows were depicted as confused and ill-equipped to offer effective leadership to their marriages and their families. Other than providing financially, both men were assigned the role of another child in the family. Their recommendations regarding family dynamics were either ignored or made fun of, and their wives reminded them how to dress and eat.

A sad commentary is that it looks like men have colluded with the conspiracy, settling for grandiose illusions of running the world. Women, in spite of feeling alone and sabotaged by our abdication of leadership, may also have colluded in order to secure power in the home, since they were excluded from power in the workplace. Men's most intimate relationships with their spouses and children go on without their leadership, and in many cases, with their willingness to remain significantly underdeveloped, lacking in mature Sovereign energy.

Another skill of the mature Sovereign is the ability to define and implement support. One form of support is interior, and it includes affirming our own goodness, and the ability to comfort ourselves in stressful situations.

As we access mature Sovereign energy, we look toward ourselves for confirmation of our personal value. More importantly, we accept the responsibility for holding our goodness, rather than deciding our spouses are responsible for reminding us that we are okay.

Mature Sovereign energy knows how to actualize self-care in a regressive moment, rather than simply reacting in a fight-or-flight pattern. From the Sovereign, we can "re-parent" ourselves by employing necessary boundaries, offering ourselves the encouragement we need, nurturing ourselves, or engaging the necessary discipline that will allow us to access allies.

Radical self-responsibility is another way to support ourselves. It simply means that we will muster as much power as we can to define ourselves and create who we are. Radical self-responsibility can manifest itself in three distinct ways. First, it means that we continue to see ourselves as responsible for our own emotional lives, including the status of our happiness. Our sadness, our anger, and our joy are our own creations. Secondly, it means that we are accountable for our own desire. Whether we are getting what we want is up to us and the choices we make. Lastly, it means that we are willing to speak our truth to our partners. We say what we want, what we don't want, and how we have not adequately taken care of ourselves in our relationships.

This last aspect of radical self-responsibility is a most crucial element of intimacy maturity. It tends to prohibit fusion by claiming the responsibility for self-care, rather than giving it to our spouses. It also is an impediment to avoidance, because it implies that we are willing to learn how to take care of ourselves within the context of the marriage, rather than take our ball and go home.

Accessing allies is another area where men are at a considerable disadvantage. Unfortunately, rugged individualism remains powerful in male psychology. Men often report that their biggest resistance to marriage counseling is that real men should not need the help of a stranger with such a personal aspect of their lives.

Men and women who are attempting to create intimate relationships with their partners need same-gender support. We need a place to express our frustrations and our appreciations, a place where we can bring our shadows and get the help we need to endure and learn from our nuptial initiations.

There are many workshops and training courses that can help to focus our learning and facilitate the deepening of intimacy maturity. Marriage counseling with a therapist who has chosen marriage as an initiatory container can also be extremely helpful. Defining and implementing support calls for the insight to notice what needs strengthening and the courage to ask for help.

We can summarize the gifts of the mature Sovereign:

*The ability to live desire
*The ability to delight in diverse expressions of creativity and generativity
*The ability to take marital leadership
*The ability to define and implement support

Here are some helpful Sovereign questions: What kind of appreciation am I willing to extend to myself for my efforts in my marriage? What kind of appreciation am I willing to extend to my partner? How can I support myself to take some necessary risk in my marriage? Who can I employ as a supportive ally? What is the purpose of my participation in this marriage? How can I gain something from one of the principle struggles in my marriage? What do I need to do in order to view my nuptial initiation more creatively?

In this chapter we examined two extremely powerful forces in human psychology: the longing for connection and bonding, and the need to sustain the core of our individuality. We explored how the longing for connection often leads to fusion, a shadow of intimacy, and how the need to remain a separate individual can lead to another shadow, which we identified as avoidance.

Both of these states can be dissatisfying, since fusion entails the loss of self and avoidance involves the loss of the other. They may be preferable to the perils and challenges presented by intimacy, which we defined as the unity of two separate and unique individuals. Intimacy is a ruthless call to the self that can only happen when two people are willing to visit their own depths and be accountable for what they find.

We explored intimacy maturity by way of the four archetypal energies: the Warrior, the Magician, the Lover, and the Sovereign. We identified sixteen competencies that can guide and enrich our maturation if we are willing to surrender to the initiation of intimacy. Intimacy is not meant for everyone, no more than mountain climbing is. For those feeling bold enough to venture forward, it may be important to be clear about the hazards inherent in the landscape and what resources will be necessary on the journey.

# 8

## *Nuptial Diversity and Accompanying "Isms"*

Some of the great challenges in any marriage are the ways a couple deals with their diversity and the accompanying "isms" of sexism, classism, and ageism. Typically, partners allow these four challenges to go underground as shadows in the unconscious; however, if they remain denied and forgotten, they have the power to send a marriage into irretrievable collapse. A shadow marriage calls these four petulant forces to the surface, seeking new and creative ways to understand them and integrate them into the relationship.

Nothing drives fear into a marriage more profoundly than a couple possessing diverse beliefs, values, or desires. Couples often fear that the expression of too much uniqueness will inevitably erode their connection. Also, the emerging diversity might show that our spouses are not really who we thought they were. Maybe we made a gross error in judgment. Why do we react with such fear when diversity shows up in our marriages?

It is often considerably easier to tolerate the diversity of coworkers, neighbors, and the folks who live on the other side of town than it is to accept the differences between us and our partners. After all, wasn't it what we have in common, our shared beliefs and interests, that brought us together in the first place? What kind of marriage would we have if we had little or nothing in common? Why should we even stay together?

## Disillusionment and Catastrophe

When partners begin to realize just how different they are from one another, they often react by feeling significantly disillusioned and exhibit a need to catastrophize their situation. They most likely came together initially because they believed they had found their spirit mate; that is, the person who would put an end to loneliness and emptiness for good; the one who would truly understand them because they saw things the same way. They were convinced that their longing to belong was finally realized by a partner who joined them in an unremitting bond. And then, the bad news: they saw that their partners were much more different from themselves than they ever imagined! They found themselves deeply disillusioned, contemplating the best avenues of escape.

A shadow marriage learns to welcome disillusionment without being naive about the accompanying disappointment. As was mentioned earlier, disillusionment is a powerful initiatory tool. It is an opportunity to inventory our beliefs to find the ones that have outlived their service. We very well may need to grieve dying beliefs, since part of our identity dies with them. However, recreating ourselves and our relationships can be the gift of disillusionment, if we do not allow ourselves to fall victim to cynicism and excessive self-pity.

The more a marriage learns to welcome shadows, the less likely a couple will indulge in catastrophizing as a way to cope with their diversity. The drama generated by catastrophizing is a convenient distraction from the fear that is stimulated when we discover how different our partners are from us. It is also a way of indirectly calling our partners back into a collective mind set. We send the message that if they thought they could reveal themselves as considerably different from us and get away with it, they've got another thought coming! We can get quite strategic when it comes to reminding our partners about the consequences of expressed diversity.

We often fear the diversity of our spouses because it throws us into an identity crisis. Our spousal identity begins to shift. If our partners are not who we thought they were, then we are not connected to them in the way we surmised. We are not someone who shares a common vision with our partner about the world. As the illusion of our similarity reveals itself, we understand that our definition of ourselves as spouses is changing.

The spouse who loses her husband as a hiking partner must now decide whether to seek a new hiking buddy, hike alone, or cut back on her hiking. And then, of course, there is the impact of her new choices upon her husband. He may very well experience a crisis of identity as he stops hiking and witnesses his wife's new hiking choices. The quake of identity resulting from couples facing their diversity can be far-reaching.

Each time spouses step into some expression of diversity, they remind themselves and their partners of their inevitable existential aloneness. Our identities are pushed toward the reality of the solitary nature of our lives. We are forced to decide how we will face the reality of our singularity.

Couples who prefer fusion to avoidance often have a more difficult time deal-ing effectively with their diversity. Fused couples view the meaning of their rela-tionship as being determined by the communal nature of what they share. They can respond to expressions of diversity with intense fear, and often cannot imag-ine a relationship founded upon the emerging uniqueness of each individual. Fused couples agree to be reflections of one another and are easily thrown into a tailspin when one of them decides to declare their uniqueness.

## Unconscious Fear of Diversity

When unconscious fear is driving a marriage, spouses must decide whether to suppress their own uniqueness, encourage their partners to suppress theirs, or both. In all three cases, there are dire consequences.

A debilitating malaise often afflicts a marriage when the fear of diversity remains unconscious. It is common for denied fear of diversity to gradually trans-form into anger and resentment. The human psyche is not fond of repeated betrayals of itself. Partners will usually tolerate their own inner duplicity only for so long before they begin to view their spouses and their relationship as a toxic opportunity to sell themselves out.

The most obvious consequence is an endless series of power struggles in which spouses are either attempting to exude control over the other or resist being con-trolled. These patterns are insidious and corrosive to building any meaningful intimacy. Partners will normally engage in power struggles only for so long before they become fatigued, or build such a case against their partners that they can't imagine attempting to heal their marriage.

The third option occurs more often than one might think: couples keep their fear of diversity in the unconscious and remain fused for the duration of the rela-tionship. In this condition, it is customary for one spouse to become an extension of the other, and decide to live their life out that way.

Bill and Paul, a same-sex couple, came for counseling just after they had been together for a year. Their year of blissful oneness appeared to be coming to an end when the hand of diversity banged on the door.

"Paul refuses to accept that I never really enjoyed bowling and that I'm proba-bly not going down to those damn alleys again," declared Bill.

"Sounds to me that you showed up at those alleys on one too many occa-sions," I suggested.

"Yes, I did. Paul loved to bowl, and he wanted me to join him, so I did," explained Bill.

"So you got into bowling for Paul?" I asked.

"Well, kind of. I also did it so we could be together. He insisted on bowling two or three times per week," he said.

"You thought that joining him at the alleys would afford the both of you more time together."

"Yes, and it did. But what kind of time together is it when you hate what you're doing?" Bill cried.

"You sound fairly comfortable with your decision," I said.

"I'm mostly comfortable. I'm hoping that Paul will bowl less, so we can spend more time together."

"I'm hearing that you want Paul to pull back on his bowling and join you in some other activity."

"Yes, that seems reasonable, especially after all the time I spent down at his damn bowling alleys," Bill insisted.

"You seem to be suggesting that Paul should undergo some sacrifice, since it's what you did," I explained.

"Yes, why not? After all, we do want to have our time together. And isn't that what partnership is all about?" he said, giving a "you'd better agree" look to his partner.

Bill's choice to sacrifice himself until he couldn't take it anymore is relatively common. Couples often have difficulty distinguishing necessary from unnecessary sacrifice. In Bill's case, he believed that it was necessary to sacrifice his preferences in order to generate time spent with his partner. He was now willing to claim his uniqueness in regard to bowling, but he was also strategizing to redeem his time spent at the alleys in order to secure the time and activities he preferred to spend with Paul.

Luckily, Paul did not bite. He refused to sacrifice his bowling time in the face of Bill's invitations to guilt. Bill slowly began to see that his self-sacrifice had not really been necessary and had only led to some unwanted fusion.

He initially felt some fear as he stayed home while Paul headed for the alleys. They both experienced a crisis of identity as they chose to honor their diversity. The issue was pushed even further when Paul stayed home from bowling with a cold, expecting that he would spend the evening with Bill. But Bill had been going out with his friend Marie on one of Paul's bowling nights, and this was one of those nights. Bill told Paul that he planned to keep his date with Marie, and true to form, Paul accused him of not supplying their relationship with the time and energy it needed.

Paul was able to catch his accusation, and he reminded himself that it probably meant that he was scared. He went on to explain how he had just assumed that Bill would be at home when he stayed home from bowling, especially when he had a cold. He had anticipated that Bill would want to be there, nurturing him through his nasal congestion. And when he wasn't there, he became scared of his different preference and the implication that he might not be able to have Bill the way he wanted.

Paul and Bill were learning a great deal about the challenge of allowing for their diversity while they each experienced a crisis of identity and remained conscious about their fear. They each saw how they faced their diversity by initially being excessively accommodating, then moving toward attempts at converting the other to their position.

In one of our sessions, they both decided to minimize the bowling issue by suggesting that it simply reflected how petty they could become. I quickly reminded them that bowling was not really the issue; rather, they were addressing how they would respond to their diversity and the fear stimulated by such a decision. I went on to encourage them to suspend judgment of the many ways that their fear of diversity would find its way into their relationship.

Paul and Bill were getting more competent at expressing their fear, rather than allowing it to unconsciously drive them into excessive accommodation or attempts at influencing the other. Paul started to accept just how much fear drove his need to be right. He understood how the diversity that showed up in regard to their beliefs left him feeling inadequate, and at times unlovable. He needed Bill to sacrifice his own beliefs in order to reassure him that he was okay.

They were working hard at supporting the diversity of their beliefs, values, and desires when they began to face a new level of challenge.

"Something happens every now and then, when we're having a discussion, that I just don't understand," explained Paul.

"My guess is that you're not simply confused about this thing that is happening, but you're also having some feelings about it," I pushed, since it appeared to me that there was enough trust in our relationship for him to handle my prodding.

"Well, yes, I guess it makes me angry and a little scared," Paul admitted.

"Can you say some more about your anger and fear?" I asked.

"We'll be driving along, and I'll have a creative inspiration and want to share it with Bill. So I do and he simply nods and says nothing. I know he's bright enough to understand what I'm saying. When it happened once or twice, I assumed he was in a bad mood. After a dozen times, I started to get pissed!" Paul said angrily, and with a sincere interest in understanding what was going on.

"Can you give me an example of what you are talking about?"

"Sure. Last week we were driving along, and I was thinking about the different ways that people empower themselves and the impact it has upon the system in which they work. When I turned to Bill with my enthusiasm, he stared straight ahead and nodded," explained Paul.

"What did you want from Bill?" I asked.

"I wanted him to respond—to be curious about what I was saying and engage me."

"I'm assuming that you did not ask Bill to engage you in the moment."

"No. He looked bored."

"Were you feeling bored?" I asked Bill.

"I don't think so. I guess I wasn't sure what Paul was wanting from me. If he wanted some discussion, then I needed him to let me know that. Anyway, Paul is an organizational consultant, and I don't spend time thinking about the stuff he thinks about," responded Bill, attempting to legitimize his uniqueness.

I proceeded to ask them if they would be open to taking an inventory aimed at delineating the unique way each of them organized their thinking. They were both very receptive. I went on to explain how couples not only differ in what they believe, but also in how they construct their beliefs.

I employed an inventory from the mind styles research of Anthony Gregoric of the University of Connecticut. The results indicated that Paul was primarily an "abstract random thinker," characterized by a comfort with abstraction as it relates to feeling and emotion. Paul enjoyed focusing upon the emotional components of human relationships. He actively employed his imagination and readily spoke in metaphors.

Bill, on the other hand, was primarily a "concrete random thinker." He comfortably focused upon the concrete world and enjoyed addressing practical considerations. He preferred using language that was concretely informative. While Paul relied upon his inner voice to validate new data, Bill needed practical demonstration. They were beginning to develop an appreciation for the depth of diversity that existed in their relationship.

"I feel like my eyes are changing. I used to watch Bill attend to the different items in our home and think that he was wasting his time on trivialities. The other day, I was walking upstairs and noticed Bill delicately pruning a Christmas cactus that sat in the living room. I was immediately filled with appreciation for the tender care he brings to our home," Paul shared, his face bright with the glow of his gratitude.

Bill discovered that he was quite intuitive as a concrete random thinker. He explained to Paul that he was quite willing to engage him in one of his inspirational moments. He noted that he would probably not respond spontaneously and that he needed Paul to ask for feedback, which would cue him in. With an invitation to join him, Bill was readily able to stretch toward Paul's abstract way of perceiving the world.

# Welcoming Diversity

From a naive perspective, it would appear that couples engaging in avoidance would have an easier time with diversity than fused couples. Recalling our definition of intimacy as the unity between two distinct and unique individuals, we can easily see how critical the role of diversity is in the building of intimacy.

Avoidant couples are not welcoming diversity in order to build unity. Their diversity is just another way to remain separate. They may have greater ease with it, but only because they are not attempting to create anything with their diversity.

Any couple who takes their unity seriously, and wants it to be intimate and not fused, will need to learn how to welcome diversity. We can access resources from the four archetypal energies of the Lover, the Magician, the Warrior, and the Sovereign in support of diversity.

The Magician can offer us an awareness of our fear, which may help us to avoid acting out from fear. Our awareness of fear can serve to clarify our reaction to our partner's uniqueness. The Lover can help us to simply feel our fear without moving into blame or attempts at influence. The Warrior offers a boundary that lets us see our spouses as simply different, without a need to catastrophize the situation.

When we are willing to access these resources again and again in support of diversity, a depth of Sovereign energy begins to develop. This energy allows us not only to feel less frightened by our marital diversity, but also to begin to bless it. We start to see our partner's uniqueness as a gift and an opportunity to create a relationship with resolve and possibility. This mature Sovereign energy lets us view our partners as evolving mysteries, capable of showing us an endless number of faces. We receive our spouses with curiosity and wonder, rather than with complacency and a false sense of security.

There is no real security in pretending that our spouses are much like ourselves. We infuse our commonness with the power of always keeping us together. From the depths of Sovereign energy, we acknowledge that our partners may only travel with us for a short time, and we delight in the limited time we have together.

We can make choices that either obstruct diversity or welcome diversity into our marriages. One of those choices is the way we communicate. I do not believe that a couple should enter therapy to better their communication, since poor communication is typically a symptom and not the problem. However, it serves a couple well to be aware of what kind of language supports their diversity and what kind obstructs it. As a general guideline, any language that suggests there is a right way and a wrong way will not facilitate the capacity to honor diversity in a marriage.

Addressing issues of diversity is about attitude. We will respond to diversity with a belief, an emotion, and a behavior. We have seen that the most prominent emotional reaction to diversity is fear. The most common belief is that we are wrong, that we are not okay, or that we will be left and ultimately forgotten. The most prevailing behavior is language that suggests a right and a wrong way.

Couples can make diversity an inside job by beginning to talk about their fear and their beliefs when diversity considerations arise. They can also make it an outside job by tracking how they speak to one another, and by letting go of language that implies someone is right and someone is wrong.

Here are some examples of right/wrong language. Moralizing and ridiculing are obvious indicators that the speaker is attempting to secure the high ground, as are shaming, blaming, preaching, lecturing, advising, and teaching; the latter is often driven by the best of intentions. Ordering, commanding, and threatening also send the message that diversity is not welcome in a marriage.

I do not recommend using the language of agreeing and disagreeing. It subtly sends the message that there is a right, rational, and logical position as well as a wrong, irrational, and illogical position. I have never experienced my uniqueness being invited into a conversation when someone declares, "I disagree with you." Striving to be rational and logical can be a terrific office pastime, but a strong attachment to reason can be deadly in a marriage.

## Positioning, Not Persuading

When spouses engage in attempts at persuading their partners to adopt their views, they strongly inhibit the life of their diversity. Persuasion communicates the following message: "I'm not really interested in your position. I'm going to give you some really good reasons to accept my position and abandon your own." Spouses employing persuasion not only alienate their partners and discourage diversity, they also are investing in being the object of sabotage.

Partners who are the targets of persuasion understand that their partners have no interest in their beliefs and values. If they defer to their spouses and adopt their views while sacrificing their own, they will likely act out in some passive-aggressive manner aimed at sabotaging their persuasive spouse. The persuaded spouse sends the message: "You can give me eight good reasons why I should adopt your position, but you're crazy if you think that your eight good reasons are going to be the last word on this issue." Essentially, persuasion means everyone loses.

What is the difference between positioning and persuading? Positioning is attempting to be clear about what a spouse values or believes. Positioning encourages diversity and collaboration. Persuading supports the exercise of influence and discourages collaboration. Persuading is divisive and inhibits diversity.

The following is an example of a dialogue between spouses that reflects positioning and is not persuasive.

"I want to go to a concert at the casino together this Saturday night," suggested Beth.

"I personally don't enjoy the casino," replied Mark.

"What is it about the casino that turns you off?" asked Beth.

"I don't like the cigarette smoke, the noise, and all the drinking. What do you like about it?" inquired Mark.

"I like the concerts, the restaurants, and occasionally playing some blackjack," said Beth.

"I don't like gambling at all. But listen, I don't want you to not go because of me. How can we work this out so that you can go and I can avoid the casino?" wondered Mark.

"I can go to the concert Friday night with Laura, and we'll do something else together on Saturday," suggested Beth.

Positioning includes clarity about one's own position, curiosity about the partner's position, inclusion of the partner's position, exploration, and collaboration.

The following is an example of a persuasive dialogue about the same topic.

"I want to go to a concert at the casino and maybe play some blackjack," declared Beth.

"No way am I going down there!" exclaimed Mark.

"The casino is a great place to spend a Saturday evening. They have live entertainment, free drinks when you gamble, great restaurants, and they've added some specialty shops. Try opening up and being flexible. I'm sure that you would enjoy yourself if you just let yourself," said Beth.

"I'm plenty open. Being pregnant, you should think about taking in all that secondhand smoke. There are probably not any good seats left for the concert, and it's too late in the week to get a babysitter," explained Mark.

Persuasion is non-collaborative, as it is an attempt to build a case against the other's position. Logic is a poor way to welcome someone's uniqueness. Spouses who run into attempts at persuasion over and over again do not believe that their uniqueness is welcome in the marriage and quite often stop actively positioning themselves, dropping out of discussions and often out of the marriage either emotionally or physically.

Consistently not having a position can be as debilitating as persuasion. Collaboration and intimacy depend upon the expression of two unique positions. Creating a marriage is dependent upon both positions being clearly represented and explored.

It can be very helpful to intentionally breathe deeply when hearing a spouse express a belief that is radically different from our own. Sometimes it can be challenging to give them the air time they deserve, as urgency builds in us to declare our incredulous reactions. Rather than simply acting out our reactions, we can speak them. "Wow! I'm surprised! I didn't expect to hear this! I didn't realize how important this is to you! It's hard for me to believe we are this different!"

Once we have given our partners the opportunity to fully express themselves and declared our reactions (rather than acting them out), we can use the language of diversity to support our own uniqueness. "I have a very different view. I'm wondering if you might be open to hearing my position. I'm aware that we have very different opinions. I want to express a position that is quite different from yours."

Language that welcomes diversity is driven by curiosity and acceptance. There is no one perfect way to communicate. Whatever language says, "I want to know your unique self as well as my own, and I'll do my best to accept each of us," goes a long way toward welcoming diversity in a marriage.

# Communication Is Not the Real Problem

Learning how to use language that welcomes diversity certainly can be helpful. However, it is like taking an aspirin for a headache caused by a brain tumor. Quite often, the language we use is simply the symptom of a greater problem.

Essentially, there are three problems which lead to ineffectual communication. **The first is the inability to consciously identify and cope with feelings of hurt and fear.** When these feelings remain unconscious, they can be expressed through blame, ridicule, criticism, preaching, teaching, disagreements (competing within a win-lose dynamic), analyzing and diagnosing. When the feeling is specifically fear, the resulting communication may be afflicted by vagueness, ambiguity and in some cases, long prolonged silences.

**The second problem is the inability to employ effective boundaries.** The communication symptom of this problem is often an over reactive listener who defends, explains, justifies and attacks.

**The third problem is being overwhelmed by shame.** The communication symptoms of this problem often show up in speakers who are vigorously attempting to influence their partners, or in listeners who defend, distract, explain, justify, or attack.

**The fourth problem is regression.** The communication symptoms of this problem include threatening, preaching, lecturing, name-calling, interrogating and withdrawing.

If couples want to genuinely enhance their communication and their ability to deal creatively with the diversity in their marriages, then they will need to address one or more of these problems directly. However, concentrating on these problems which show-up symptomatically in a couple's communication can begin as an outside job by exploring communication skills that support diversity.

Focusing on the symptom of communication can be helpful in two ways. First, it often happens that couples who where raised in shame-based family systems simply have no idea what shameless and blameless communication sounds like. They need to hear examples of language that supports diversity in a marriage. Secondly, being acquainted with effective communication skills can help bring attention to the real problems when couples begin to employ language obstructive to honoring each person's uniqueness.

For example, utilizing *I-messages* rather than *you-messages* can either facilitate communication or point toward the underlying problem. The statement, *I'm feeling disconnected from you and I want to spend more time together*, keeps the focus on the speaker. Where the *I-message, I'm fed-up with your insensitivity and your need to continually ignore me,* places a blameful focus on the listener. This second statement is likely to lead to a breakdown in communication and is suggesting one of the three problems. The speaker is either using blame to defend against shame or attempting to influence the partner.

Two effective listening skills include *non-verbal attention* and *paraphrasing,* where listeners summarize in their own words what they hear speakers saying. These skills are effective if they are authentic ways to attend to the message of the speaker and then enter the conversation. However, they can be used to disengage, in which case the real problem is probably the listener not knowing how to engage while holding a semi-permeable boundary which allows for both partners to express their separate truths.

The most obvious problem involving shame which affects communication happens when the speaker attempts to hold the listener non-blamefully accountable and the listener defends against being held accountable. Although the speaker is communicating non-blamefully, the listener is probably defending against feeling shame.

Most over-reacting communication is the result of ineffectual boundaries. When boundaries are too permeable, listeners will inevitably hear the speaker as defining them and in turn, utilize language aimed at defending against the definition.

Communication is symptomatic of a larger problem, and therefore it does make sense to approach the problem as an inside job by addressing the feelings we are having a problem legitimizing, dealing with our shame or learning to employ more effective boundaries. But we can also approach the issue as an outside job where we learn the difference between ineffectual communication and constructive communication. As we stumble back into more dysfunctional ways of communicating, one of the four major problems will begin to show itself for our examination and learning.

# Belonging

Recently, I was lying in bed comfortably, holding my wife in my arms. Suddenly, I noticed tears gently dropping from her cheeks. I asked her what she was experiencing.

She said, "I want you to take me with you."

At first I wasn't quite sure what she was talking about, since I didn't have a trip planned in the near future. I decided to simply listen. Connie went on to describe what she cherished about my uniqueness. She described how she loved belonging to our marriage. Connie described how my uniqueness and our diversity called her to parts of herself she would not simply walk to on her own. The depth of belonging is one of the sacred gifts of diversity.

Our difference becomes an opportunity for all of us to be invited into areas of ourselves we would never have dreamed of visiting. Connie's unique appreciation of nature, her bold adventurous spirit, her eagerness to travel, and her receptiveness to what is new and different all call me to places I simply would not feel motivated to visit on my own. Because of the differences between us, I have the opportunity to expand my own identity and belong to a marriage with greater richness.

Belonging means that our essential uniqueness is welcomed. It may be accompanied by fear, anger, and confusion, but the welcome is unfaltering. The welcome must begin with us. If we do not welcome our own uniqueness into our marriages, we will never feel welcome there. Our values, our beliefs, and our preferences must be invited into our marriages by us, sometimes at the risk of creating tension, disruption, and conflict.

Once we possess some comfort at welcoming ourselves, we can begin to welcome our partners. Belonging deepens as these two processes weave into the fabric of our marriages and we experience the delight of saying to our spouses, "Take me with you."

## Sexism

Sexism is an inherent shadow in any marriage. Because our institutions are sexist, it may be impossible to be educated, receive religious training, and not be sexist. What is sexism, and how does it affect a marriage? Sexism is an attitude that defines people by gender, with accompanying duties and privileges.

We might begin by suggesting that marriage is a sexist institution. Over ninety-five percent of the appointments made for marriage counseling at my office, over a twenty-five-year period, have been made by women. Close to one hundred percent of the time, the wife sets the agenda in therapy, with the identified problem being some unmet need of the woman's.

Our culture defines marriage as a female institution, which means that women are supposed to define, design, and support the wellness of a marriage, which translates into the power and responsibility to make a marriage happen. Marriage is a dyadic experience, and to give that much power and responsibility to one person is to set that person up for failure, and to set the marriage up for failure. Both spouses lose.

It is naive to think that sexism leaves one party at a great advantage while the other is seriously deprived. Women may be comfortable with the power, but feel significantly burdened by the responsibility; while men may feel relieved to defer responsibility to their wives, but feel deeply dissatisfied about their powerlessness. Consequently, a marriage in which the wife's commitment to work on the relationship is wavering runs a much greater likelihood of collapse.

In order to effectively cope with the sexism in a marriage, a couple will need to pay attention to how they assign power and responsibility to one another based upon gender. Women need to be willing to let go of power and responsibility while men need to be ready to claim more. The common fear many women face is that if they do not attend to the needs of the relationship, no one will. The fear men regularly face is: how do they remain real men while holding power and taking responsibility for the welfare of the marriage?

Because of the efforts of feminism in the past thirty years, many women experience flexibility regarding the different roles they might play in a marriage and in a family. Unfortunately, men have not had such a profound emancipation of gender roles. Many men continue to experience their gender identity as being quite fragile. Consequently, men exhibit more rigidity in regard to roles that culturally define their maleness. Men are simply more resistant to exploring roles that are not traditionally ascribed to men.

It can be extremely beneficial for men to find training, workshops, and groups that affirm a wide range of roles for men; however, this kind of personal growth is defined by the culture as female. I recently approached several personal-growth learning centers with proposals for workshops that would support the liberation of men from rigid roles in their marriage. The marketing departments at these institutions saw my proposal as unacceptable, and explained that eighty percent of their participants were women!

Men are not supposed to be needy, so it is extremely challenging for men to even think about accessing support. Men are a long way from finding the "sacred masculine" in their aggression, in their loving, in their tenderness, in their resolve, and in their sensitivity. Men are often ill-equipped to be stewards of their inner worlds and of their marriages until they learn to welcome more of themselves into their own lives.

Women are often more aware of the oppression of sexism than men. As long as men are doing what is defined as culturally appropriate for men, they are often unaware of the price they are paying for the cultural buy-in. Men are often locked into the "good provider" role, working excessive hours, harming their health, and isolating themselves from their families and friends. They can remain unconscious of the pain, as long as it is an activity that the culture validates as a "real man" activity. They often don't understand that they are hurting themselves and those whom they love the most.

Sexism is far more prevalent in a marriage than the simple definition of women as nuptial caretakers. Many of the roles husbands and wives play in their marriages have been properly sanctioned as gender-specific by the culture. Stereotypically, men are supposed to attend to outdoor work, while women are in charge of the inner sanctum of home. Women are defined as responsible for the acquisition and preparation of food, as well as the after-meal cleanup. Women parent children, while men are often described as babysitters.

Sexism also affects how many men view sex. Men often decide that the significant woman in their lives should not have a rich sexual past, filled with a variety of partners and varied experiences. Of course, they do want to have a fulfilled sexual life with a partner who has little or no sexual savoir faire. I call this attitude the "Chasing Amy Syndrome," named after the film *Chasing Amy*.

Obviously, the Chasing Amy Syndrome is based upon a double standard. Men are entitled to an exhaustive sexual life and are in no way sordid for embracing their carnality. Men are seeking lustful virgins! It's a precarious quest, one that may reflect men's preoccupation with the goddess or the Great Mother. In order to have passionate partners, men may need to be willing to let go of their need to be mothered and move out of the sexist dilemma that demands that a wife be both sexual and chaste.

Men are responsible for maintaining automobiles and other mechanical appliances, while women typically attend to the interior decor. Women are quite often in charge of creating celebrations on holidays, birthdays, and anniversaries; they also tend to be responsible for the couple's social life. Men are commonly responsible for providing the necessary funds to support these events.

One client reported purchasing her own birthday and Christmas gifts, wrapping them, and signing them with her husband's name. This procedure went on for twenty-two years. She explained her behavior as making sure that she was recognized on her birthday and at Christmas. She learned that she was colluding in her husband's incompetence. What a benefit it was to her husband and to herself when she finally announced that she would no longer be buying her own gifts and that she expected gifts from her husband.

Obviously, these stereotypes do not automatically define all spouses; however, because we are all touched by the sexism of our social institutions, some degree of sexism will inevitably touch a marriage. Sexism, like all shadow material in a marriage, lies hidden and unrealized. It will take work for a couple to unearth their sexism. The digging will likely be disruptive. Both partners have to nonverbally agree in order to maintain sexist dynamics in a marriage.

Why do couples allow themselves to be defined by sexist stereotypes? One reason is that it simply feels easier to adopt a cultural definition, rather than take the responsibility to create our own identities as spouses. It is seductive to think we can get away with not doing all the work involved in creating a marriage. We also want to "get it right," and if our relationship appears to adhere to some cultural norm, then we must be "doing it right."

Another alleged benefit is that we get to feel like we belong to the "husband club" or "wife club." It can be somewhat frightening to be out there on our own, trying to put together a marriage without a clue about what it is supposed to look like. There is an illusion of security when we define ourselves in accordance with some preconceived norm.

What happens when we allow sexism to define marriage? Sexist definitions place a lid upon individual potential. Spouses stop exploring their innate possibilities, leaving their growth stunted as they succumb to a stifling complacency. Over time, we forget we are much more than the cultural stereotypes that constitute our identities. The challenge to be true to ourselves dries up, and we live according to convention, no longer willing to risk stewarding our personal gifts.

Resentment and cynicism replace passion and adventure. No matter how much we attempt to deny the fact that we are betraying ourselves, we are reminded by those around us who are determined to live their life's purpose; we are reminded that we have stepped away from ourselves.

Sometimes our compliance with prescribed gender roles can leave us feeling deeply inadequate. This is a common occurrence when spouses attempt to satisfy certain gender criteria instead of expressing their innate strengths.

Lastly, a marriage suffers immensely when spouses bring their appropriate gender postures to the relationship rather than their natural potency. All marriages face adversity, and in order to respond with fortitude, each partner must bring their best.

What happens when a couple allows themselves to move away from sexist stereotypes? Spouses often feel insecure about their gender identity when they begin to find their identity within. We no longer receive reassurance from neighbors, church groups, and the media about the appropriateness of our identity. We must legitimize our own choices, since we no longer have the culture to do it for us.

Spouses normally do not let go of sexist stereotypes at the same time. Consequently, it may be threatening to the partner hanging onto stereotypes when the other decides to find his or her gender definition within. A wife may decide to do less cooking and housecleaning and take more responsibility for household finances and yard work, while a husband decides to let go of maintaining the family computer and claims to be tired of the weekly runs to the town dump. This latter change can be quite significant, since dumps are traditionally defined as male turf. I have been told by dozens of spouses how threatening it was for them when their partners moved out of traditional gender roles.

One husband reported, "How will I know I'm the man of the house when my wife insists upon having a thousand dollars' worth of her own tools?"

Quite often, spouses who are clinging to cultural stereotypes will attempt to influence their partners to give up their liberation and return to what is socially proper. Consequently, emancipating spouses may face some abandonment issues as they move toward their own freedom.

It is typically extremely disempowering when we attempt to be someone we're not. It creates a constant inner struggle, casting us further and further into self-betrayal. It prohibits us from identifying and living our life's purpose. It makes our uniqueness unavailable to us and to our partners, making intimacy just about impossible.

When both spouses are willing to confront their affinity with gender stereotypes, they go a long way toward deepening their power and their intimacy. Couples return to who they were meant to be. Rather then attempting to "get their marriage right," in accordance with some external standard, they let their hearts define the beat of their relationship. They give their authenticity to themselves and to their relationship, rather than living by the lure of social conformity.

# Classism

Classism defines members of a particular social class by ascribing to them certain duties and privileges. Classism is a much more subtle shadow than sexism in most marriages. There is a tendency to view ourselves and our partners from the current socioeconomic perspective; hence, we are inclined to see a common education and a similar financial status as equalizers, placing us and our partners in the same class. What goes unappreciated is the influence of the class in which each of us was born and raised.

There are four significant differences between spouses raised in the upper middle class and those raised in the lower middle class: directness of communication, entitlement, view of money, and the role of self-reliance.

I was working with Tom and Ann, a middle-aged couple who had been married for ten years; both were in their second marriage. They were focusing their counseling on their diversity when the issue of classism began showing itself.

"I was shocked the other day when I described my discussion with our landscaper to Ann," Tom explained.

"Was there something about Ann's response that confused you?" I asked.

"Confused? Shit, I was damned surprised! Our landscaper normally treats our lawn with fertilizer, and I mow it. He suggested that the lawn was not up to snuff, and he wanted to mow it for awhile. I told him I needed to think about it. I went into the house and recounted my talk with him to Ann. I told her that all the men in my family always mowed their own lawns. I went on to describe how my eighty-year-old grandfather actually dropped dead from a heart attack while mowing his lawn. Ann looked a bit confused and said, 'I don't think I ever saw one of my family members mowing grass.' I knew right then that we grew up in very different homes," concluded Tom.

Tom was right. He and Ann came from very different social classes. Ann had been raised in a wealthy family from Georgia, while Tom came from a blue-collar family that worked in the local textile mill for generations. The more we explored the diversity of their class, the better they understood what lay behind their negative reactions to one another.

Tom had a strong resistance to hiring anyone to do work that he was capable of doing, while Ann preferred to hire someone regardless of her ability to perform the task. Tom had some doubt about his entitlement to great service and fine things, while Ann believed that she deserved the best, and whether in a restaurant or department store, she never hesitated to let people know. Ann believed there would always be enough money for their needs. Tom had some real doubts about always having adequate funds. Tom was quite clear about what money was coming in and what was going out, while Ann remained quite oblivious to the status of their financial resources.

Money became an area where they exercised their power by positioning themselves strongly. Each thought that the other had some real problems with money. Ann found Tom's tendency to worry unfortunate. Tom found Ann's nonchalant attitude about money to be financially irresponsible.

The more they were willing to view their money issues as an opportunity to learn, the less antagonism surrounded their diversity. Ann had accumulated financial debt, and she eventually became appreciative of Tom's ability to oversee his finances. Tom began to appreciate Ann's capacity to hold the belief that there would be enough money, rather than indulge in excessive worry.

In Tom's background, people spoke their minds.

"You always knew where people stood in my neighborhood. Nobody pulled any punches. You knew exactly how people felt," explained Tom.

Ann found Tom's directness very unlike the more genteel and indirect way of communicating used by her family and their friends. Ann eventually learned from Tom how to communicate more clearly, and Tom learned discretion and discernment from Ann.

When couples can accept that there are strengths and weaknesses in every class, they can begin to learn from one another. Curiosity, acceptance, and learning will allow couples to transform classism from something quite divisive to something that deepens their connection.

# Ageism

Ageism delegates certain duties and privileges to people based upon age. Since we are a culture that denies death, we devalue aging and adore youth. We empower youth with images of vitality, efficacy, and the illusion of being immune from death. We view aging as unfortunate—and unnecessary, if science can fulfill its destiny.

Ageism has a similar impact upon both men and women. They are both prone to judge themselves negatively as they age. Their judgments usually tell a story of the loss of physical beauty, stamina, sexual potency, physical strength, and self-esteem. To me, women seem somewhat more gracious when dealing with these losses, even though our culture tends to be more punitive with women in regard to aging.

Our culture gives men more permission to age, whether they accept it or not. Men are perceived as "maturing" as they wrinkle and turn gray, while women are viewed as "over the hill." Many of my female clients in their early fifties find it impossible to find men their own age willing to date them. These women often take up with men aged sixty-five and older.

Men appear to have a higher need to strategically deal with aging. One of their maneuvers is to affiliate with younger women. There is a wonderful scene from the movie *Moonstruck,* starring Cher as a daughter with aging parents in an Italian family. She and her mother, played by Olympia Dukakis, are returning from the grocery when the daughter turns and says, "Why is Pop having an affair with a younger woman?"

Her mother replies, "Your father is afraid to die."

Aging does entail losses as well as gains, but our acculturation leaves us blind to the beneficiaries and victims of our ageism. We overlook the possibility of a greater capacity for acceptance, empathy, wisdom, grace, and tolerance accompanying the aging process.

Marriages that have longevity or simply begin later in life will undergo the losses and the benefits of spouses aging. There are two important focuses for spouses experiencing aging. Internalized ageism can affect the way we see ourselves and it can affect the way we see our partners. In both cases, we may be preoccupied with the losses of aging and completely lose sight of the benefits. My work suggests that men are more concerned about the losses inherent in aging and almost never talk about their worries about getting older.

It can be critical to give a voice to our ageism, especially as it relates to the losses we incur by aging. It may be challenging to accept the physical losses that accompany aging, but under the influence of cultural ageism, it can be almost impossible. More wrinkles and less hair can be talked about and worked with as specific losses; however, under the influence of ageism, more is happening than some particular physical losses. Ageism moves us to turn against our bodies in shame and disgust. We are no longer able see our own beauty and worth, which can drive us to create a relationship with someone younger than ourselves, or invest in products that promise eternal youth.

Moving through ageism calls for a great deal of honest talk. We need to talk about our feelings about our own bodies and our feelings about our partners' aging bodies. Obviously, this latter discussion needs to be delicate. Keep in mind two dynamics. First, the more peace we make with our own aging bodies, the easier it will probably be to be accepting of the impact of age upon our partners' bodies. Secondly, females are conditioned to believe that they should have perfect bodies, which is impossible, and deeply hurtful to women.

The goal is not to launch an indictment upon our partners because of the losses we experience in regard to their aging; rather, we want to simply identify what we were so attached to; *e.g.,* tight abdominal muscles, smooth skin, thick hair, or firm buttocks.

Like all shadows, aging has its gold. Once we have some degree of acceptance over our losses, we can begin to identify the benefits of our own aging and learn how we profit from our partners' aging. The stronger the internalized ageism, the more challenging it will be to unearth the gold of our aging. Ageism dictates the illusion that there is no gold associated with aging and that all beauty dies with the decline of youth.

It calls for a fresh vision and resilience to own our ageism and allow ourselves to relinquish cultural stereotypes of aging. Remaining young is not an option. We either die or age, and eventually we die. We are called to make peace with aging and offer our marriages a youthfulness that is not meant for the young. We come of age, no longer striving to make our marriages "right," but rather finding the songs of our marriages, and more importantly, allowing ourselves to sing them. We approach one another more lightly, less severely, and with more compassion; without a need for crisis, we create more room for our diversity.

# 9

## *The Shadow Dance of Sex*

Sex is the most insidious of all shadows haunting our culture, and what haunts the culture, haunts each and every one of us. Upon first glance, it would appear that our approach to sex is anything but shadowy. After all, we sexualize everything—how we talk and walk, how we sell automobiles, and even how we entertain during halftime at football games. Our culture is obsessed with weaving sex into most of the fabric of social life. So where's the shadow? What's being denied and cast into the unconscious? How does the shadow nature of sex affect our marriages?

Before addressing these questions specifically, it may be important to explain the context within which sex slips into the depths of shadow. I want to suggest that the story of sex in our culture begins with death. In Greek mythology, Eros is the god of human sexuality, and his twin brother, Thanatos, is the lord of death and dying. The Greeks obviously found it fitting to have sex and death come from the same womb, bound genetically together. What do the Greeks convey by this coupling of sex and death?

What sex and death have in common is the human body. Sex and death demand the presence of a body; without a body, they do not happen. Both sex and death raise important questions in regard to having a body. How do we maintain the uniqueness of our personalities while having bodies like other members of the species? For that matter, when it comes to dying and sex, our bodies reflect a deep connection to all animals.

What does it mean to be in a body that guarantees finitude, an end to our selves as we know them? How do we live a life guided by personal values and longings while limited and constrained by physical bodies? How do we live with the fears of having a body that is vulnerable to disease and injury, as well as unpredictable death? How do we live with bodies that make it easy to be seen, heard, and possibly rejected by others?

Death and sex reflect what Ernest Becker referred to as our "creatureliness" in his book entitled *The Denial of Death*. It is that place where our bodies define us. We will have sexual relations, and we will die. It appears that the worlds of sex and death move to us and through us, regardless of our intentions. In fact, if we attempt to control sex and death by forcing them to comply with our wishes, they appear to become even more powerful and unpredictable.

We see this boomerang effect in the Catholic Church, where celibacy appears to guarantee sexual aberration. Holy men determined to control their sexual desires are driven to sexually abuse children. An agoraphobic patient protects himself against unsafe situations by reducing the world to a one-room living space where the possibility of dying is seriously reduced; in reality, that person has turned life into a living death. It appears that the more we attempt to control sex and death, the more we are defined by them. It may be that only through a profound willingness to surrender to the powers of death and sex can we learn to make peace with these two immense forces.

Surrendering to sex does not mean allowing ourselves to be hedonically driven by every erotic impulse and acting out whenever possible. Surrendering to death also does not suggest living recklessly, since dying is inevitable. Surrendering to sex and death means welcoming them as essential to the human condition, as heralds of what it means to be truly alive. Such a statement is blasphemy in our death-denying culture.

One of the core beliefs of our culture is the illusion that the more death can be denied, the more life can be welcomed. Just as young children hold their hands in front of their faces and claim they cannot be seen, we childishly hold our hands in front of the face of death and pronounce it nonexistent.

Our insistence upon dominating and denying death, by dismissing it as an option, guarantees that we infuse the culture with a ubiquitous sense of morbidity. We can see the hand of death in the pollution of the air, the rivers, and the oceans, in the burning of the rain forest, and in the generic nature of our malls, which inhibit the unique expression of the goods and tastes of the local inhabitants. Our schools have become battlegrounds where our children are killing one another. Our office buildings house millions of workers who remain at unfulfilling jobs in order to secure retirement, and they die prematurely because of the years of stress created by working at unfulfilling jobs. We can see the death of viable government as we vote for politicians whom we neither know nor trust. It is in our families, where we have forgotten how to talk to one another.

Our need to deny death places us in denial of what truly serves life. In order to keep death at bay, we move fast, talk fast, attempt to do much more than is healthy for us, and then take medications so we can sleep. In our need to deny death, we inhibit the fullness of life. We forget about what we truly love, how to nurture ourselves, how to quietly listen to ourselves, how to exercise our freedom so that it maximizes the quality of our choices, and how to make peace with the mystery of being alive. As we push death aside, so do we push life aside, and nothing is more at the core of life than sex.

Sex is about procreation, pleasure, passion, love, longing, and the experience of our own vitality. There are two common approaches to denying the potency of sexuality. The first is morality, which was vividly depicted in Hawthorne's *The Scarlet Letter*. The moral agenda is simply to drain sex of its power by making it bad. As we said earlier, sex will not be denied its potency. It will simply find more covert and perverse ways of expressing itself.

The second attempt to render sex helpless is to pathologize it, or to make it sick. This tendency became very popular in the eighties, when anyone interested in sex ran the risk of being identified as a sex addict. I recall participating in a workshop in which a woman confronted one of the men, claiming that he was standing with his pelvis thrust forward, and described how she felt violated by such a posture. The gentleman looked down at his hips, shamed and dejected, as if he had contaminated the workshop. As in when it is moralized, when pathologized, sex will find more clever and subversive ways to express itself.

Most of us will not escape the bite of our sexuality getting moralized or pathologized, and we will experience that pain in the form of shame. Sex often summons the shame shadow. It is an unusual home, school system, or religious training that teaches us to celebrate our bodies and honor our sexual lives. Often the shame is simply about having a body that isn't perfect or about giving a voice to what pleasures us.

The tendency is to either deflate or inflate the way we integrate sex into our lives. When we cope with shamed sexuality by deflating, we appear unavailable for sex, we diminish its importance, we don't talk about it, and we appear generally indifferent or antagonistic. When we cope with the shame of our sexuality by inflating, we often aggrandize sex in a typical adolescent fashion. Our language is filled with references to buttocks, breasts, and genitals. The strategy here is to make sex bigger than life, and to represent ourselves as perfectly comfortable with this bigger-than-life endeavor.

# Surrendering to Death

How curious it is that the place to start making peace with sex is with its twin brother. Instead of approaching sex by way of some new positions, gadgets, or techniques, we step closer to our sexuality and to life by surrendering to death; that is, only by making peace with death will we open to the depths of life and become receptive to living the fullness of our sexuality. As we welcome death as part of life, our capacity to live expands, and we become more capable of experiencing our sexuality as something larger than the friction produced by a pair of genitals. We can say that our capacity to die determines our capacity to live, which in turn determines the robust nature of our sexuality.

We can begin facilitating our surrender to death in several ways. One is the use of what I call "death language" in our thinking and in our conversation. A death-denying culture strives to eliminate language that makes any direct reference to death and dying. It substitutes euphemisms such as "change," "ending," "passed away," and "moved on" in lieu of candid death talk. We are under the illusion that if we don't think or talk about death, then there is no death.

We can go a long way toward reclaiming death by thinking in terms of dying: a calendar year dying, a job dying, a relationship dying, a childhood dying, time spent in a certain place dying, and even today dying. All change is a process of dying. Indigenous peoples knew this about the nature of change, and it made it easier for them to make peace with death. It is a common experience to feel awkward initially when speaking directly about death. The key is to feel the awkwardness and the tension and do it anyway.

A second strategy in the death-surrendering process is to ritualize our dying experiences. Recently, a couple called me, sobbing and convinced that there was something seriously wrong with them. Ruth and Ed went on to describe how they were moving from the home where they had lived for the past twenty-five years. I suggested that they were grieving and that they think seriously about ritualizing the death of living in their home. Their reaction told me that they were quite confused about what it would look like to ritualize their experience.

I recommended gathering friends, neighbors, and family members for the purpose of supporting their ritual. Another idea was to light a candle in each room of the house, bring the group to that room, and for a few minutes, tell some stories about the importance of each room, extinguishing the candle in the room just before walking out. I also proposed that they gather as a group in the living room, reading poetry, telling stories, or singing songs about family life and home. Ruth and Ed appeared to be somewhat open to my recommendations, while remaining skeptical about their value.

They met with me two weeks later for a regular therapy session and went on and on about the value of the ritual, both for them and their children. Ed explained how they had already begun to design a ritual aimed at blessing their new home.

The need for ritual lives in our cells. We live in a ritual-barren culture. Many of us have a few faint memories of some religious experience that felt essentially irrelevant; however, our DNA carries the profoundly intimate connection that our ancestors had with ritual. They understood ritual as a way to bring action to the sacred stories of their lives, and, in doing so, they viewed death and life as sanctified.

The third way to facilitate surrender to death is to acknowledge and express our grief. Life guarantees loss. When we attempt to ignore the losses of life, we ignore all life. Grief is a great testimony to the devotion and fervor with which we lived. It tells a story of just how important a place, a pet, a person, or some experience was for us. Grief is life-affirming!

Grief helps us let go of old life and prepare for new life. The fire of our anger and the water of our tears incinerate and wash away the old and prepare us for more life. Grieving is a way to live life, and it makes us ready to be intimate with life.

It is certainly overly simplistic to say that a couple who grieves together stays together; however, couples who grieve together bring the depths of themselves to one another. In their sorrow, they not only share their losses, but they allow for the diverse ways each of them grieves. Actively grieving may be the single most significant prerequisite to unleashing life and passion in a marriage.

Tina and Luke came to their first counseling session complaining about their sex life. Each of them spoke about the lack of fulfillment they had experienced in the bedroom over the past year. I asked them what was going on in their life about a year ago. They initially reported that life was pretty much status quo, when Tina paused, her eyes becoming moistened.

"Well, I did have a miscarriage ten months ago," Tina said, her eyes cast downward.

"Tell me how that experience was for you," I encouraged.

"Oh, I don't know. Everything was going so well, and then all of a sudden, I'm sitting on the toilet losing my baby. I carried her for seven months!" she yelled, then paused and offered an apologetic glance at Luke.

Tina went on to describe how she felt like she had failed Luke because of the miscarriage, and how she had been withholding these feelings for ten months. Luke was able to reassure her that he did not experience the miscarriage as Tina's failure. His comfort prompted her to sob uncontrollably, as if she finally had permission to let go and begin to find the strength to forgive herself.

Tina explained how she had been holding her grief silently to protect her three-year-old daughter from the experience. I encouraged Tina to go home and tell the story to her daughter, welcoming her into her grief. Tina was concerned that her daughter would not understand. I reassured Tina that her daughter would understand her tears, and told her to let her daughter know that she was getting all the support she needed from Luke and her friends.

I then turned my attention to Luke, who, unless he was supporting Tina, appeared quite stoic. He talked about being strong for Tina. I pointed out that everyone was trying to be strong for someone else. There were some extended silences as Luke spoke about how he had coped with the miscarriage.

After listening for some time, I decided that the silences were telling their own story, so I asked Luke if his experience of the miscarriage reminded him of anything. The silence that ensued seemed deeper and longer, and then he described the death of his one-year-old brother from spinal meningitis when Luke was seven.

Luke's parents had been separated, and he took it upon himself to support and comfort his mother, while sequestering his own grief to the recesses of his psyche. Tina's miscarriage had resurrected Luke's old grief, along with the pattern of ignoring his own loss while attending to the significant female in his life.

The warmth and the passion in their relationship had been replaced with Tina's guilt and Luke's frozen grief. There was no room for new life in their relationship. But as each of them took responsibility for their own grieving process and clearly asked for what they needed from the other, the warmth quickly returned. Within months they reported crying in one another's arms, and told about how easily they would gently slip into making love. I pointed out that crying in one another's arms *is* making love. Actively grieving is a blessing of life and an act of loving life.

When we are not actively grieving our losses, we are constructing a dam that holds back the waters of our grief and smothers the fire of our desire. Sometimes the fire finds a way of getting out of control, because there is not adequate water to maintain it, which results in addiction. When we either extinguish our fire or allow it to burn unrestrained, we move away from life and closer to death.

# From Necrophilia to Biophilia

We have seen how our denial of death puts us in more death. We can employ addictions, medications, depression, and hyperactivity to help suppress and deny death; however, these strategies inevitably place us against life and closer to death, or what can be described as necrophilia, or "love of death." We have also seen how our denial of death diminishes our capacity for life, and therefore for sex.

It's no wonder we are a society obsessed with translating the sexual into images of death and violence. Where death is denied, expressions of life become inundated with morbidity. It becomes literally impossible to have a thriving sex life while consistently moving away from life. When death is denied and pushed into the unconscious, it acts like any other shadow, projecting itself onto anything and everything, until life is mostly about dying.

The denial of death throws us into death's embrace. We become accustomed to feeling depressed and detached from our passion, speaking in cliché and innuendo instead of expressing our personal truths, and reducing sex to something mechanistic. Necrophilia touches all aspects of our lives, especially sex. Couples living in the depths of necrophilia forget what they love about themselves and one another, and what they love about life.

Luckily, our capacity for biophilia does not go away; it simply slides into a state of dormancy. I highly recommend traveling and attending retreats, workshops, and training programs in order to awaken biophilia. We can use our awareness of the presence of necrophilia as a way to step closer to ourselves. The dissatisfaction accompanying necrophilia can be a great wake-up call to the choices we need to make in order to bring the love of life back into our lives. Nothing brings the love of life back to us more robustly than the awakening of eros.

# Eros, Aphrodite, and Hephaestus

According to Greek mythology, Eros was the son of Aphrodite, but his paternal genealogy is not as clear. Some accounts suggest that his father was Hephaestus. The god Eros can be seen as a metaphor for passion and sexual desire.

Our culture is inclined to reduce eros to the erotic, making it a genital energy; however, the arousal of eros is much larger than sexual excitement. It is the awakening of the human spirit that occurs emotionally, intellectually, intuitively, sensually, and creatively. It is common to see writers and other artists practice sexual abstinence, which directs their eros toward the creation of magnificent art. But to awaken on all these levels also entails the experience of pain, longing, frustration, and disillusionment; hence, we often turn away from eros and settle for a rush of blood to the penis, provoked by the ingestion of Viagra. If we want a full sexual life, instead of merely an engorged penis, we will need to learn what it means to invite eros into our lives.

It may be helpful to ask how we can become more inviting to eros. Foremost, we can be willing to learn how to carry the tension of being awake. To be aroused intellectually and emotionally means that we understand and feel with depth. Life is no longer a childish undertaking, where mystery is ignored by insisting upon remaining innocent and naive. A life moved by eros knows the tension of self-doubt, guilt, grief, and anxiety. It means being willing to learn how to comfort ourselves while our life choices evoke tension. It means mostly depending upon ourselves for comfort, instead of holding our spouses responsible for our succor.

We can be invited to live from eros and welcome its energy. There are many faces of eros within the human condition. The spirit of eros lives in our play, anger, curiosity, competition, sex, and adventure, as well as in stirring experiences of beauty, and in culinary delights.

It also might be helpful to examine the nature of Aphrodite, who gave birth to Eros, in order to better understand how we might birth eros in our lives. Aphrodite was considered to be the goddess of beauty. We can begin by asking about our relationship to the beautiful. Do we seek beauty? Do we linger enough to notice and appreciate the beautiful? Do we pay attention to beautifying our homes and offices? Do we pay attention to beautifying our own bodies? Do we actively acknowledge the beauty of others? Are we able to speak to others about our experience of the sublime? Obviously, calling Aphrodite energy into our lives has a great deal to do with our relationship to beauty. And later, we will see how important it is when we wish to bring romance into our lives.

Aphrodite was also granted charge over laughter and hoaxes, sweet lust, love and loving kindness, and the whispering of maidens. We can treat Aphrodite's responsibilities as a metaphor of what gives rise to eros.

We are told that Aphrodite's son Eros is extremely mischievous and is represented as an adolescent, rather than being granted the full maturity of other gods. In both mother and son there is a tendency toward impishness. Aphrodite's charge over laughter and hoaxes goes a long way toward suggesting that sexual energy greatly depends upon playfulness. The seriousness often attributed to sexuality by morality and psychology drains eros of its vibrancy. Somber conversation is better suited for the living room or the kitchen, leaving the bedroom for play and lightness.

How does a couple become more receptive to Aphrodite's laughter and Eros's playfulness? Learning not to take personally what is said and done greatly facilitates the presence of lightness in a relationship. We can see our partners' choices as their attempts at navigating their way through life, rather than as assaults upon our pride.

It also helps to put points of contention to rest. We can do this by applying the principles of creative empowerment. The first is problem ownership, which we employ by identifying our unmet need, taking responsibility for meeting that need, and moving on. Sometimes we can ease the force of discord by becoming more accepting of what is out of our control, rather than expending hours attempting to influence our partners. Sexual energy is commonly not aroused by constant struggle.

It is said that Aphrodite is responsible for sweet lust. We can understand sweet lust as being an appetite for sensual pleasure. Our culture often confuses genital sexuality with sensuality. I recently listened to a client describe himself as having an adverse response to his partner's scent. Following the session, I was more keenly aware of how much I enjoy my wife's scent. I also realized that I seldom allowed myself to be cognizant of how pleasant I find her fragrance, and almost never acknowledged it to her. If we are to have an appetite for sensuality, then we will need to pay attention to the smells, sounds, tastes, and touch of our partners.

The following poem by Galway Kinnel celebrates the body as not simply an expression of carnality, but rather as an incarnate manifestation of divinity.

## Last Gods

She sits naked on a boulder
a few yards out in the water.
He stands on the shore,
also naked, picking blueberries.
She calls. He turns. She opens
Her legs showing him her great beauty
and smiles, a bow of lips
seeming to tie together
the ends of the earth.
Splashing her image

To pieces, he wades out
and stands before her, sunk
to the anklebones in leaf-mush
and bottom-slime—the intimacy
of the visible world. He puts
a berry in its shirt
of mist into her mouth.
She swallows it. He puts in another.
She swallows it. He puts in another.
She swallows it. Over the lake
Two swallows whim, juke, jink,
And when one snatches
an insect they both whirl up
and exult. He is swollen
not with ichor but with blood.
She takes him and talks him
more swollen. He kneels, opens
the dark, vertical smile
linking heaven with the underearth
and murmurs her smoothest flesh
more smooth. On top of the boulder
they join. Somewhere
a frog moans, a crow screams.
The hair of their bodies
startles up. At last they call out
in the tongue of the last gods,
who refused to go.
Chose death, and shuddered
In joy and shattered in pieces,
bequeathing their cries
into the human throat. Now in the lake
two faces float, looking up
at a great maternal pine whose branches

open out in all directions
explaining everything.

We are told that Aphrodite watches over love and loving kindness. From this, we can draw upon the images of compassion and generosity. Compassion invites our partners to forgive themselves for their shadows, as we also accept them for their imperfect humanity. The more we attend to our own shadow work, making peace with our own humanity, the less likely we are to occupy the self-righteous high ground.

What engenders a capacity for generosity? Refusing to live in self-sacrificing deprivation goes a long way toward deepening our ability to be generous. The more we move out of victimhood and take responsibility for our own needs, the more we find ourselves rejoicing at the possibility of our partners acquiring what they desire. Our choice to extend compassion and generosity to our spouses is a grand invitation for them to open to us on numerous dimensions.

We should also note that the free expression of anger is a wonderful way to facilitate compassion and generosity. As we saw earlier, blocked anger readily translates into resentment, which significantly inhibits the expression of compassion and generosity.

Lastly, we are told that Aphrodite holds dominion over the whispering of maidens. Although we are working within a heterosexual paradigm, these metaphors are also aptly suited to homosexual and lesbian relationships.

"Maidens whispering" is an image of what is shy, girlish, and retiring. When we can see the face of a girl or a boy in our beloved regardless of their age, we extend the kind of tenderness that furthers the possibility of openness.

The origin of the word "maiden" also suggests the image of "first time." If we want our sexual encounters to possess some of the intrigue and excitement of first-time experiences, then we need to act with warmth and tenderness, in the spirit of whispering maidens, long before we get to the bedroom.

Let's turn our attention to Hephaestus, the father of Eros. We are told that Hephaestus is deeply connected to the instinctive, the libidinous, and "the fire down below." Much of the human psyche is fueled by the fire down below. This is the place of longing, desire, anger, ruthlessness, decisiveness, lustiness, and tenacity. We can step into this subterranean fire in any of these places as a way to ignite its flame and encourage the life of eros.

Hephaestus was born disabled. We can see this as a metaphor for our own wounds and the power we acquire when we welcome these wounds. Resistance to our wounds makes us defensive; where our hearts are closed, we act excessively severe and extremely vigilant, doing whatever we can to prevent feelings of vulnerability. When our mission is not to be witnessed in our emotional nakedness, we inhibit the likelihood that we will be genuinely witnessed in our physical nakedness. Our sexual life pays a price.

When we are able to carry our wounds lightly, we define ourselves as much more than our wounds. The issue is not how badly we have been wounded, but rather how we relate to our wounds, and how we carry them.

The mythology surrounding Hephaestus suggests that his mother, Hera, abandoned him because of his deformity. It may very well be that before we can fully welcome eros, we will need to attend to some wounding by parental rejection. It is common to project onto our partners the abandonment we experienced in the past. We are convinced that our spouses do not really love us and that rejection is inevitable. When this experience from the past overlays our present relationships, we will actually defend ourselves against the love and desires of our partners, claiming that we are simply bracing for the unpreventable abandonment.

The image of Hephaestus also teaches us that we may need to learn how to love ourselves—in spite of our imperfections—if there is to be any hope of receiving the love and desire of our partners.

It is also said that Hephaestus created the first woman. In a real sense, our "fire down below" becomes the heat needed for our partners to forge a character of depth, grace, and resiliency. As our spouses feel our heat, they may make choices to open to it, protect themselves from it, create something from it, and ultimately discover who they were meant to be. Our dissatisfaction with some behavior or attitude of our partners' can reflect our heat and an opportunity for our partners to decide who they are in the face of our dissatisfaction. We have the same opportunity in the presence of our partners' dissatisfaction.

We can ask a number of potentially illuminating questions: Is my partner's dissatisfaction simply a result of his or her unmet need, and not a statement about me? Is my partner's dissatisfaction a reflection of some way I may have violated my own values? Is my partner's dissatisfaction indicative of some change I am seeking for myself? Our partners' dissatisfaction can be the heat necessary to bring about desired changes.

As heat was the catalyst necessary to transforming elements in the alchemical crucible, so is the heat of Hephaestus necessary to bringing eros forward in the container of a marriage.

The mythology surrounding Eros tells a story of fire, from the warmth of loving kindness to the burning flames of passion and lust. I am often asked what is a reasonable starting point for inviting eros into our lives. Desire in all of its subtle expressions is an excellent place to begin.

What do I want for breakfast? What time do I want to leave for work? What do I want to do at work, and with whom do I want to work? What time do I want to go to bed, and when do I want to awaken? To whom do I want to extend friendship? What do I want to give and receive from my spouse? Whom am I willing to ask for help? A life lived from desire will surely welcome the heat of eros and all the warmth and fire of his parents.

## The Fire of Eros

What happens when couples do not bring their desire to their relationship? Desire is fire, and fire provides light, warmth, and power. The luminosity of eros's fire allows spouses to see why they are in a marriage. Desire illuminates what is given, what is received, and what is longed for. The light produced by the light of desire allows us to know who we are as spouses and helps define who our spouses are. When desire's beacon grows dim, it becomes extremely difficult to know ourselves and our partners.

I often ask couples if they know their partners. After an abrupt reply in the affirmative, I continue to ask what they believe their spouses want from them. More times than not, spouses go blank, having little or no awareness of what is desired of them. It is almost impossible for spouses to really know one another if the light of desire is no longer shining on the relationship.

When a marriage is not being infused by desire, it loses its warmth. It will increasingly become cold, lacking a capacity to comfort and nurture. When a marriage becomes icy, spouses either learn to endure the bleakness, adapting to deprivation, or they turn elsewhere for their comfort.

A marriage without fire is a marriage without power. Ancient alchemists believed fire to be the only ingredient necessary to transform a combination of elements into a compound. The fire of desire has the potency to bring two unique individuals into a dynamic union. The flames of eros can burn away the walls that separate us, bringing us out of isolation and into deep closeness.

The alchemical principle also applies to separating a compound into its distinct parts. The same flames can torch excessive connective tissue, allowing us to separate and reclaim our individuality. Spouses who have lost their desire do not have the power to create union with their partners, nor are they able to embrace the uniqueness of their identities as spouses.

There are a number of significant implications of a marriage losing warmth, power, and light. The loss of power is experienced as a significant self-betrayal, because spouses no longer experience themselves as the authors of their own lives. When we are not living from our desire, we are either living from obligation or from someone else's desire, which commonly results in anger and resentment. The result is quite often some abuse of power, commonly expressed as an affair.

The loss of desire's light is frequently manifested as a loss of imagining or dreaming, which translates into the loss of a future. We often hear how important it is to have a dream. I am not suggesting that it is crucial to have a dream; in fact, I would claim that becoming attached to some dream can be a good way to cancel your current reality. My recommendation is not to get overly invested in some future reality depicted by a dream, but rather to exercise the power of dreaming and imagining as ways to call forth what is pregnant in the present moment. Active desiring fuels our capacity to imagine, stretching the present into its possibilities.

When the light of desiring grows dim, so will our values and our life's purpose. Living from our desire reminds us of what is important to us and to that which we are willing to commit. Time and time again, I have witnessed spouses wrestling with some decision, without a clue about which direction to turn. When I ask them what personal values they possess that might give them some indication of how to deal with their dilemma, their response is generally profound confusion. There is no way to be clear about personal values without living from our desire.

Without the power, warmth, and light of desire, it is almost impossible to have a creative capacity to resolve conflict. After the dust settles from the fighting, couples must be able to identify and express what they want in order for there to be any kind of reasonable resolution. Generally speaking, couples are in conflict because at least one person is not getting something that is desired, and if that something cannot be spoken clearly, there will be no resolution.

Lastly, and probably most troublesome, spouses not living their desire pass on the legacy of a life without desire to their children. When I ask couples to identify what their parents desired and how they championed their desire, they usually report confusion about their parents' desire, confusion that reflects the confusion they experience about their own desire. Obviously, there is much to gain by reconnecting to our desire. When the fire of eros is rekindled in a marriage, spouses have the power to live their love.

# Live Your Love

Many couples who take their marriages seriously ask how they can bring more love into their relationships. This is a very honorable curiosity, but one that is typically examined with a great deal of shortsightedness. Spouses limit their perspective to their marriages, seeking strategies and techniques that might enhance the flow of love between them.

Shadow marriage encourages a much larger view of welcoming love into our marriages. What does it mean to invite love into our entire lives? If we want to increase the depth and meaning of our love, then we need to learn to live our love.

Living our love does not mean that we have some life-altering religious conversion, whereby the lenses of our eyes gain a permanent rose tint. It does not mean that we need to regress to being flower children of the sixties. It does mean that we begin taking very seriously what we love, who we love, and how we are going to fill our lives with the people and the experiences we love.

Living our love calls for a ferocious spirit. We must be willing to remain self-examining, so we can identify who and what we love. We need to do the work necessary to support our deservedness to live our love. Lastly, we need to find the courage to pursue our love, even when it may not be popular with friends and relatives, or when it initially appears not to be financially feasible.

As a rule, fear calls us away from living our love. We fear failure, we fear betraying family legacies, we fear success, we fear being fully alive, and we may fear moving out of deprivation. When we succumb to fear, we often demand that our partners compensate for our failure to live our love by asking them to love us perfectly, which sets our relationships up for failure.

Ask yourself: "Am I living my love? And if I'm not, what risk am I willing to take in order to move in the direction of living my love?" These are great starting points for infusing a marriage with love.

# Getting Safe

We can think of eros as the fullness of life. It is a generative life force that longs to express itself by dancing, singing, writing, creating, building, talking, making love, decorating, and even playing. Many of us experienced our families of origin as not conducive to expressing the bountiful nature of our inner lives. We learned that it would be either physically or emotionally dangerous to show our exuberance, so we learned to contain ourselves, seeking protection from the dangers lurking behind parental displeasure. Instead of coming forward spontaneously, we got good at monitoring ourselves with a watchful eye, remaining vigilant for whatever menacing family dynamics might erupt.

No matter how effective we were at taking care of ourselves in our families of origin, there remains a longing for the one who will provide true safety for us. On countless occasions, I have heard clients who are in the beginning stages of a relationship say that a person they recently met makes them feel really safe. There is comfort in the illusion that some significant other can make us be or feel safe; however, the illusion is normally short-lived. As soon as our protectors express some adverse reaction to one of our beliefs or choices, the illusion begins to shatter, and we may become disillusioned.

In an intimate relationship, authentic safety can only be supplied by ourselves, and it is not limited to a feeling. We generate safety by being capable of employing three specific behaviors, and by being willing to do so. The first is to set whatever boundaries we need in order to make sure that no physical harm comes to us. Any form of physical abuse needs to remain unacceptable in a marriage, and unless spouses who live under the threat of physical harm learn to take care of themselves, the spark of eros will certainly be extinguished.

The second safety-promoting behavior is the ability to employ the kinds of boundaries that prevent us from being emotionally abused by being subjected to shaming, ridicule, blaming, moralizing, and any other verbal attack aimed at either diminishing our personal worth or stripping us of the right to define ourselves.

The third way safety is secured is by our willingness to remain loyal to ourselves by not being ashamed of who we are and by honoring what we need and want. The more we are willing and able to take responsibility for our own safety, the more our marriages are transformed from the insecurity of victimization to a freedom that gives rise to the expression of eros.

The art of creating boundaries that protect us while maintaining creative engagement with our partners is challenging, and at times it can be downright messy. If the boundary is too permeable, we fall prey to whatever pugnacity is coming our way. If the boundary is not permeable enough, we cut off our connection with our partner.

The flow of eros in a marriage depends upon engagement, which takes place through eye contact, verbal expression, and physical touch. Consequently, emotional or physical withdrawal can have a damaging impact upon eros in a marriage. Boundaries that are set up as part of attempts at influencing our partners are excessively impermeable, sending an offensive message to our spouses that their uniqueness is not valued. On the other hand, accommodation often leaves us in self-betrayal in setting up an excessively permeable boundary, supporting the desires of our partners while neglecting our own.

The challenge of generating safety while supporting eros involves remaining engaged while clearly communicating our own truths as we let go of the need to either influence or accommodate. We can speak the truth of what we want, what we value, what we believe, and what is unacceptable to us. We can remain focused upon ourselves, while inviting our partners to speak their own truths. If eros is to thrive in a marriage, we will need to learn how to hold on to ourselves, back ourselves up, stay engaged, and invite our spouses to join us in self-focused truth-telling.

## Sex As Ritual

In his book *The Soul of Sex*, Thomas Moore defines sex as the primary ritual. Ritual is a behavioral way to tell a story; as a primary story, sex is a collection of behaviors telling an essential story. Sex tells a story about our bodies: how we relate to our bodies, how we relate to our partners' bodies, how we relate to the environment, how we relate to our own emotional lives, and how we relate to the emotional lives of our partners. Sex tells the richest and most evocative of all human stories; it can reveal the subtle and hidden areas of our souls.

Sex can expose those parts of us that we wish to remain veiled. Our bodies tell candid narratives, truths that have not been spoken—in some cases, not even conceptualized. We have the choice to listen to the stories told by our sexual bodies, or to reduce the messenger to a simple deliverer of pleasure and excitement. If we choose the latter, we strip sex of its potency and stop inviting its wholeness into our lives. We then wonder why we are left with rudimentary gyrations that lack passion and intimacy.

When we are willing to open to the fullness of our sexuality, we open to ourselves. The challenge is whether or not we will allow our sex to teach us about ourselves. It's too easy and trite to suggest that sexual inhibition reflects a fear of intimacy with our partners. The real issue is whether or not we are going to allow our sex to bring us intimately close to ourselves. Can we dare to witness both how brilliant and how petty we are? In reality, this is the only important sexual question, because our sex will reveal both expressions of our shadow.

Anita and Colby, a couple in their mid-forties, came to their first session complaining about their sexual life. They both possessed enough emotional maturity to remain relatively self-focused. Anita talked about her inability to remain present while making love with Colby.

"I immediately start thinking of work, the kids, my friend who was recently in a car accident, and a myriad of other current happenings in my life," explained Anita.

"How do you deal with your drifting out of the bedroom when you're making love with Colby?" I asked.

"I just pretend it's not happening," she replied, visibly embarrassed.

"What would happen if you simply declared to Colby that you were not present?" I inquired.

"That would be very hard to do," she quickly responded.

"What would make it so difficult?"

"Well, I'm not supposed to be drifting all around when I make love with my husband," she explained.

Anita went on to talk about how much she lived by certain prescriptions and just how shamed she felt about not staying focused when she was making love. It was not appropriate for her to be distracted during sex, so she kept it a secret, wandered, and continued to feel shame about it.

Anita learned that unless she told her secret in the moment, she would continue not being present and feeling ashamed about it. Anita's sexuality was telling her shame story, and luckily she was willing to listen and start telling the truth about wandering out of the bedroom during sex.

The more Anita was willing to talk about not being present while making love with Colby, the less shame she felt; however, her tendency to be distracted was telling a narrative about her fear. She began to see how scared she was of the possibility that her lovemaking with Colby would not be satisfying for him. As she opened up to feel her fear and talk about it, she discovered she was taking responsibility for Colby's sexual satisfaction. Anita was willing to learn how to give back to Colby the responsibility for his sexual fulfillment. It helped that Colby was willing to accept the responsibility.

It is critical that we not see Anita's difficulty in being present, her shame, and her fear as an indication of some kind of pathology that needs fixing. There was nothing wrong with Anita. She was simply allowing her eroticism to bring her to her fear, from which she had drifted away. She was letting her sexuality bring her closer to herself, and eventually closer to her husband. As she allowed her sexuality to teach her about herself, she felt more satisfaction in her sexual life. When we grant sex its power to bring us closer to ourselves, it renews itself through the permission we give it to be all it was meant to be.

Colby was eager to tell his story. He explained how he had the tendency to get his sexual needs met without paying much attention to Anita. Colby's sexual behavior confused him and Anita, since in all other areas of their relationship, Colby was extremely considerate of Anita's needs. He was hard on himself, referring to his behavior as "sexual looting," in which his intention was simply to get his sexual needs met.

Finally, I asked him about his sexual life in his first marriage. He described himself as significantly sexually deprived during a fifteen-year marriage. I pointed out to him how common it is for severe deprivation to lead to "looting." Colby's sexual ritual was telling a narrative about a man who was angry and determined not to sacrifice himself unnecessarily; however, in his attempt to avoid deprivation, he was creating deprivation, as he used Anita's body to satisfy himself while losing Anita.

Colby understood that he had some work to do regarding letting go of his anger about his past deprivation. The more he allowed himself to sink into the issue, the more he felt angry at himself for allowing it to happen. He began to more fully see Anita as an ally of his sexual fulfillment and not at all interested in depriving him. They both began to prioritize being present with themselves and with one another during sex. They understood that their commitment to a satisfying sexual life meant being willing to endure tension and pay attention to the stories being told by their sexuality.

In his seminal work, *Resurrecting Sex,* David Schnarch states, "There's a lot more anxiety involved in turning sexual problems around than performance and anxiety or guilt about sex. Couples frequently have anxieties about facing their relationship, or changing sexual behaviors, or being better known."

What Schnarch refers to as anxiety, I am calling tension. Schnarch is saying that the ritual of sex inherently generates a great deal of tension. Much of this tension is due to sex telling a larger story about the status of the relationship, such as shifts in how couples are relating sexually; it also reflects us simply becoming more transparent to ourselves and our partners.

Thomas Moore says that "one of the main purposes of sex is to be palpably present to the other." How difficult it is to hide from our partners as we lie naked, breathing heavily, sweating, openmouthed, and insatiably hungry. We are stripped of our normal protocol, social convention, and well-developed ways of hiding ourselves behind everything from sophistication to sarcasm. So much tension accompanies this kind of primal transparency, yet it is only the beginning, as our sexuality tells a larger story of our relationship to our hearts, our wounds, and our longing.

The sexual ritual ushers in these larger narratives, creating an opportunity for us to step closer to ourselves and to our partners. The moment we are invested in our sex being fulfilling or meaningful, we begin surrendering to the larger stories being told by our sexuality. It's quite a conundrum.

We only want a little pleasure and maybe a release of some tension, and before we know it, we are facing the tension of some challenging shadow work. Some denied and forgotten part of us begins to stir, moving closer to consciousness as we allow ourselves to be confronted by our sexuality.

## Tension Abounds

Sometimes the tension has to do with our sexual ritual-awakening stories about how we are either fused or avoiding our partners. We feel the comfort of the status quo slipping through our fingers as the tension of a new way of relating begins to emerge, in addition to a new identity for ourselves.

Nothing provokes tension more than some part of us dying and some new part struggling to be born. One of the great gifts of the sexual ritual is that it tells a story about a man or a woman who wants to reclaim what has been forgotten or step toward the frontier of the self, a place deep within that has not yet been visited.

Schnarch points out that those new sexual behaviors stimulate a great deal of tension. We subdue the tension by comforting ourselves with a sexual routine. We get used to being seen by our partners in certain postures and behaviors. It is tension-provoking to step out of those patterns in order to become exploratory.

One of the greatest challenges is to allow ourselves to be the recipients of our partners' delight. Nothing can create more tension than noticing that our partners are delighting in our touch and in simply being in contact with us. Being the recipient of delight is a grand opportunity to access the golden shadow of our worthiness.

Fulfilling sex greatly depends upon learning how to carry tension creatively. Talking about the tension helps us to get more creative with it. Becoming playful is a wonderful way to move the energy of the tension, rather than allowing it to bind us up from head to toe. Breathing fully also helps to move the energy. And suspending expectations, with the focus being our willingness to be present with ourselves and with our partners, is a powerful way to deal with tension.

It also helps to learn to carry tension out of the bedroom. The more we practice truth-telling out of the bedroom, the more comfort we gain with experiencing the tension of our uniqueness being juxtaposed with the uniqueness of our partners. We can also be assisted by remembering that the tension we experience is not so much about us as it about the larger myth of human sexuality. No one gets to be completely comfortable in the sexual arena.

Let's return for a moment to this idea of being present to ourselves. What does it mean? How does it happen? It is a meditative state, in that it is a quieting down. The quieting down happens when we close our eyes and breathe fully. As the breathing becomes rhythmic, we can first notice what expectations or demands we may be placing on ourselves, and begin offering ourselves some permission to let go of them. Then we might take a body inventory, noticing where tension is residing in our bodies and giving each of those body parts permission to be at peace, while we sustain deep, rhythmic breathing.

It is noteworthy that becoming more present is mostly about giving ourselves permission to breathe, feel, and be at peace. Becoming more present gets us closer to ourselves, and so we actually have our selves to bring to our partners. I highly recommend integrating this practice of becoming present as an essential part of lovemaking.

# The Romantic

Our culture is inclined to reduce the romantic to either a lusty strategy aimed at disarming our partners' sexual reservations, or a quixotic quest having little or no relevance to real life. Three ancient Latin meanings of "romance" translate into "love charm," "friendship," and "love," so we can say that the romantic has the power to charm or lure one toward friendship and love.

It may be very useful to expand our understanding of the romantic to include friendship, rather than simply love and sex. A call to friendship may be considerably more alluring, since it invites the whole person, rather than making a plea to mere body parts. This perspective of the romantic can be especially important in a marriage. What does it mean to sustain a capacity to allure our spouses to friendship and love?

Unfortunately, we're inclined to depend heavily upon what is fashionable to call our partners to us. As we employ conventional strategies of romance such as flowers, candy, and candlelit dinners, it is only too easy to overlook whether or not these parochial gestures have any meaning for us or our partners. We employ them because they allegedly have some social credence, and we are afraid to fail.

A call to friendship and love may need to be very particular to the participants; consequently, employing conventional expressions of the romantic may be a setup for failure. We are much better off being candid about our fear of failure.

We can move away from pedestrian expressions of the romantic by asking: What kind of relationship do I have to beauty? What do I find beautiful? How do I feel about my own beauty? What does my partner find beautiful?

In his recent book, *Beauty*, John O'Donohue writes: "When beauty touches our lives, the moment becomes luminous. These grace-moments are gifts that surprise us. When we look beyond the moment to our life journey, perhaps we can choose a new rhythm of journeying which would be more conscious of beauty and more open to inviting her to disclose herself to us in all the situations we travel through."

We can say that infusing our marriages with the romantic means choosing a new rhythm of journeying that is more conscious of beauty. This consciousness of beauty goes beyond knowing what our partners find beautiful and appropriately producing it. More importantly, it means living our own lives as beings more conscious of beauty.

Nothing is more alluring than our partners witnessing us having an active and endearing relationship with beauty. It places us in beauty! It invites our partners to join us in friendship and love by suggesting that they will be immersed in beauty when they join us.

Our experience of beauty is both an outside job and an inside job. As an outside job, we can explore ways to bring beauty to our environment and search out different expressions of male and female plumage.

It can be as simple as deciding to add a plant, a picture, an ornament, or a lamp to a particular room. I recommend being especially attentive to bringing beauty into the bedroom. When exploring plumage to adorn our bodies, we can try wearing new colors, some jewelry, makeup, different kinds of clothing, or new hairstyles. Beauty can be added to our lives by reading poetry the first thing in the morning, or maybe writing a poem. Playing recorded music or playing an instrument can stimulate the presence of beauty. I strongly suggest starting the day with some activity that calls in the beautiful, such as experiencing poetry or music.

As an inside job, we can explore bringing beauty into our lives by exercising compassion and generosity. We can ask ourselves about the places where our responses to our partners fall short of being compassionate. We can also ask questions about being generous sexually, financially, and with our time and energy.

Speaking our truth is another internal way to support the presence of beauty. When we clearly describe what we want or how we feel, we create access to the beauty of our own souls. This is especially true when our utterances are not draped with attempts to influence, defend, or manipulate. For a moment or two, we let go of attempting to impress or persuade. There is great beauty in the simple articulation of our truths. We relax into ourselves and release the tension accompanying our resistance to simply saying who we are.

I have been privileged to see the physical changes that often take place when we speak personal truths. Cheeks soften and eyes brighten with a general luminosity that surrounds the person's entire body. It is as if we relax into ourselves, no longer needing to resist who we are. As we bring compassion, generosity, and truth to our marriages, we summon an immense amount of beauty.

There is also beauty in our wildness. Our wildness is that part of us that refuses to succumb completely to cultural protocol. Our wildness can be seen in the uniqueness of our language, our values, our beliefs, and our lifestyle. We can see our wildness in living what we love, rather than what is deemed appropriate. I have often witnessed brightness in the eyes of those who live what they love. A life of wildness offers constant testimony to our anomalous nature in a way that sets us free from the bondage of cultural norms.

## Sex in the Bedroom

In his book *Resurrecting Sex*, Schnarch offers us three strategies for maximizing sexual fulfillment:

*Optimizing your body's ability to respond
*Optimizing the physical stimulation you receive
*Optimizing your feelings, emotions, and thoughts, including your relationship to your partner

Optimizing our bodies' ability to respond means being willing to take responsibility for our bodies' wellness. We can do this by having regular medical exams. Western medicine rates extremely high in regard to acute care. It is much less laudable when it comes to preventive medicine and chronic care. I highly recommend having a team of physicians, a MD and an ND, with the latter being proficient in herbal or homeopathic medicine.

Understanding what medications we are taking and their impact upon our sexual lives is critical. Often there is a natural alternative that will not have the adverse reaction to our sexual functioning a pharmaceutical supplement might have.

It is also important to pay attention to diet and exercise. When either of these is askew, it can be challenging to properly stoke the fires down below. There is also sound research suggesting that middle-aged males who regularly exercise have a greater propensity for sex than middle-aged men who do not regularly exercise.

Optimizing the physical stimulation we receive means taking responsibility for being physically and emotionally present to ourselves and to our partners. We can ask some questions that help guide our intention to be physically present with our partners: Am I willing to create times where there will be an opportunity to have physical contact with my partner? What will it take to create these times? Do I want to receive sexual or nurturing touch? What kind of contact am I willing to give? What kind of environment tends to support physical contact with my partner? What do I want my touch to communicate to my partner? Am I able to identify what my partner's touch communicates to me? Responding to these kinds of questions with our spouses can greatly add to the quality of physical stimulation we receive.

Whenever we are able to identify what we are feeling emotionally, we become present to ourselves and communicate that we are emotionally present for our partners. Sometimes it simply means crying, shaking our bodies, or raising our voices. We can ask some questions that can guide the process of being emotionally present as we encounter our partners: What kinds of emotions am I carrying into my encounter with my partner? How do I feel about making physical contact with my partner? How do I cope with becoming distracted while making love? How challenging is it for me to acknowledge the distraction? How do I feel if my partner becomes distracted and acknowledges it?

Optimizing our feelings, emotions, and thoughts, including our relationship to those of our partners, means being willing to stay self-focused and self-examining while seeing how we contribute to fusion and avoidance in our relationship. Essentially, this means living a commitment to intimacy with ourselves and with our partners. It means being willing to track our relationship to power and the myriad of ways we abuse and abdicate power. It suggests a willingness to integrate creative self-empowerment into our lives. In doing so, we can craft a lifestyle that supports our desires while remaining accountable for choices that diminish the creative spirit of our relationship. We can also claim ownership for our situations, refusing to define ourselves as victims of our spouses.

Optimizing our thoughts means that we are willing to exercise reality checks with our partners. It is common to create stories about what our spouses are feeling and believing and what motivates them. We do our relationships a great service when we check these stories out with our partners, allowing them to define their own reality.

Schnarch suggests that when we have both feet in a relationship, sex in the bedroom will reflect who we are out of the bedroom. The sexual ritual will tell its larger narrative, and that story will inevitably bring us closer to or farther from ourselves and our partners.

We have been discussing the shadow dance of sex. Our sexual life reveals the rhythm of how we confront and avoid who we are. The primal ritual of sex will blatantly reveal the faces of our hidden selves. We saw that as we are willing to make peace with death, we open to greater life (or biophilia); and that our love of life is a grand invitation to our sexual energy. We examined the mythology surrounding the parents of Eros and the images and energies of what it means to birth eros in our lives.

We looked at sex through the perspectives of Thomas Moore and David Schnarch as they described the challenge of opening to the stories our sexuality can tell about who we are in our shadow places. We acknowledged the role of tension and the challenge to accept the golden shadow of being the recipient of delight. Finally, we looked at romance as an invitation to friendship and love, and at the role beauty plays in that invitation.

It would be grossly misleading to suggest that we have captured the essence of human sexuality. John O'Donohue says that "the essence of a thing is always elusive and hidden. We manage merely to live in the neighborhood of things. Their essence remains beyond our reach." And so we stroll through the neighborhood of human sexuality, hoping to capture an image or two that will help to remind us of who we are. But there is no penetrating the mystery of sexuality. At best, it can point us toward the impervious nature of the mystery surrounding the entire nuptial journey.

However, the mystery does invite us to listen to the call of our sexuality and decide how much life we want to live. No other aspect of our humanity thrusts us so intimately into the human adventure. We can intensely gaze at, touch, and taste our partners, allowing ourselves to salaciously dine on life.

We can open to desire, surrendering to its course, allowing ourselves to be carried to depths and heights we faintly remember. When we live our fire, we boldly choose life and enter into a sacred love affair with the journey. There may be no greater blessing than a life lived from desire.

# 10

## *The Mystery of Marriage*

One ancient meaning of the word "mystery" is "secret service," and an equally ancient interpretation of the word "marriage" is "connection." So one thing we can say about marriage is that it is the connection of two people who are engaged in a secret service to themselves, to one another, and maybe to whatever they refer to by the word "God."

In his work entitled *Marriage—Dead or Alive*, Adolf Guggenbuhl-Craig addresses what it means to surrender to this secret service: "A marriage only works if one opens himself to exactly that which he would never ask for otherwise. Only through rubbing oneself sore and losing oneself is one able to learn about oneself, God, and the world. Like every soteriological pathway, that of marriage is hard and painful."

We are engaged in a secret service to ourselves as we surrender to the mystery and the power of our nuptial initiations. We can allow marriage to take us to the depths and frontiers of ourselves, places we would only unwittingly wander before. There is no way to know what our initiations will awaken in us. There is mystery and at the same time a great service in allowing ourselves to be provoked away from the familiar.

The unfamiliar is ushered in along with countless questions begging to be asked in our marriages. We wonder if our boundaries will be permeable enough to allow ourselves to be touched by the passion and tenderness of our spouses, and impermeable enough to secure our individuality. Are we able to be clear with our partners about what we want from them, while maintaining the kind of support that prevents us from being an excessive drain upon them? Do we carry personal power in a way that brings our values and beliefs to bear upon the relationship, without attempting to invalidate the inherent diversity in the marriage? Are we able to bring a playful spirit to our sexuality, while being able to track threads of shame that may be woven through the fabric of our passion? Are we able to open our hearts in order to give and receive love, while being able to protect our hearts when our partners are regressed or emotionally unavailable? The mystery of marriage is not only reflected in the above questions that we live over and over again; it is also about the process of recreating ourselves. We are involved in a "secret service" of our own deepening and self-discovery, offering our partners an opportunity to create themselves and join us in the co-creation of the marriage.

## The Mystery of Creation

An authentic marriage happens when we are willing to surrender to the creative energies of the relationship. Nothing obstructs our possible surrender more than the desire to be happy. Guggenbuhl-Craig says: "A writer who creates meaningful works does not want to become happy, he wants to be creative. Likewise married people can seldom enjoy happy, harmonious marriages, as psychologists would force it upon them and lead them to believe. The image of the happy marriage causes great damage."

How does the image of the happy marriage cause great damage? The goal in seeking our spirit mates is happiness, while the motivation to find our soul mates is creativity. In most cases, happiness is defined as the absence of tension. Consequently, spirit mates run a high risk of moving into a fused state or engaging in avoidance. Fusion and avoidance are effective tension-reducing as well as creativity-reducing strategies. As we saw in an earlier chapter, fusion dulls the uniqueness of one or both spouses, while avoidance prohibits unity. Avoidance also restricts our surrender to the impact our spouses might have upon us. Through avoidance, we keep ourselves immune from the potential transformative potency of the marriage.

The willingness to support our own individuality while remaining engaged with our partners often stimulates a great deal of creative tension. An authentic marriage continually asks us to step into the mystery and the paradox of choosing ourselves and choosing our connection to our partners.

Of course, the more regressed we become, the more we're convinced that we must choose either ourselves or our relationships. It can be very useful to track the either/or thinking, allowing it to remind us of possible regression; we can then get the support we need in order to "grow ourselves back up" and return to the mystery of choosing ourselves and our marriages. We are only able to step back into the mystery and the paradox when we have mustered enough internal resources to hold the inevitable tension.

There are several internal strengths that allow us to work with the tension, deepening our capacity to create with it, rather than simply feeling overwhelmed. As mentioned above, confronting our regression, using the steps in the chapter on regression, is of foremost importance, as is doing what it takes to support our goodness. Once we forget that we are valuable, we inevitably feel unsafe. Having no value translates into being abandoned and dying. It helps to get clear about reclaiming our power and letting go of places where we identify ourselves as victims of our partners' choices. We strengthen ourselves by employing boundaries that support the uniqueness of our beliefs and values while remaining engaged with our partners. Those boundaries allow us to give voice to our views without deferring to or attempting to influence our partners. It is also helpful to detach from our partners' reactions to our boundaries.

Nothing mucks up the water more than needing our spouses to react favorably to our boundaries. Our partners have the right to express displeasure with our boundaries. Our boundaries are not meant to make our partners happy. They are meant to support the identification and expression of what we really believe. The value and meaning of our boundaries is our responsibility alone.

Another valuable internal resource is to loosen the grip upon the need to be happy. Our determination to be cheerful frequently leaves us feeling victimized by our spouses. Their frustration and anger in response to our choices can create tension and, consequently, the suspension of our desired bliss. If, in the name of happiness, we insist upon a tension-free marriage, we practically guarantee the demise of the marriage and put in place serious impediments to accessing our own depths.

The presence of tension declares an opportunity to unleash the creative spirit of a marriage. Nuptial unrest typically indicates that at least one spouse is moving toward truth: a truth about some unmet need, a reaction to diversity, or maybe a feeling of betrayal. In any case, tension announces the possibility of some emerging truth.

Even if the initial stirrings are as primitive as a temper tantrum, some truth is likely lurking close to the surface. Significant personal truths are often announced by blaming, shaming, ridiculing, analyzing, and the use of sarcasm. Within the deepening of a shadow marriage, these painful and annoying reactions can be seen as proclamations of some emerging truth. Even these communication pests can be used to track the presence of some truth being announced with intense reverberations. Strong emotional reactions are the mainstay of soul mates, and their challenge is to learn to carry the tension produced without creating catastrophe. As your spouse's truth makes its way to the surface, it will inevitably be a call to you.

How can your spouse's dissatisfaction be a call to yourself? If you take both your relationship to yourself and your relationship to your partner seriously, then you will be called to yourself. You will be prompted to define who you are based upon your partner's malcontent. The common tendency is to employ some strategy aimed at diminishing tension.

Tension-reducing strategies usually include deprecating either ourselves or our partners. There's got to be something wrong with us or those we love. Often spouses move back and forth, first discrediting themselves and then their partners. But we discover that this belittling process only temporarily helps to lessen the pressure; soon the tension is back with more force than we ever imagined.

If we are going to learn how to hold the tension and let it call us to our own deepening, as well as to the strengthening of our relationship, then we may need to access counseling support in order to mobilize our creative energies. It can be very challenging to see how we are attempting to avoid the tension of our marriages, and in doing so, sending our relationships into a downward spiral of estrangement and hopelessness.

Jonah and Samantha had been dating for a year when they came to their first session, complaining of feeling frustrated and stuck. Their creative energies were stymied, resulting in both of them feeling helpless and hopeless.

"I just can't stand it anymore. He belittles me and yells, and he doesn't care who's nearby," explained Samantha.

"Tell me, what do you do when he starts yelling?" I asked.

"I don't know. I guess I pull away. I don't want to be part of it. It feels awful!" she declared.

"Does it get you angry?"

"Well, yes," she replied.

"What do you do with your anger?"

"I guess I get quiet and withdraw," explained Samantha.

"You pull away and shut down. I'd like to check something out with you. My hunch is that you heavily rely upon being sweet and loving in negotiating your relationship with Jonah, as well as in making your way in the world," I pointed out.

"I'm not sure what you mean by sweet and loving," she responded.

"You don't? I mean that you rely upon your capacity to be sensitive, warm, and understanding in order to deal with life's challenges, especially as they arise with people, and especially Jonah," I explained.

"Well, I think that I do," she said, with a tone and a look that suggested that her best-kept secret was no longer a secret.

Samantha's desire to protect herself from Jonah's tendency to come on strong, coupled with her desire to maintain her relationship to Jonah, created the container for her creativity. Her father had abandoned the family when she was six months old. Somewhere in her psyche, she was convinced that if she was loving and sweet enough, she would never need to know the bite of abandonment again.

Initially, Samantha was very lost, with no idea of how to cope with life and intimacy without the use of her cherished sweetness. She began to learn that being excessively gracious and agreeable was leaving her ill-equipped to fight for herself and her relationship. She also discovered that when "sweet and loving" didn't work, her inclination was to quit.

Samantha understood that while creating an intimate relationship with Jonah, she could not adequately back herself by either being extremely pleasant or by grabbing her ball and going home. She began to create a fiery Samantha, one who could express anger and even fight. Because she did not want to lose herself or Jonah, she was able to ignite her creative spirit and bring her fire to the relationship.

Jonah was also finding his way to deeper levels of creativity. The more Samantha deferred to him, the more he got into attempting to influence her by indulging in short lectures. Her deference was an invitation for Jonah to get into teaching. Up until now, the more he attempted to be instructive, the more Samantha would withdraw. Jonah was becoming extremely frustrated and was inclined to blame Samantha for not appreciating the value of his mini-seminars.

"Aren't you getting tired of offering Samantha these 'lecturettes'?" I asked.

"Well, yeah. They don't seem to be doing any good," Jonah responded, suggesting that the real issue was Samantha's obstinacy.

"My hunch is you're not sure why you have been attempting to teach her, and you're not sure what the option to teaching her might look like," I suggested.

"Maybe I'm trying to control her. Men are always hitting on her, and she doesn't handle it well," Jonah pointed out.

"You mean she's not dealing with these overtures men make toward her in a way you want her to. You think you can actually teach her to act the way you wish her to."

"Yes, that's it. I'm trying to get her to do what I believe is best; that is what is in her best interest," said Jonah.

"And if you were to simply state how her behavior makes you feel, what would that sound like?" I asked.

"I feel angry and scared," Jonah announced, looking a bit disoriented without his podium.

His helplessness was calling him to a deeper level of truth within himself. Like Samantha's sweetness, his lecturing was not getting him what he desired. Jonah was learning to have a deeper relationship with himself in Samantha's presence. She might or might not respond favorably to the disclosure of his emotional truths; however, he was honoring his truth, and offering her an opportunity to do likewise.

They were each allowing their relationship to deepen their awareness of choices that did not serve them. Their willingness to postpone their pursuit of happiness allowed the relationship to work on them, moving them to unearth new strengths and resources.

## Betrayal Everywhere

Nothing characterizes the mystery of shadow marriage more than a couple accepting the many faces of inevitable betrayal. Of course, the most popular take on betrayal is the tendency to see ourselves in the victim role, where some act of duplicity is perpetrated upon us.

There are four significant expressions of betrayal operating in every marriage. We've already mentioned the first: some act of disloyalty directed at us. The second is deceit or violation that we inflict upon our partners. The third is the deception created by the culture regarding the nature of marriage, and the fourth is our own disloyalty to ourselves.

The betrayal of ourselves seems to receive little or no attention, yet it is the most prevalent form of betrayal in a marriage, and the one we have the most power to prevent. We betray ourselves when we act against what we believe is in our best interest, or when we deceive ourselves. Acting in our best interest and committing to being vigilant about self-deception are two proficiencies that reflect the depth of a person's emotional and spiritual maturation. They cannot be mastered, only learned; this means that we will be constantly invited to notice how we deceive ourselves and to indulge in shabby self-care.

There is probably more opportunity for self-betrayal or self-loyalty in a marriage than in any other social institution, including a monastery! The self-loyalty challenge is charged in a marriage because of the constant dilemma of how to choose ourselves while doing what is in the best interest of our relationships. We will explore more closely how marriage bears down on this issue of self-loyalty in the next section.

Fear and temptation of all kinds call us away from being loyal to ourselves. A husband frequents a local pub after work, telling himself that a few drinks allow him to decompress and reenter the home less stressed and more able to engage his wife. Ironically, his wife is contemplating leaving him because of his chronic problem with alcohol.

It is not always easy to decide whether or not we are acting in our best interest, but it can be helpful to live close to the question. It is also very beneficial to have an ally or two who is willing to assist us with our self-inquiry. Several valuable considerations reflecting the possibility of self-betrayal include: Are we giving a voice to what we want or need? Are we prone to excessive deference or compliance? Are our boundaries excessively permeable or impermeable? Are we susceptible to excessively seeking the approval of our spouses?

We can push the shadow element a bit further by pointing out that spouses often collude with their partners' particular tendencies toward self-betrayal. Why might we unconsciously support the betrayal our spouses bring down upon themselves? The best reason is that it typically creates an illusion of power or a feeling of being needed.

This form of collusion is in place when one spouse defers his self-care to the other spouse, putting himself in a child role; and the partner agrees to the deal, placing her in a parent role. A parent-child dynamic is created, with one spouse abdicating responsibility for self-care and the other spouse acting as if their partner is actually better off depending upon their direction and support, rather than relying upon himself.

The stage is set for a landslide of betrayal. Spouses moving into the role of a child have obviously betrayed themselves, while spouses in the parent role are actually living under the illusion that they know what's best for their partners, and so they are betraying themselves while colluding with their partners' self-betrayal.

The story becomes a bit more complicated when the spouses in child roles act like most kids do: sooner or later, they act out. The spouse in the child role will likely come to reclaim power with a vengeance.

Another expression of betrayal is violation or deceit enacted by us toward our spouses. I once heard my friend and colleague Jeffrey Duval say, "If you befriend me, the one thing you can be assured of is that you will be betrayed." I sat there shocked, mostly because I had vaulted myself to high moral ground, convinced that I was beyond reproach when it came to betrayal. I came to discover that my tendency toward impunity was shared by many. We seem to be much more comfortable with seeing ourselves as victims of betrayal than as perpetrators.

It might help us to have a more accepting and creative relationship with betrayal by lessening some of the drama we are inclined to attribute to it. Betrayal does not only occur in catastrophic dimensions, where you come home and find your partner in bed with your best friend. It also happens in more subtle and ordinary ways.

Some relatively routine expressions of betrayal are: breaking an agreement without renegotiating with our partners; making a unilateral decision when our spouses believed they would be included in the process; revealing something to a third party that our spouses expected we would hold in confidence; being misleading about how we really feel about something; and lying.

It can be very helpful to begin entertaining the idea that we betray as well as get betrayed while in a marriage. There are several important implications of being able to accept our capacity to betray. The first is that our acceptance positions us to possibly be more honest about betrayals we've enacted, rather than simply succumbing to denial. It also helps to restore our integrity.

When we betray another, we inevitably betray our own integrity, since the betrayal entails acting against some declared intention or agreement we made. The willingness to see our duplicity puts us closer to getting right with ourselves. When we accept our propensity to betray, we place ourselves in a more likely position to initiate the healing process after we have perpetrated some form of betrayal. Lastly, it adds to our trustworthiness, as we limit our need to place ourselves above betrayal.

There are normally two distinct elements to a betrayal. The first is some form of violation of a promise or agreement, and the second is the deceit with which the violation is enacted. Often the agreements are assumed or understood and not actually articulated: *We will do our best to support our marriage and not simply walk away.* Most spouses appear to have a much easier time being the victim of some violation than being the recipient of deceit. It is the deceit that becomes such a burden to heal.

We don't have to lose our integrity when we betray our spouses. I occasionally work with clients who are contemplating having an affair. On some level they are seeking my permission to engage in a wanted sexual interlude. After listening to a host of reasons why they believe the affair is an acceptable alternative, I often say, "It sounds to me like you have some great reasons to go ahead with the affair. I would simply suggest that before you do so, you tell your partner about your intention." They normally react as if I am crazy or being extremely sarcastic.

I go on to explain that I am being completely serious. I further point out that by telling their partners, they eliminate the deceit, making any further healing of trust much easier, and they maintain their integrity. Almost no one ever takes my advice. On one occasion a client did, and announced to his wife that he was going to have an affair with a woman from his office. Several weeks later, when his wife asked where he had been, he explained that he had been with his lover, which stimulated a violent reaction from his wife.

When the smoke settled, he asked her why she was so shocked, when he had told her his plan some two weeks prior to the incident. She responded that she simply had not believed him. She, like most of us, did not expect integrity from her spouse.

Besides acting with integrity, what can spouses who betray their partners do to address the need for healing in their marriages? The next best thing we can do is to be clear about the impact the betrayal of our partners will have upon ourselves. Unless the betrayal is simply a way of blasting our way out of a marriage (or we have strong sociopathic tendencies), we will likely experience shame, guilt, remorse, grief, and feelings of inadequacy. If the betrayal has already been perpetrated, then we will need to get right with ourselves. Getting right with ourselves does not entail a confession to our spouses in order to elicit their sympathy or forgiveness. Our forgiveness is our responsibility.

I am often asked, "Should I tell my spouse about my affair?"

As I mentioned, if the affair has not yet taken place, it is an ideal time to act with integrity and declare the intention to have the affair. If the affair has already taken place, the choice will call for discernment and reflection. If there is no norm in place for spouses to be accountable for common expressions of betrayal, then expect a great deal of drama when disclosing an affair.

Another question is: Will irreparable harm come to anyone because of the disclosure? Irreparable harm includes suicide, homicide, or physical injury to someone. The next question is: What do I hope to gain by the disclosure? If the hope is to move into deeper levels of truth with the intention being the healing of trust, then I recommend the disclosure. If the exercise is an effort to gain the other's forgiveness, then I discourage the disclosure.

I am often asked, "What if my spouse decides to leave me?" I respond by asking if they are willing to take the risk, and by asking whether they want to attempt to rebuild a relationship after deceit.

My best wisdom suggests that it's often in the perpetrator's best interest to disclose betrayal. The presence of betrayal usually tells an even bigger story about neglect, deprivation, anger, abuse, and passive-aggression. The more important question is: Are you willing to address the issues in your marriage that will likely surface once the betrayal disclosure has been made?

The healing of the betrayer rests upon the question: What does this betrayal say about me and my marriage? It will take a great deal of work to continue to come back to this question.

There will be temptation to wander away from this healing question. There will be a tendency to invite our spouses to punish us in order to cope with shame and guilt, as well as a pull toward becoming obsequious. There may also be a tendency toward self-righteousness on behalf of the betrayer in order to deal with the darkness of the betrayal. The goal for the perpetrators is to find authentic compassion for themselves and allow the betrayal to drop them into the depths of themselves and their marriages.

Another way of getting right with themselves is for perpetrators to make amends to spouses. This has two distinct components: the first is a sincere apology, and the second is a commitment not to reproduce the betrayal. The reparation is not principally for the violated spouses, although they may benefit from it; it is an opportunity for perpetrators to support their own integrity.

The third perspective of betrayal is from the position of the betrayed. The overwhelming tendency is for the betrayed to experience themselves as deeply victimized. They often feel beguiled and misled. The more entrenched the betrayed are in victimhood, the more helpless they are to understand their betrayal experience, identify their role in the betrayal, and access the energy needed to heal. Victimization is a natural reaction to being betrayed. The key is simply not to stay there too long.

There are a number of conditions lending themselves to keeping the betrayed stuck in victimization. It can be very seductive to get into punishing the perpetrator or exercising revenge; however, this keeps the betrayed one impotent and unable to initiate healing and learning. Betrayed partners remain unable to allow the betrayal to take them to a deeper place when they are stuck blaming the perpetrators.

The betrayed can begin to loosen their grip on being victims by remembering that their partners are not the only ones capable of generating betrayal. It is also helpful to let go of employing moral judgments that allow one to fall on the side of righteousness. Morally judging the perpetrator is a strategy aimed at making the betrayed one appear irreproachable and beyond such unscrupulous deeds.

If the betrayal stirs old childhood betrayals that have not been addressed, it may be more difficult to shake the embrace of victimization. Feelings that have not been accessed around these old betrayals can freeze spouses in their victimized identities. In order to separate the old betrayals from the current one, intense grief work is usually called for.

Once spouses who have been betrayed begin to shed the shroud of victimization, they also can begin to ask the healing question: "What does this betrayal say about me and my marriage?" Working with this question begins to restore power to the betrayed. They can sustain control over their own lives by remaining self-focused and continuing to gain power. They can begin to position themselves to discover how they may have colluded with the betrayal. Those betrayed can consider how they may have subtly conspired to support the betrayal they vehemently denounce—once they let go of being victims.

What are common ways that the betrayed collude with their betrayers? The betrayed can participant in the betrayal in a number of ways. They may have denied their partners something they deeply desired, setting the stage for their partners to pursue their wants elsewhere.

The betrayed may have a need to be punished for some prior transgression, employing a number of behaviors that practically invite their spouses to betray them. Or the betrayed may have been looking for an excuse to end the relationship, conveniently placing themselves in a vulnerable position that encourages their partner to violate some form of trust.

The last dimension of betrayal impacting a marriage is the betrayal imposed upon a marriage by the culture. Our culture seriously misrepresents the nature of marriage. Why would a society distort the essential personality of marriage, which is so fundamental to its very fabric?

My best understanding is that because our culture denies the nature of life itself, then any significant expression of life, such as a marriage, will also be open to distortion. As I mentioned in an earlier chapter, our culture defines life as understandable, secure, and predictable, as long as we have the "right stuff." The "right stuff" includes education, financial investments, the right neighborhoods, and whatever clubs and associations serve to prop us up so we can pretend that we are immune to life's inevitable afflictions, including death.

The culture insists upon denying the essential mystery, insecurity, and unpredictability of life; hence, it denies the mystery and insecurity of marriage. We end up with a sterilized version of wedlock, filled with idyllic nonsense.

We are promised a spirit mate who brings happiness, fulfillment, and an opportunity for everlasting love. We are told marriage is a natural part of life, one that anyone over twenty-one years of age should know how to master.

In order to be released from being a victim of the cultural betrayal, we will need to be disillusioned over and over again. The challenge is not to direct our disillusionment at ourselves or our spouses, but rather toward a culture that insists upon generating useless myths. Unfortunately, many of us believe that our nuptial discontent is due to our own incompetence or a lack of marital adroitness on behalf of our partners.

How do we heal the betrayal perpetrated upon us by the culture? Working with a good marital therapist can be very helpful. We need assistance to identify the cultural myths we have bought into, and to experience the grief that accompanies letting them go. We have integrated many false beliefs that need to be recognized while allowing ourselves to feel the anger, the sadness, and the fear generated by our disillusionment. As we grieve and replace the old myths with an acceptance of marriage's mystery, we can gradually stop being victims of the culture.

We need to create our own beliefs about marriage. We can replace cultural illusions of marriage with creative beliefs that deepen our capacity to endure the nuptial adventure. We can view marriage as a grand opportunity to grow up, as an invitation into our own depths. We can identify the internal resources necessary in order to accept marriage's invitation to descend into the unknown regions of our own souls while creating intimacy with our partners. We can see marriage as an intense spiritual quest teaching us how to make peace with the essential mystery of being alive.

## Marriage Makes Good Religion

In his book *The Soul's Religion*, Thomas Moore describes religion as "a constructive means for being open to the influence of mystery." Moore's definition raises several important questions: Why might we want to be open to the influence of mystery? And if we want to be open, how would we do such a thing? And what does being open to the influence of mystery have to do with marriage?

As I said earlier, to take marriage seriously means to confront the popular cultural myth that life is understandable, secure, and predictable. If we attempt to "get marriage right," we will be thrown back again into life's inherent mystery and insecurity. We can't "get marriage right"! And if we are not attempting to "get it right," then what are we doing in a marriage?

Rather than be caught up in the self-defeating task of "getting marriage right", we allow ourselves to be influenced by its mystery. The challenge is to let go of our drive toward achieving marital bliss, accept the unknowing involved in stepping into a mystery, and surrender to the power of marriage. Our job is to continue to choose ourselves and our relationships; this commitment will influence the mystery and the power of marriage.

The deeper we hold ourselves and our relationships in our hearts, the more open we become to marriage's mystery, and the more we will allow a marriage to take us to our depths. We become lost and confused when we attempt to remain loyal to ourselves while our marriage asks for sacrifice; we seek joy while our marriage presents opportunities for trauma.

Suffering and loneliness often bring us to our spiritual depths more than any other human endeavor. We are hurt, and we scramble as old beliefs and values render little or no comfort. This is the fork in the road where we must decide. We either choose to stand against ourselves or against our partners, or we allow ourselves to be open to the mystery of marriage.

If we are determined to choose ourselves and our partners, then we will likely suffer. As our spouses make choices or hold beliefs that we do not advocate, there will be tension, and possibly suffering. When we hold our own positions while refusing to turn our backs upon our partners, we are letting go of the idyllic longings of spirit mates. We hold ourselves and our relationships, which allows us to deepen our capacity to love and be loved, and empty ourselves of illusions in preparation for wisdom. We begin to see that although we do not look forward to suffering, it aids in the death of naïveté, diminishes pride, and can ignite curiosity and wonder.

Marriage is a constructive means to open to the influence of life's mystery; it is not meant to bring us to our knees, although it very well might do that. The purpose of the influence is to bring us into a deeper relationship with ourselves, our partners, and life itself. This deepening can only be done by learning to accept that we suffer, we delight, and we die.

Adolf Guggenbuhl-Craig says, "The central issue in marriage is not well-being or happiness, it is salvation." Our marital salvation happens as we remain open to ways of creating more life for ourselves and for our relationship. Our salvation often depends upon our willingness to experience the brokenness of our wills and our hearts, and experience the loss of faith; however, most of us resist welcoming that much life. Instead, we rely upon spurious formulas aimed at reducing marriage to a social and legal contract.

Once our perfunctory nuptial recipes prove to be disastrous, we may be ready to surrender to the influence of marriage, rather than simply standing in protest of what does not meet with our satisfaction. If we can let go of our need to intellectually drive our marriages, then we may be able to summon enough imagination to see marriage as a mysterious force inviting us to the salvation of who we were truly meant to be.

Marriage demands that we become students of suffering, delight, and death. It is this nuptial demand that drives so many of us into divorce court.

# Divorce

The end of a marriage is as mysterious as the life of a marriage, or, for that matter, as mysterious as the beginning of a marriage. How do spouses decide to move on and accept the death of that to which they were once devoted?

In so many cases, spouses have not remained focused on themselves during the life of the marriage, so they die the way they lived, blaming and accusing one another for the demise of their relationship. In a real way, marriages that lack self-focus (where each partner takes responsibility for his or her own happiness) never have a chance. Without taking responsibility for their own fulfillment and their own shadow, each partner remains a victim of the other. The creative energies of the relationship remain stymied, unable to infuse the marriage with passion and insight.

The death of a marriage can offer spouses an opportunity to open to a new and powerful initiation. Their separation launches the initiatory process, with the accompanying grief and life changes thrusting them into a series of challenging trials. The anticipated relief of a divorce soon transforms into a series of challenging initiations. Most divorcing individuals believe they are choosing to get away from their truculent and obstinate partners. The truth is that they are attempting to gain a reprieve from a troublesome initiation, one which most definitely will not go away.

# A New Faith

We have been describing marriage and intimacy as a mysterious initiation. This portrayal of marriage asks us to give up childhood fantasies of the nuptial life and consider opening to a new faith.

The old faith was about "happy-ever-aftering", while the new faith is about the courage to create ourselves as we co-create our marriages. The new faith requires us to take our emotional and spiritual maturation quite seriously. The old faith pursued comfort in marriage, while the new faith seeks the challenge of remaining radically self-responsible. The old faith offered an alleged asylum from shadow; the new faith fosters an embrace of shadow. The old faith suggests that we can manage marriage without giving up beliefs and attitudes entrenched in childhood. The new faith demands that we grow up and believe in the power of marriage to guide us toward that end.

Just when I am convinced that I have evolved into marital enlightenment, the hidden forces of marriage call me back to my learning. Recently, Connie and I were shopping at one of our favorite grocery stores. I proceeded to confront Connie about a purchase she intended to make. She quickly countered with several remarks meant to back me off. I skittishly made my way out of the store, determined to take it up further in the car.

"I've asked you not to raise your voice at me in public," I declared.

"I don't think I raised my voice, but what if I did?" responded Connie.

"Well, I don't like it," I offered.

"You don't like it because you don't want to stand there and fight, and you don't like how it looks to walk away!" Connie asserted.

There I was, holding the bag, the bag of old faith, believing that it is my spouse's responsibility to make my choices easier for me.

The new faith holds the belief that marriage is a viable container for reclaiming ourselves. Inevitably, we will lose ourselves in our marriages. Whether we are prone to unconsciously influencing our partners, accommodating them, or withdrawing, we will lose ourselves. When we find the courage to reclaim ourselves, we will be ready to meet our partners with increased depth and creativity. A marriage constantly offers opportunities to steal ourselves back, not just from our spouses, but from parents, schools, religion, and maybe even from the gods.

978-0-595-3884⁹
0-595-38849-3

Made in the USA
Lexington, KY
25 July 2010